Reform and Punishment

Cambridge Criminal Justice Series

Published in association with the Institute of Criminology, University of Cambridge

Published titles

Community Penalties: Change and Challenges, edited by Anthony Bottoms, Loraine Gelsthorpe and Sue Rex

Ideology, Crime and Criminal Justice: A Symposium in Honour of Sir Leon Radzinowicz, edited by Anthony Bottoms and Michael Tonry

Reform and Punishment: The Future of Sentencing, edited by Sue Rex and Michael Tonry

Reform and Punishment
The Future of Sentencing

edited by

Sue Rex
Michael Tonry

WILLAN
PUBLISHING

Published in association with the Institute of Criminology, University of Cambridge, by

Willan Publishing
Culmcott House
Mill Street, Uffculme
Cullompton, Devon
EX15 3AT, UK
Tel: +44(0)1884 840337
Fax: +44(0)1884 840251
e-mail: info@willanpublishing.co.uk
Website: @www.willanpublishing.co.uk

Published simultaneously in the USA and Canada by

Willan Publishing
c/o ISBS, 5824 N.E. Hassalo St,
Portland, Oregon 97213-3644, USA
Tel: +001(0)503 287 3093
Fax: +001(0)503 280 8832
Website: www.isbs.com

First published 2002

ISBN 1-903240-94-8 (cased)

British Library Cataloguing-in-Publication Data
A catalogue record for this book is available from the British Library

Typeset by TW Typesetting, Plymouth, Devon
Printed and bound by T J International Ltd, Trecerus Industrial Estate, Padstow, Cornwall

Contents

Notes on contributors

David Faulkner, Senior Research Associate at the Centre for Criminological Research, University of Oxford, was the principal architect of the Criminal Justice Act 1991 and for many years a senior civil servant in the Home Office.

David A. Green has an MPhil from the Institute of Criminology in Cambridge and is now studying for a PhD there.

The Honourable Judge Peter Jones is a circuit court judge in Sheffield and a member of the Sentencing Advisory Commission for England and Wales.

Thomas P. LeBel is Lecturer in the School of Criminal Justice, State University of New York at Albany.

Alison Liebling is University Lecturer in Criminology, Institute of Criminology, University of Cambridge, and Director of the Institute's Prison Research Centre.

Shadd Maruna is Lecturer in Criminology, Institute of Criminology, University of Cambridge.

Rod Morgan, Chief Inspector of Her Majesty's Inspectorate of Probation, was for many years Professor of Criminology, Faculty of Law, University of Bristol.

Sue Rex is Senior Research Associate in the Institute of Criminology, University of Cambridge, an ESRC Fellow and Director of the Institute's Cropwood Programme.

Julian V. Roberts is Professor of Criminology, Faculty of Social Sciences, University of Ottawa.

Michael Tonry is Professor of Law and Public Policy and Director of the Institute of Criminology, University of Cambridge, and Sonosky Professor of Law and Public Policy, University of Minnesota.

Andrew von Hirsch is Honorary Professor of Penal Law and Penal Theory, Institute of Criminology, University of Cambridge, and Director of the Institute's Centre on Penal Theory and Penal Ethics.

Preface

This volume explores the implications for English sentencing policies, practices and institutions of the proposals set out in the 2001 Halliday Report and memorialises discussions at the 26th Cropwood Round Table Conference on 'Sentencing Policies and Possibilities in Britain' which was convened in Cambridge in November–December 2001, with support from the Barrow Cadbury Trust. The Halliday Report was prepared by John Halliday with support from a small, full-time Home Office team. It drew upon extensive consultation: a core working group which met monthly for 18 months; an external reference group of 50 people; a series of mid-course and final conferences held throughout England and Wales to elicit reactions from informed practitioners and others; extensive interviews with influential people and stakeholders; and visits to jurisdictions in the United States and Europe which were believed to have undertaken ambitious and successful sentencing innovations in recent years. The Report proposes a comprehensive overhaul of law, practice and institutional arrangements for dealing with convicted offenders in Britain. Among other things, the Report proposes replacing existing sentencing statutes, the establishment of a sentencing commission and sentencing guidelines to govern imposition of all sentences imposed in magistrates' and higher courts, and the creation of a 'sentence review' function in the judiciary under which judges oversee not only the imposition but also the implementation, amendment, revocation, and final termination of all community penalties. It may be the single most ambitious and comprehensive set of proposals for reconstituting the sentencing system of a common-law country ever presented. Its closest competitor is the model Penal Code developed by the US American Law Institute over a period of 13 years, from 1949 to 1962, involving a much larger cast of characters.

So ambitious a set of proposals deserves close attention. The Cropwood Conference on Sentencing Policies and Possibilities was convened to provide that kind of examination in prepared papers, in discussions, and finally in this volume which contains revised and more fully elaborated versions of the papers that were presented and discussed. The conference was stimulating and constructive, and we are most grateful to the participants. Like all Cropwood Conferences, this one was attended by a mix of policy-makers, senior practitioners, and scholars:

Mr Robert Allen (Esmée Fairbairn Foundation)

Mrs Maureen Bateman (Chairman of the Sentencing Committee, The Magistrates' Association)

Professor Anthony Bottoms (Institute of Criminology, University of Cambridge)

Mr David Faulkner (Centre for Criminological Research, University of Oxford)

Ms Cecilia French (Home Office)

Dr Stephen Goode (Chief Officer, National Probation Service Headquarters)

Mr John Halliday (Home Office)

Mr Keir Hopley (National Probation Directorate)

Professor Mike Hough (The Criminal Policy Research Unit, South Bank University)

Professor Neil Hutton (The Law School, University of Strathclyde)

Professor Roxanne Lieb (Visiting Fellow, Institute of Criminology, University of Cambridge)

Dr Alison Liebling (Institute of Criminology, University of Cambridge)

Dr Shadd Maruna (Institute of Criminology, University of Cambridge)

Dr Amanda Matravers (Institute of Criminology, University of Cambridge)

Professor Rod Morgan (HM Chief Inspector of Probation, Home Office)

Mr Nigel Newcomen (Sentence Management Group, HM Prison Service – Headquarters)

Ms Anne Owers (HM Chief Inspector of Prisons, Home Office)

Mrs Nicky Padfield (Institute of Criminology, University of Cambridge)

Hon. Judge Christopher Pitchers (Circuit Court, Nottingham)

Professor Julian Roberts (Criminology, Faculty of Social Sciences, University of Ottawa)

Ms Christine Stewart (Home Office)
Mr Robert Street (Home Office)
Mrs Sukhvinder Stubbs (The Barrow Cadbury Trust)
Professor Andrew von Hirsch (Institute of Criminology, University of
  Cambridge)

The two days' exploration of Halliday's proposals, their implications
and their practicability illuminated their intelligence, sophistication
and ambition and some of the formidable challenges that must be
overcome if they are to be adopted and successfully implemented.

The Cambridge Institute of Criminology has been receiving support
from the Barrow Cadbury Trust since 1968 to underwrite the convening
of Cropwood Conferences. The Trust also supports the Cropwood
Fellowship Programme, which enables Fellows, selected in a competitive process, to spend up to three months in Cambridge working on a
research-related project, advised by a member of the Institute's
academic staff. Cropwood Fellows are typically mid-career practitioners
drawn from throughout the criminal justice system. Many of the reports
distilling the results of their work have been published by the Institute
and elsewhere. Ideas generated in those reports have often had an
impact on policy and practices in the agencies to which Fellows return.

The Institute is enormously grateful to the Barrow Cadbury Trust,
and to Eric Adams and Mrs Sukhvinder Stubbs from Barrow Cadbury,
for their support of the Cropwood Programme in general and, in
particular, for their support of the Conference on Sentencing Policies
and Possibilities. In addition, we pay tribute to Helen Griffiths, without
whose commitment and cheerful, kind-hearted and efficient work the
Conference would not have been possible nor would have been such a
success. Helen Griffiths is secretary to the Institute's Cropwood
Programme and organises both the Cropwood Conferences and the
Cropwood Fellowship Programme. She is a joy to work with, as we
and participants in the conference unanimously testify. Sara Harrop
edited the papers in this volume and co-ordinated its production.

We believe the papers in this volume provide a comprehensive and
intelligent overview of sentencing policies and possibilities in England
and Wales. Readers will decide for themselves whether they concur in
that judgment.

Sue Rex and Michael Tonry
April 2002

Chapter 1

Reconsidering sentencing and punishment in England and Wales

Michael Tonry and Sue Rex

Sentencing and sanctions in England and Wales are likely to undergo substantial refashioning in the next few years. Background conditions make change inevitable. The prison population, 70,266 in March 2002 (plus 1,965 prisoners under Home Detention Curfew), has risen steadily since December 1992 when it stood at 40,600 (www. hmprisonservice.gov.uk). Decisions must soon be made either to reduce prison use, and thereby head off further increase, or to accept continued growth and make substantial new investments in physical plant and personnel. The reorientation of the Probation Service mission from coordination of social services and provision of support to risk management and surveillance continues, as does the consolidation of formerly autonomous county services into a centralised national agency. The movement for accreditation of prison and probation treatment programmes continues and is likely to gain added vigour and momentum. The movement toward rationalisation and reorganisation of the courts, including reconsideration of the role of the magistracy, also will continue whether or not along the lines set out in Lord Justice Auld's recent report (2001). In the name of evidenced-based policy-making, hundreds of millions of pounds have been invested since the first Blair government took office in piloting and evaluating new programmes in the juvenile and adult justice systems. Those results are steadily accumulating.

Kenneth Clarke, Michael Howard, Jack Straw and David Blunkett, the last four Home Secretaries, each in his own way expressed dissatisfaction with sentencing laws and practices. Clarke oversaw the repeal and revision of key provisions of the Criminal Justice Act 1991.

1

Howard proposed and achieved the enactment of mandatory minimum sentence laws, and famously declared that 'Prison works.' Straw put Howard's mandatories into effect, repeatedly reiterated his lack of concern about prison population growth, was careful not to let the Tories get to his right on crime control issues, and appointed senior Home Office civil servant John Halliday to lead a review of the sentencing framework. Blunkett, in office at the time of writing for less than a year, has so far been sending mixed messages. Sometimes, as with the February 2002 proposals for 'custody-minus' sentences, he appears to want to pull back from Howard and Straw's emphasis on deterrent and incapacitative crime control strategies in general and imprisonment in particular. At other times, as in his speeches in March 2002 on street robbery in London and policing issues, he appears to want to move towards increased reliance on tougher sanctions.

The probability of change is high, but its likely direction is far from clear. Partly, this is because it is much easier to agree that problems exist than on what should be done about them. Partly it is because reasonable people disagree fundamentally over what sentencing is about – reassuring the public, preventing crime, imposing deserved punishments, rehabilitating offenders. Partly it is because of governmental inertia and resistance to change; 'Reform, reform, don't speak to me of reform,' pleaded one Victorian civil servant; 'things are bad enough as it is' – no doubt still a widely shared sentiment. Partly it is because of the perceived political salience of crime control policy. To be taken seriously, substantive policy proposals must pass muster with some or all of tabloid editors, focus groups, and political advisers.

For the past year, and probably for the next few years, the starting point for consideration of changes to English sentencing and sanctions will be the final report from the Home Office Review of the Sentencing Framework for England and Wales headed by Halliday (Home Office 2001). Most of the papers in this volume attend to analyses, arguments and proposals in the Halliday Report (some also consider the Auld report). Rather than anticipate or reiterate what their writers have to say – readers can find that out for themselves – in this introduction we say a little about the process from which the Halliday Report emerged and its major themes and proposals. We conclude by exercising the editors' prerogative of setting out our own brief agenda for the reconstitution of English sentencing.

The Review of the Sentencing Framework, though intelligently, ambitiously and professionally executed, was misconceived. Too much was expected from too few in too little time. In addition, the Review's lack of independence from Home Office politics compromised its ability to carry out its ambitious agenda. In particular, the need to accommodate Jack Straw's policy preferences for 'seamless sentencing', close community supervision, 'custody-plus' sentences and punishment increments for successive offences, and to avoid Straw's forbidden ground of the reconsideration of mandatory minimum penalties, distorted the proposals that were made. We believe there is considerable merit in Halliday's recommendations of limiting retributivism as a guiding principle, of sentencing guidelines to assure consistency, of rationalisation of authorised sentencing options, of increased investment in treatment and supervision, of increased coordination of community and institutional penalties, and of increased judicial involvement in the implementation of sentences. We also believe that much more thought needs to be given to how such recommendations should be elaborated, improved and implemented.

Before we move to detail, a disclaimer. One of us was a member of an 18-member project group that met monthly with Halliday and his staff as the report was being developed and written. There is nothing of the exposé in this chapter and, we believe, there is no impropriety in a project group member writing about the report. From the outset – and this was repeatedly made clear in project group meetings – the final product was envisioned as a report written by John Halliday with support from assigned Home Office staff, and not as a statement of the views of the project group. The group, which is identified in the appendix to this chapter, represented a wide range of views and institutions and discussed successive iterations of Halliday's work plan and draft report. Individuals expressed personal views and sometimes at least appeared to express the official positions of the organisations for which they worked. At no time, however, was the group asked to express its collective view.

The process

Halliday's assignment, at least as he interpreted it, was extraordinarily large and ambitious. The 'sentencing framework', as the object of a governmental policy review, could have been defined in a number of ways. At its narrowest it might have been deemed to refer to the statutory framework that specifies the sentencing powers of judges. More broadly it might include the procedural rules and processes that relate to the imposition of a sentence. Successive further broadenings might encompass the body of appellate case law on sentencing, the implementation of sentences, the functional purposes of sentencing and sentencing's guiding philosophy. The Halliday Report addresses all these subjects, and takes on some – the establishment of a sentencing commission and the promulgation of comprehensive sentencing guidelines – that are unprecedented in the UK.

The report's ambitious compass is all the more impressive given that it was substantially the work of one man in less than 18 months, albeit ably assisted by a small staff and with research and statistical support from the Home Office Research and Statistics Directorate. A similarly ambitious effort in the United States, the development of the sentencing and corrections provisions of the Model Penal Code, involved upwards of 100 people and unfolded over ten years (American Law Institute 1962). A second edition of those portions of the Model Penal Code began early in 2002 under the direction of Professor Kevin Reitz of the University of Colorado, and is expected to take 6–10 years. So leisurely a process is not imaginable in government, but the contrast remains striking and raises the question of whether it was realistic to ask one person to undertake so large a job in so short a time.

The related question is raised as to why for so large a job the government did not appoint a Royal Commission or similar body and give it a sizeable staff, substantial resources and a realistic timetable. We have no inside knowledge with which to answer that question and can only speculate. Perhaps Jack Straw was not really interested in reform of the sentencing system and the establishment of the Halliday review was meant to allow him to appear to be doing something while doing nothing. Appointing a committee is a classic way to buy time. Perhaps Straw regarded sentencing issues as so politically salient that he was unwilling to risk appointing a review body that was beyond political control. Perhaps Straw thought the issues easier than they are and believed that one person in a little over a year could adequately consider and authoritatively address them.

The assignment in any case was as it was and Halliday made a serious, professional effort to consult widely, draw on empirical data and research, and learn from the experience of other jurisdictions. In addition to meeting regularly with the project group to discuss issues, position papers and draft chapters of the final report, Halliday created an external reference group of 40 or so people with which he met on several occasions to explore particular subjects. At those meetings participants broke into smaller groups and developed responses to questions posed by Halliday and his staff. When the draft report was nearing completion, Halliday and his staff convened regional meetings of practitioners in Buckinghamshire and Yorkshire to elicit responses. In order to be sure that the views of approximately 25 senior practitioners and scholars were taken into account, rather than assume such people would attend external reference group or regional meetings to which they were invited, Halliday travelled round the country to talk with them one by one. Finally, to try to draw on the experiences of other countries that had recently made major changes to their sentencing systems, Halliday and his senior support staff visited a number of European countries and American states.

Similarly extensive efforts were made to canvass available data and research findings and in some cases to arrange for major new surveys and data analyses to be completed. To the maximum extent possible the report cites and relies on empirical data. In study group meetings Halliday often explained draft proposals on the basis of data on offending or criminal career patterns or findings from evaluation research. Substantial new efforts were made by Home Office economists to develop and then to refine projections of the likely effects of alternative policies under consideration and related cost-benefit analyses. Other Home Office researchers conducted new surveys of public and practitioners' opinions about the operation of the criminal justice system and about sentencing policy. The appendices to the final report, half again longer than the report itself, are a treasure trove of otherwise unavailable information. Anyone seriously interested in English sentencing policy will profit from a few hours' investment of time in working through the appendices.

Major themes and proposals

True to its ambitious scope, Halliday offers major proposals on every element of the English systems of sentencing and sanctions. At the broadest level, he proposes adoption of 'limiting retributivism' as the philosophical premise for English sentencing: the framework 'advocated in this report . . . is described as "limited [sic] retributivism" i.e. one which seeks utilitarian goals within limits based on proportionate punishment' (Home Office 2001: 163). As described by Halliday, limiting retributivism sets outer, particularly upper, limits of deserved punishment. Within those limits instrumental purposes can be taken into account. Halliday then identifies three functional goals: punishment, reparation and crime reduction. So that sentences can be designed to maximise the realisation of those goals in policy terms and in individual cases, Halliday proposes the promulgation of presumptive sentencing guidelines for all offences. The guidelines, set by an administrative agency, would indicate starting points for consideration

5

of sentences for particular cases and indicate the criteria on the basis of which sentences should be made more or less severe. To simplify policy-making and eliminate rigidities in current laws governing particular existing sentencing options, Halliday proposes the repeal of current statutes and the enactment of new ones establishing a small number of sentencing options: fines, 'community punishment orders', short stand-alone prison sentences up to three months in length, 'custody-plus' sentences of up to twelve months of which no more than three could be to prison, and 'custody-plus' sentences of twelve months or longer, of which half would be served in prison and half in the community. The mandatory life sentence was not addressed and extended sentences for particularly dangerous offenders were proposed. To assure the adequacy and continuity of implementation of sentences, Halliday proposes substantially increased investment in treatment and supervision, closer working cooperation between the Prison and Probation Services, and, more radically, much closer and more continuous judicial oversight of the implementation, modification and revocation of community penalties.

Space does not allow us to discuss all these proposals in detail. We highlight four of them – limiting retributivism, sentencing guidelines, simplification of sentencing options and judicial oversight of sentence implementation – and briefly discuss the others along the way.

Limiting retributivism

Limiting retributivism includes two main ideas.

- *Outer Limits*. Retributivist considerations establish outer limits beyond which any punishment for a particular crime is unjustly severe or unduly depreciates the seriousness of the offence.

- *Parsimony*. Within those limits the least severe punishment should be imposed unless a more severe punishment would demonstrably achieve net public benefit, taking the offender's interests into account.

Although Halliday explicitly claimed a limiting retributivist rationale for his proposals, the proposals themselves are consistent only with a weak version of the outer limits idea and an even weaker version of parsimony.

The term 'limiting retributivism' was coined by Norval Morris (1974) though the ideas closely correspond to those set out by H.L.A. Hart in his *Prolegomenon to the Philosophy of Punishment* (1968: chapter 1).

Morris works essentially within a utilitarian philosophical framework but acknowledges that widely shared intuitions and prudential considerations argue for the incorporation of retributive ideas into punishment theories. Morris argues that retributive notions cannot convincingly explain why any particular absolute level of punishment is deserved but that within any society broad agreement can be reached about punishments that are undeservedly severe or unduly lenient. Within those limits, consistent with the Benthamite idea that everybody's, including criminals', suffering is undesirable, punishments more severe than the least deserved can be justified only if more suffering will be avoided through crime prevention than will be caused by the incremental punishment.

The Halliday Report adopts the stance in relation to 'persistent offenders' that every successive crime should result in an additional increment of punishment. This is a view Straw often expressed (Faulkner 2001: chapter 12). In explaining limitations and problems with current sentencing, Halliday indicates that 'the most compelling of these [is] the unclear and unpredictable approach to persistent offenders' (Home Office 2001). Whether on normative grounds Halliday agreed with Straw or whether on other grounds he believed the Report should adopt that view we do not know. In any case, the Report cites the failure of current practice to deliver such incremental penalties as a major deficiency. Major deficiency or not, as Judge Peter Jones explains elsewhere in this volume, practitioners find repeat minor property offenders particularly perplexing and many do not believe a monolithic strategy of deterrence through successively harsher sentences a sound one.

The Report also adopts a conception of proportionality that would apportion deserved punishments to the seriousness of the current offence and prior convictions:

[S]everity of punishment should reflect the seriousness of the offence (or offences as a whole) and the offender's criminal history ... The severity of sentence should increase to reflect a persistent course of criminal conduct as shown by previous convictions and sentences. (p. 21)

It is difficult to imagine the argument by which 'recent and relevant previous convictions' (p. iii) are *a priori* measures of deserved punishments. The three prevailing views are that prior convictions are not at all relevant (e.g. Singer 1979), they are only negatively relevant (e.g. their absence justifies less-than-deserved punishments; von Hirsch 1985), or they are relevant only when in the particular

case demonstrable and ethically justifiable crime-preventive considerations allow them to be taken into account (Morris and Miller 1985).
Elsewhere in this volume Andrew von Hirsch recounts various
unpersuasive arguments that might be put forward for making prior
convictions a component of the calculus of deserved punishment for a
new crime.

The Halliday Report is also inconsistent with limiting retributivist
premises in three other respects. First, although Halliday proposes
three scaled levels of minor offences for which community penalties
might be imposed, he proposes starting points (p. 41) but no meaningful limits on sentencers' authority to cumulate conditions attached to
community penalties. As a result, people who commit offences of the
lowest level might easily receive more burdensome community penalties than less troubled or threatening offenders who commit offences of
the highest level. This could easily happen when sentences of middle-
class people who have committed highest-level offences are compared
with those of disadvantaged people of troubled backgrounds who
commit lowest-level offences. For the former, fines alone or community
service might be deemed to suffice while for the latter drug treatment,
a curfew, electronic tagging and community service might appear
called for. Without meaningful upper limits for low-level cases such
disproportionate results appear inevitable.

Second, the Halliday Report proposes the extension of sentences on
grounds of dangerousness beyond the maximum justifiable in relation
even to the current offence and recent and relevant prior convictions.
That also cannot be reconciled with limiting retributivism. If retributivist concerns set limits, they set limits. The possibility that we may
live among risky people who have completed their deserved punishments is a price we pay to live in a free society.

Third, in the conceptually most mysterious passage in the Report,
Halliday calls for '[c]onsistent application of explicit principles and
standards, recognising that these may result in justifiably disparate
outcomes. The goal is consistency of approach not uniformity of
outcomes' (p. 16). Literally interpreted, this is a call for procedural rather
than substantive consistency. Concerns for equality and proportionality,
however, are implicit in retributive punishment theories; the point is to
attempt to assure that comparably undeserving offenders receive
comparably severe penalties. Halliday may be arguing here against too
great a rigidity in comparing cases solely in terms of the offence of
conviction. That is a valid concern, but as worded the way the point as
made must be music to judicial ears: consistency in outcomes is not the
issue but whether judges have considered the appropriate principles.

Halliday nonetheless deserves credit for setting out a philosophical rationale for the Report and its recommendations. Few sentencing commissions or policy-review committees are prepared to do that, but opt either for silence in the matter or unhelpfully point out that sentencing serves diverse purposes and implicates diverse principles and let it go at that (e.g. US Sentencing Commission 1987: introduction). Were there to be a next version of the Halliday Report, the features described in this subsection could fairly easily be revised to make them consistent with limiting retributivist ideas.

Sentencing guidelines

Except for the Dutch prosecution service's sentence recommendation guidelines (Tak 2001), and guidelines under consideration in some Australian states (Freiberg 2001), the only extensive experience with numerical sentencing guidelines of the sort Halliday envisages is in the United States (Tonry 1996; Reitz 2001). That experience shows that presumptive sentencing guidelines can achieve credibility among judges and lawyers, can reduce sentencing disparities in general and in relation to race and gender, can provide a tool for successfully implementing changes in sentencing policy and can make sentencing sufficiently consistent and predictable that correctional resource needs can be predicted reasonably accurately. However, that guidelines can achieve those results and in some places have does not mean that they will. Most American guidelines systems have failed to achieve those results. Sometimes this is for political reasons; some powerful constituency opposes guidelines and effectively uses that power to stop them. More often, failures result from lack of sophistication and political acumen on the part of guidelines developers or from failures in the creation of the administrative body (in the US called a commission so we use that term) charged to create the guidelines. This is an area where the Halliday Report merely sketches possibilities and leaves the detail for others later.

The successful development and implementation of sentencing guidelines is fundamental to the achievement of the goals of Halliday's proposals. This is a subject that unfortunately could not be adequately explored because of limitations of time, staff and resources. The Report's failure to say more about the detail of proposed guidelines might be justifiable if plausible proposals were offered concerning the leadership, composition and authority of the body that would create them. None of these are discussed except hypothetically and no concrete proposals are offered. The Report merely loosely sketches

9

three possible mechanisms for developing guidelines. All contemplate the commission either as the Court of Appeal under a different name or under the effective control of the Court of Appeal.

Presumptive sentencing guidelines were first proposed by an American federal district court judge, Marvin Frankel. He was concerned that the absence of established rules governing judges' exercise of sentencing discretion inevitably produced unwarranted disparities and made sentences turn as much on the identity of the judge as on the crime and defendant. Frankel believed that development of sentencing guidelines would require the creation of specialised administrative agencies that could develop specialised expertise and institutional memories that legislatures cannot and, further, would be better insulated from short-term political pressures and better able to carry out ongoing programmes of research, evaluation and training.

Many sentencing commissions have been established in the United States and some have successfully functioned as Frankel suggested they might. More have failed, however, than have succeeded. All of the successful commissions have satisfied four conditions. The first two are managerial: they have had adequate material and personnel resources, and they have been ably led. The other two conditions are that judges have not been able to dominate the commission or the process, and that guideline-setting within the commission be accepted to be a political process. 'Political process' does not refer primarily to partisan politics, though these are unlikely to be absent from any governmental effort to develop sentencing policies, but to institutional and personal politics. These last two conditions go together and demonstrate why Halliday's proposals for guidelines and a commission are inadequate. If judges control the commission and are determined to protect practices and values widely admired by judges, little genuine political compromise is likely. Judges, prosecutors, defence lawyers, researchers, probation officers, prison officials and former offenders are all likely to have distinctive points of view and to attach greater and lesser importance to various issues, considerations and goals. All of these things need to be brought into the open and discussed and, where necessary, compromises need to be negotiated.

Judges tend to be less dissatisfied with sentencing than other people and often to be wedded to the belief that they have a unique understanding of sentencing issues. As a result, commissions comprised entirely or mostly of judges tend to attach great importance to preserving judicial discretion and less importance to the achievement of such goals as increased consistency and predictabilty, reduced disparities, successful implementation of new policies and resource management. And, when judges are in charge or are a majority of the commission, they are generally unprepared to engage in horse-trading to produce compromises. Thus Halliday's options of having the Court of Appeal in effect be the commission or of having a judicial or judicially selected commission are not unlike asking a fox to provide hen-house security. Judicial participation is essential to effective guideline development. Most successful commissions have included a sizeable minority judicial presence and many have had as chairs judges who had come to believe that sentencing needed changing. A chapter by one of us (Tonry) in this volume discusses these issues in more detail.

Commissions constituted, selected or led as Halliday proposed are unlikely to produce guidelines of the sort he envisioned. Should the decision be made to create a sentencing commission, there is plenty of experience elsewhere on which to draw.

Sentencing options

Halliday proposed a complete overhaul of sentencing options, repealing existing statutes and adopting a small number of flexible authorised sentences. Reasonable people will differ in how persuaded they are. Halliday linked sentence types to purposes and was unafraid to conclude that evidence for deterrent ('[T]here seems to be no link between marginal changes in punishment levels and changes in crime rates', p. 8) and incapacitative ('[T]he prison population would need to increase by around 15 per cent for a crime reduction of 1 per cent', p. 9) effects of sentences is weak. Mandatory life sentences and mandatory minimums were not considered and incapacitative sentences for dangerous offenders were assumed to be politically necessary. He considered and rejected, we think unwisely, the authorisation of sentences of intermittent (weekend, evening, discontinuous periods) confinement. He did not consider day fines but should have. One of us, but not the other, also thinks he unwisely rejected re-authorisation of suspended prison sentences.

A single new generic community punishment order would replace existing authority for probationary sentences, community service, drug treatment and testing orders and combination orders. Sentencers could tailor the conditions of community penalties to offenders' treatment needs and reoffending risks and would retain jurisdiction to revise those conditions as circumstances change. One of us believes the concept of a single sanction that can be adapted to individual circumstances is a clear improvement over existing policy. The other fears that a generic community order would lead to what Halliday calls 'condition creep' (Home Office 2001: 43), as sentencers are attracted to the possibilities offered by multiple conditions, and that it would be difficult to preserve proportionality limits, especially given the lack of meaningful limits proposed on the power to cumulate conditions.

Halliday proposed the use of short prison sentences of not longer than three months. His rationale is that retribution may require prison terms for some types of cases, but unless the case is so serious that a term of at least a year is needed, three months is long enough and sentences longer than three months can only damage offenders with no offsetting benefit. Since proposed longer prison sentences would be at least twelve months, of which half would be served in prison, Halliday would effectively forbid prison terms of three to six months time served.

Other prison sentences would be to 'custody-plus'. Three-month prison sentences could be, but need not be, augmented by a period of community supervision of up to nine additional months. Fifty per cent of longer prison sentences would be served in institutions and 50 per cent in the community. Judges would have the same discretion to set and alter individualised treatment, surveillant and punitive conditions for custody-plus sentences as for community penalties.

The political set-asides are as they are. Halliday characterised mandatory life and mandatory minimum sentences as outside his charge and fairly perfunctorily proposed incapacitative sentences for dangerous offenders. The latter are difficult to justify in principle.

Halliday might be faulted for lack of imagination concerning suspended prison sentences, intermittent confinement and day fines. Suspended prison sentences were dismissed because they have previously been unsuccessful, in the sense that judges dislike them and did not often impose them. Many continental European countries use suspended prison sentences extensively, to general satisfaction. We are of different minds about suspended prison sentences. One of us, working from the parsimonious premise that prison sentences should never be imposed when some other sanction will do, favours them as an almost ideal punishment for generally law-abiding persons who have committed a serious out-of-character crime. The prison sentence can express strong censure while the suspension spares unnecessary expense to the state and unnecessary damage to the low-risk offender and his or her loved ones. The other is concerned that the power to suspend a prison sentence could lead to discrimination in favour of affluent and middle-class offenders, and that, where a prison sentence is inappropriate, a community-based penalty should usually be used instead.

Intermittent confinement was rejected because Prison Service representatives vigorously opposed such arrangements on grounds of logistical impossibility: prisons are already crowded and budgets are stretched; the prisons, primarily rural, are in the wrong places to accommodate offenders, primarily urban. That Halliday was mistaken to defer to this view is demonstrated by the February 2002 calls by David Blunkett, backed by Prison Service head Martin Narey, for programmes of intermittent confinement. Switzerland uses such penalties heavily and has found that they satisfactorily balance state interests in imposing retributive punishments and avoiding unnecessary damage and disruption to offenders.

Finally, the rejection of day fines was predicated on the unhappy story of unit fines under the Criminal Justice Act 1991. There appears to be wide agreement that the unit-fine legislation was repealed too soon and for the wrong reasons. Particularly in a country that uses suspended prison sentences only exceptionally, there is a need for a retributive penalty for moderately serious crimes that do not require imprisonment (Faulkner 2001).

Judicial sentence review

Perhaps the most ambitious proposals in the Halliday Report call for a vast increase in judicial involvement in the oversight and implementation of community penalties and the community part of a custodial sentence. Halliday's Chapter 7 proposes a new 'sentence review function' in which courts would not only as now impose sentence but also deal with breaches of community sentences, hear appeals against recalls to prison, engage in pre-release planning of the conditions affecting prisoners when they are released after serving half of a prison sentence of a year or more, and review the performance of, and when necessary revise the terms of, community punishment orders (p. 49). Halliday suggests that it would be desirable for judges to oversee sentences they have imposed, though he recognises that this may often be impracticable.

This proposal is an acknowledgement of the logistical implications of a number of other ambitious proposals. Halliday supposes that a very substantially increased investment in treatment and surveillance can reduce reconviction rates by as much as 30 per cent (from the present 56 to 40 per cent). For this to happen, though, there will have to be substantial improvements in coordination between the Prison and Probation Services, and substantial investments in expanding the Probation Service. Judicial sentence review is meant to tie this all together and make it possible continuously to supervise offenders' progress and, drawing on professional correctional know-how and advice, to adapt sentence conditions as needed. The American drug courts, in which judges play roles not unlike that proposed by Halliday, may be a model, as, in a weaker form, may be drug treatment and testing orders.

At least as originally proposed, the judicial sentence review proposals are unworkable. One reason is cultural. English judges are much less accustomed than are American judges to being programme developers and entrepreneurs, and so may be less ready to take on the sentence review function and the new tasks it envisions. In addition, even though US drug courts have proliferated rapidly, and in 2001 existed in nearly 1,000 judicial districts, many of the judges who work in them are self-selected. When the time comes to replace the enthusiastic pioneers, it is often difficult to find others who wish to do so and there is widespread concern that the movement may suffer as a result (Gebelein 2000).

The English part-time lay magistracy creates another enormous obstacle. They impose more than two-thirds of sentences and yet most work only a few days a month. Continuity in magistral oversight of sentences would be logistically impossible. In addition, the greater complexity of continuously overseeing and adjusting sentences, compared with the substantial demands of imposing sentences in the first instance, would inevitably produce even greater inconsistency in magistral behaviour than sentencing now does.

The idea need not be abandoned, however. If sentence review were restricted to a small percentage of serious cases in which there were reasonable grounds for believing judicial sentence review might make the margin of difference, the participating judges could be restricted to volunteering District and Circuit Court judges. The American drug court experience shows that some judges derive great satisfaction from the rewards of participating in sentence review and having a part in helping people change their lives. A toe in the water may be the best law reform strategy here.

Next steps

Halliday's impressive report by itself does not show the way forward but has laid solid and useful foundations on which others can build. The proposals for the refashioning of English sentencing options, for the creation of a sentencing commission, for sentencing guidelines, for increased investment in treatment programmes and for improved coordination of effort between the Prison and Probation Services are important and constructive.

It appears, alas, that more preliminary work is needed if the main elements of Halliday's proposals are to be pursued. In relation to sentencing narrowly considered as what judges do, sentencing guidelines are the key innovation, but work on them cannot be started until plausible arrangements for the creation of a sentencing commission are in place. The sentencing commission, however, cannot seriously begin the work Halliday envisaged until the statutory framework of authorised sentences is in place. Sentencing guidelines encompassing newly recast sentences cannot be used until new programmes and facilities are in place. Judicial review of sentence implementation cannot effectively begin until coordinated programmes are in place.

Other than abandoning the momentum Halliday's Report created and continuing business as unsatisfactorily as usual, there appear to be two ways forward. The first is now to constitute a royal commission on sentencing and the penal system and ask it over 18–24 months to examine Halliday's proposals, to refine and build on those it believes have merit, and to propose concrete plans and schedules for effecting necessary legislative changes and implementing programme proposals.

The second is to work in parallel tracks, viewing guidelines as Halliday's core proposal and developing plausible plans for a commission to develop them, having the Home Office move legislative proposals forward for recasting the statutory sentencing framework and having the Prison and Probation Services continue their efforts at improved coordination and development of new programmes.

Neither way forward offers a high probability of success. Even if a royal commission did good work, its creation and operation would consume three or four years, and by then the moment may have passed when widespread sentiment supports a major overhaul of the sentencing and penal systems. And it might not get off the ground at all or do good work.

However, it is hard to imagine maintenance of momentum if authority is diffuse and each part of the system receives a general charge to improve itself. Under the best of circumstances the creation of a sentencing commission is risky (though the risk is of failure and waste of resources rather than of concrete harms). The political influence and power of the judiciary may just be too great to allow the creation of a successful sentencing commission. Even if that proves too pessimistic a view, many commissions appointed under reasonably congenial conditions have failed and this one would have a very large agenda. It would, for example, have to work simultaneously, with the Home Office, on refashioning the statutory framework and on the development of guidelines.

Our vote is for the appointment of a royal commission. Its prospects for success are far from certain and the danger of loss of momentum is inevitably present. Given, however, the likely resistance of the judiciary to major changes in how sentencing is carried out, the likelihood that Home Office attention will shift to other issues and the likelihood that business as usual will get in the way of the Prison and Probation Services' best-laid plans, the appointment of a royal commission gives better odds of success. If it fails, it fails. If it successfully builds on Halliday's solid foundations, it may show the way forward and revive the momentum necessary to get there.

Appendix: Sentencing project group – membership

Maureen Bateman	Magistrates' Association
Victoria Baum/Harry Carter	Legal Advisers' Branch, Home Office
Paul Cavadino	NACRO
Scott Dickinson	Audit Office
Pat Dowdeswell	Crime and Criminal Justice Unit, Home Office
Philip Geering	Crown Prosecution Service
Keir Hopley	Probation Unit, Home Office
Gill Mackenzie	Chair, ACOP
Michael Mettyear	Judge – Hull Combined Court Centre
Graham Parkinson	District Judge (Magistrates' Courts)
Icah Peart	Barrister
Paul Henderson	Economic Resource Analysis Unit, Home Office
Christine Stewart	Sentencing and Offences Unit, Home Office
Paul Stockton	Lord Chancellor's Department
Nicole Smith	Sentence Enforcement Unit, Prison Service
Michael Tonry	Institute of Criminology, Cambridge
Helen Tuffs	Treasury
Jim Barker McCardle	Assistant Chief Constable, Kent Constabulary

References

American Law Institute (1962) *Model Penal Code* (Proposed Official Draft). Philadelphia: American Law Institute.

Auld Report (2001) *Report of the Review of the Criminal Courts of England and Wales*. London: HMSO.

Faulkner, D. (2001) *Crime, State, and Citizen*. Winchester: Waterside.

Freiberg, A. (2001) 'Three Strikes and You're Out – It's Not Cricket: Colonization and Resistance in Australian Sentencing', in Tonry, M. and Frase, R. (eds), *Sentencing and Sanctions in Western Countries*. New York: Oxford University Press.

Gebelein, R. (2000) 'The Rebirth of Rehabilitation: Promise and Perils of Drug Courts', *Sentencing and Corrections: Issues for the 21st Century*, No. 6. US Department of Justice.

Hart, H.L.A. (1968) *Punishment and Responsibility: Essays in the Philosophy of Law*. Oxford: Oxford University Press.

Home Office (2001) *Making Punishments Work: Report of a Review of the Sentencing Framework for England and Wales*. London: Home Office Communications Directorate.

Morris, N. (1974) *The Future of Imprisonment*. Chicago: University of Chicago Press.

Morris, N. and Miller, M. (1985) 'Predictions of Dangerousness', in Tonry, M. (ed.), *Crime and Justice: An Annual Review of Research* (6). Chicago: University of Chicago Press.

Reitz, K. (2001) 'The Disassembly and Reassembly of U.S. Sentencing Practices', in Tonry, M. and Frase, R.S. (eds), *Sentencing and Sanctions in Western Countries*. New York: Oxford University Press.

Singer, R. (1979) *Just Deserts: Sentencing Based on Equality and Desert*. Cambridge, MA: Ballinger.

Tak, P. (2001) 'Sentencing and Punishment in the Netherlands', in Tonry, M. and Frase, R.S. (eds), *Sentencing and Sanctions in Western Countries*. New York: Oxford University Press.

Tonry, M. (1996) *Sentencing Matters*. New York: Oxford University Press.

US Sentencing Commission (1987) *Guidelines Manual*. Washington, DC: US Sentencing Commission.

von Hirsch, A. (1985) *Past or Future Crimes*. New Brunswick, NJ: Rutgers University Press.

Chapter 2

Public opinion and sentencing policy

Julian V. Roberts

Achieving a satisfactory level of public confidence is an important goal of sentencing, and the framework of sentencing needs to support that goal. (*Report of the Review of Sentencing Framework for England and Wales,* Home Office 2001: 1)

If state penal codes prescribe punishments well below public standards, then they should be re-written and brought into line with public opinion. (Bessette 1997: 71)

Introduction

The link between public opinion and sentencing policy can be situated within the broader context of the relationship between law and public opinion. That relationship has been explored in both directions: does the law influence public opinion, or do the views of the community determine the shape of criminal policy? Writers going back to Dicey at the beginning of the last century have discussed the ways in which legislation and opinion relate to one another. The aim of Dicey's review of the evolution of law and opinion in eighteenth- and nineteenth-century England was to understand the relation between 'legislation . . . and the varying currents of public opinion'. His research led him to conclude that 'The true importance, indeed, of laws lies far less in their direct result than in their effect upon the sentiment or convictions of the public' (Dicey 1914/1962: 43).[1]

In addition to specific legislation, the criminal law influences public opinion in a number of ways. Andenaes (1971), for example, discusses the moral or educative influence of the criminal law, by which public attitudes towards crimes are shaped by factors other than the fear of legal punishment. Individual sentencing decisions, according to some views, are also aimed at changing public attitudes. Indeed, one view of sentencing holds that 'the main duty of the court [in sentencing] is to *lead* public opinion' (*R*. v. *Sargeant*, 1974, emphasis in original). The sentence conveys to the public a sense of the wrongfulness of the criminal conduct, and perhaps the degree of culpability of the offender.

There is a clear connection between community sentiment and sentencing policy, although the nature and strength of the relationship varies from country to country. Public opinion is often cited by politicians as a justification for introducing sentencing reforms, particularly punitive legislation. By showing that they are 'doing something' about rising crime and lenient sentencing, politicians may reap some electoral benefit therefrom (see Beckett 1997; Roberts *et al.* 2002). For this reason, they are quick to cite public support for tougher sentencing proposals such as mandatory sentences. However, the 'research' politicians typically use is mail from 'concerned constituents' or unrepresentative polls rather than the results of scientific surveys.

A recent example of the link between public opinion and sentencing policy relates to the mandatory sentencing laws in the Australian Northern Territories. Prime Minister Burke stated that 'he was not surprised at the overwhelming support [Australians] have shown for the introduction of mandatory sentencing laws in their state' (Burke 2000), and added that: 'The poll figures justify the government's decision to stand firm against a campaign to scrap the Territory's laws.' The Minister concluded: 'The public want sentencing to reflect community attitudes . . .'[2] In England and Wales, the former Home Secretary Michael Howard made the link between public opinion and sentencing policy when he introduced his package of proposals for harsher sentencing. Mr Howard stated that his reforms were 'vital if public confidence in the criminal justice system is to be maintained'.[3]

Outline of chapter

The purpose of this chapter is to describe the current state of public opinion regarding sentencing and to draw some conclusions about the effectiveness of employing statutory reforms to increase public confidence in the courts. Throughout the chapter I draw upon research from several common law jurisdictions. I do not deal with the way in which to incorporate the views of the public into sentencing policy, although there is a literature on this thorny issue (see Freiberg 2001; Lovegrove

1998; Tomaino 1997 for further discussion). Nor do I review the voluminous literature on the media coverage of crime and punishment, although clearly the media play an important role in shaping public perceptions.

The first section below reviews the limited evidence pertaining to the relationship between sentencing practices and public opinion: are judges affected by community views? In the next section I summarise findings from the international literature on public knowledge and opinion regarding sentencing. In the third section I review the specific statutory reform proposals of the Home Office Sentencing Review. With respect to the Sentencing Review's Report, this chapter poses two questions. First, is the assumption that sentencing reforms can affect public opinion justified? Second, even if this assumption were correct, will the specific reforms laid out in the report actually increase public faith in the sentencing process?

To anticipate the conclusions, I respond to both questions in the negative. In my view there are important limits on the ability of the sentencing process to influence public confidence and difficult questions to be answered about the propriety of attempting to promote public confidence by modifying the statutory framework of sentencing. The experience in other jurisdictions indicates that statutory reforms have little impact on public views of sentencing. In addition, it is not clear, on the basis of the extant public opinion literature, that the Review's proposals in this regard are in fact consistent with the views of the public. The chapter concludes with a brief discussion of specific strategies with which to respond to the long-standing crisis in public confidence in sentencing.

Report of the Home Office Sentencing Review

The Sentencing Review Report (Home Office 2001) emerges in an atmosphere of widespread public criticism of the sentencing process. Indeed, a central aim of the Review's proposals is to increase public confidence in the courts. These proposals include a more systematic attempt to explain sentencing to the public and a modification of the statutory principles of sentencing to make them more consistent with community expectations. If these proposals are enacted, the role of an offender's criminal history will become more important. The Review argues that this change is consistent with public support for a more utilitarian sentencing framework and public intolerance for crime committed by recidivists.[4]

The Sentencing Review Report is permeated with references to the importance of public opinion in sentencing. For example, it is noted that the proposed changes to the sentencing framework 'should increase the contribution of sentencing to . . . public confidence' (Home Office 2001: i). Thus the Review makes the assumption that modifying the sentencing framework can affect public confidence in sentencing. In discussing the costs and benefits of the proposals, the Report notes that 'the framework is intended to *earn and deserve public confidence*' (Home Office 2001: 63, emphasis added).

The clear implication of these quotes is that the public does not fully share the just deserts philosophy underlying sentencing at the present time, and that modifying the current Act to promote crime prevention considerations will increase confidence in the courts. Finally, the Review ties its reform recommendations specifically to the views of the public when it notes in the report that: 'The Review's assessment of public views on how sentencing should operate has informed its recommendations for a new framework' (Home Office 2001: ii).

The current Home Secretary appears to share the Review's concern regarding public opinion. In his first major speech touching upon the proposals, he placed the issue of public opinion front and centre by referring to public frustration with sentencing and stating he was 'determined to hammer out what they deserve . . . because public confidence is the key. The law must reflect the will of the people . . . we need genuine trust and confidence in the criminal justice system as a whole, and in sentencing policy in particular' (Blunkett 2001: paragraph 41).[5] He has also stated that there has been 'a serious loss of public confidence in the system. And that confidence must be re-gained' (Blunkett 2001).

Increasing public confidence: goal or consequence?

The position taken by the Home Office Review report makes a striking contrast with the other major Review of the Criminal Courts undertaken by Lord Justice Auld. The Auld Report published the same year as the Halliday Report argues that 'Public confidence is not so much an aim of a good criminal justice system, but a consequence of it' (2001: 18), and further: 'public confidence is not an end in itself . . . if public ignorance stands in the way of public confidence, take steps adequately to demonstrate to the public that it is so' (2001: 106).

Influence of public opinion on sentencing practices

There are two important questions to be addressed with respect to the influence of public views on sentencing practices. First, what statutory authority or case law precedent exists for these views to affect the nature or quantum of punishment? And second, even if the propriety of incorporating public opinion were beyond dispute, how accurate are judicial perceptions of community views of punishment? Judges do not have the time to keep abreast of even opinion surveys on sentencing, let alone the scholarly literature. As has been pointed out by a number of writers (e.g. Lovegrove 1998; Walker 1985), judicial perceptions are probably even more informal and unsystematic than those of politicians. Their interpretations are likely to be at odds with reality, and to vary considerably from court to court.

If politicians are sensitive to the views of the public, can the same be said for judges? Are sentencing patterns influenced by judicial perceptions of public opinion? The link must be speculative, since few reported judgements – and no systematic research – has demonstrated that sentencing practices are affected by evolving public attitudes (or judicial perception of these attitudes). A number of scholars nevertheless accept that judges attempt to incorporate public opinion in their sentencing decisions. As Nigel Walker observed: 'In theory, sentencing decisions are influenced only by officially approved considerations, whether embodied in statute, practice direction, case-law or circular. In real life most sentencers admit to having some regard to what they believe to be public opinion' (Walker 1985: 64).

There is some evidence, however, that judges are not totally immune to the force of public opinion. First, a number of senior members of the British judiciary have suggested that judges need to consider public attitudes. In 1997, for example, the Lord Chief Justice observed that he did 'not consider it would be right, even if it were possible, for judges to ignore the opinion of the public' (Lord Bingham 1997).

Second, Home Office research (1998) suggests that judicial practice has in the past been influenced by community sentiment. This study examined fluctuations in the incarceration rate in England and Wales over a sustained period of time. A sharp increase in committals to custody occurred shortly after the murder of James Bulger in 1993. It is possible that the widespread public outcry and media coverage of the murder (and another murder at the same time) may have encouraged judges to become more punitive. This conclusion must be very tentative, however, as other explanations for the shift are always possible in a correlational design of this kind.[6]

Finally, there is some research evidence that judges in other common law jurisdictions are affected by public opinion, at least when considering the imposition of sanctions which may provoke public criticism. This has been demonstrated in Canada, a country which, like England

and Wales, has a staunchly independent judiciary. Canada recently created a new alternative sanction to imprisonment. The conditional sentence is effectively a term of imprisonment which the offender serves in the community, similar to the suspended term of imprisonment in England and Wales.

Unlike the English sanction, the Canadian conditional sentence has generated great public concern, as some judges have imposed it in serious cases of violence, including rape and manslaughter. Offenders convicted of these offences have been permitted to serve long custodial sentences at home, under minimal conditions. A national survey found that four-fifths of the judges stated that they considered the views of the public before imposing a conditional sentence (see Roberts, Doob and Marinos 2000). Unless Canadian judges are quite unlike their British counterparts in this respect, it is likely that the English judiciary are, to some degree, influenced by their perceptions of the views of the public.[7]

Similar trends appear to exist elsewhere. For example, George Zdenkowski (2000) cites a guideline judgement in New South Wales that notes 'The courts must show that they are responsible to public criticism of the outcome of sentencing practices'. Zdenkowksi concludes that 'there is evidence of an increasing desire by the courts to take account of public opinion' (2000: 68).

Public knowledge and opinion about sentencing

The attention to public views of sentencing is long overdue, for the crisis of confidence confronting us now has been around for many years (see Cavadino and Dignan 1992). The research on public attitudes is summarised elsewhere, but a few key findings bear repeating in the present context. First, criticism of the judiciary is founded upon perceptions of leniency in sentencing. Fully twenty years ago, a representative poll found that approximately two-thirds of the public in the United Kingdom believed that sentences were too lenient, and almost as many people were of the view that tougher sentencing would result in less crime (reported in Hough and Moxon 1988). The most recent survey to pose this question was conducted by the Home Office Review, and found that 74 per cent of the British public believed that sentences were too lenient (Home Office 2001: 112).

In 1997, the British Crime Survey (BCS) included a module devoted to sentencing, and the results were revealing. The questions explored both public *knowledge* of sentencing practices as well as public *opinion* regarding sentencing and the judiciary (see Hough and Roberts 1998, 1999 for further details). Some of these findings were replicated in subsequent sweeps of the BCS (e.g. Mattinson and Mirrlees-Black 1998) as well as the public opinion research conducted for the Home Office Review in 2000 (see Home Office 2001: appendix 5).

- Most respondents underestimated the severity of sentences imposed. For example, over half the sample provided estimates of the incarceration rate for rape that were much too low. Other research has found that people have little knowledge of the sentencing process in general; for example, they are unaware of the statutory maximum penalties or minimum penalties.

- Most respondents also had little knowledge of sentencing options; for example, only a third of the public were able to identify probation as a sanction.

- Four out of five members of the public thought that sentences were too lenient, and over half responded that they were 'much too lenient'.

- An even higher proportion (82 per cent) thought that judges were out of touch, and only 20 per cent felt that judges were doing a good job. Judges received the poorest 'ratings' of all criminal justice professions; by contrast two-thirds of the public rated the police as doing a good job. It is worth noting that public evaluations of judges are more negative in the United Kingdom than in other countries.

Public knowledge of sentencing has been in a parlous state for some time now. A poll conducted for the BBC over 40 years ago found that less than 2 per cent of polled public had any idea of the number of people in prison (Silvey 1961). Fifteen years later another poll found that only one quarter of the public in Britain was able to generate an estimate of the number of people in prison (Banks *et al.* 1975). These specific questions have not been replicated recently, but it is unlikely that the result would be much different today.

The British public are not unique in this regard; opinion surveys conducted in other western countries have found the same results: most people are cynical with regard to their courts, favour tougher sentencing[8] and subscribe to a number of misperceptions about sentencing and parole.[9] (For reviews of the international literature, see Hough and Roberts 2002; Cullen, Fisher and Applegate 2000; Kury and Ferdinand 1999;[10] Roberts and Stalans 1997.) Finally, although the question has not attracted a great deal of research, it is clear that many of the attitudes (and particularly the misperceptions) about sentencing are held with a great deal of conviction by members of the public. As Leslie Wilkins once observed, 'the degree of confidence with which views are expressed tends to be inversely proportional to the quality of knowledge' (Wilkins 1974: 84).

Attitudinal stasis

Perceptions of crime and fear of victimisation

One of the most robust findings in the international public opinion literature is that public perceptions of crime trends rarely accord with either police statistics or victimisation surveys. Even after almost a decade of declining crime rates, the majority of people in the US and Canada persisted in believing that crime was increasing. For example, after six years of declining crime rates, four out of five Canadians still believed that crime rates were on the rise. The most recent survey conducted in the US (in 1998) found that more than half the public thought that there had been an increase in crime over the previous year, when in reality crime rates had fallen across the country (Maguire and Pastore 1999).

The same stability can be observed for public responses to surveys that measure fear of criminal victimisation. Pollsters in America have asked the following question for over 25 years now: 'Is there anywhere in your neighbourhood where you would be afraid to walk for fear of becoming a crime victim?' Although this period has seen striking changes in crime trends, levels of public fear of crime have been quite stable. In 1974, 45 per cent of the polled public responded affirmatively to this question; 20 years later the figure was 47 per cent. Mark Warr (1995) summarises these trends by noting that 'the most striking feature of fear trends is the relative constancy of fear during the past two decades' (p. 297).

Attitudes towards sentence severity

A similar kind of stasis of belief appears to characterise public attitudes towards the severity of sentencing. The experience in the US may well carry lessons for the current discussion underway in England and Wales. Throughout the 1980s and 1990s, sentencing and parole policies became more punitive as a result of changes to sentencing guideline ranges, the passage of mandatory sentencing legislation, including the 'three strikes' statutes at the federal and state levels, and a move towards 'truth in sentencing' laws which increase the proportion of custodial sentences that offenders spend in prison (see Tonry 1996).

25

These policies were responsible for a 70 per cent increase in the US prison population over the decade 1989–99 (Pastore and Maguire 2000: table 6.26).

Notwithstanding this shift to more punitive sentencing, the American public continued to express the view that sentences were too lenient. In fact, the percentage of respondents endorsing the view that the courts are too lenient has not fallen below 70 per cent or risen above 85 per cent between 1971 and 1998 (see Cullen, Fisher and Applegate 2000: figure 2; Maguire and Pastore 1999; Roberts 1992: figure 1). Since crime rates have changed considerably (having risen and then fallen) and sentencing/parole policies have become harsher, these potential influences cannot be responsible for the steady-state nature of public views. The most probable cause of the perpetual perception of leniency is news media coverage of crime and sentencing (see Ashworth and Hough 1996: 779).

The lesson from the US seems clear: promoting public confidence should not be used to justify changes to sentencing policy, as changes to date have had little if any impact on public perceptions. The solution to the problem of public opposition to the courts lies elsewhere, in increasing the transmission of information and perhaps ensuring greater transparency with respect to judicial decision-making, suggestions to which I shall return later in this chapter.

Canadian data on public attitudes to sentencing tell the same story. In 1986, 61 per cent of the public held the view that sentences were too lenient. A major (and well-publicised) sentencing reform was undertaken several years later. The reforms aimed to make sentencing more rational, and more consistent (Roberts and Cole 1999). In 1999, a survey revealed that 69 per cent of the public believed that sentences were too lenient. The percentage expressing this view has changed little over the past 25 years: in 1974, 66 per cent believed sentences were too lenient (see Roberts and Doob 1989: table 1).

The trends in British public perceptions of judicial leniency show a similar pattern. In 1987, just over 70 per cent of the polled public believed that sentences were too lenient (Dowds 1994). A decade later, during which the prison population escalated considerably, the figure had risen to four-fifths (Hough and Roberts 1998), and, as noted, the latest poll found 74 per cent of the polled public held this view (Home Office 2001). Tracking over time the percentage of the British public who believe the courts are too lenient produces the same relatively flat line that emerges from the American data (Dowds 1994). Clearly, public perceptions of sentence severity have little to do with actual trends in the punitiveness of the courts.

Effect of mandatory sentencing on public confidence in the criminal justice system

Further evidence of the intransigence of public opinion in the face of sentencing reform comes from England and Wales. According to section 111 of the Powers of the Criminal Court (Sentences) Act 2000, the Crown Court must impose a sentence of imprisonment of at least three years if the offender has been convicted of two previous domestic burglaries and is now convicted of a third such offence. This quasi-mandatory[11] sentence thus creates a recidivist premium for domestic burglars. In an all too rare test of public awareness of sentencing, the 1998 British Crime Survey asked respondents whether they were aware of the new sentencing provision. Unsurprisingly, only a quarter of the sample responded affirmatively. Whatever their penological merit (in terms of deterrence or denunciation), severe mandatory penalties cannot be effective if they are not publicised. Fear of the unknown may deter tourists from visiting exotic destinations, but it will not deter potential offenders from committing crime.

The same BCS posed a subsequent question on this issue. After having been told about this new mandatory sentence, respondents were asked whether they had more or less confidence in the sentencing process. Only 18 per cent of respondents stated that they had a 'lot more confidence' in the criminal justice system as a result of learning about the mandatory sentence. Almost half the sample (48 per cent) responded that the existence of this penalty would either not change, or even lower their level of confidence in the system. The most frequent response was that the mandatory sentence would not affect the respondent's level of confidence (British Crime Survey 1998). This finding further suggests that changing sentencing policies may have little impact on levels of public confidence in the courts (see Roberts 2002a for further discussion).

Effects of specific sentences, specific maxima on public perceptions

If statutory reforms appear to have little effect on public evaluations of the sentencing process in general, do specific sentences affect public opinion in any way? A few years ago, Nigel Walker conducted some research to test the 'expressive' function of sentencing (Walker and Marsh 1988). The hypothesis, derived from the Sergeant judgment, was that individual sentences can influence public perception by changing public evaluations of the seriousness of the crimes for which they are imposed.

Walker used experimental manipulations to explore the effects that the severity of particular sentences had on public attitudes to the

27

offences for which they were imposed. The results were clear – and negative: subjects' disapproval ratings were unaffected by the severity of sentences. Professor Walker summarised this line of research in the following terms: 'The results did not provide any support for the belief that disapproval levels ... were raised or lowered by information about the sentence or about the judge's views' (Walker 1985: 102).

Similar findings emerged in Canada with respect to the effect of maximum penalties on public views of the seriousness of crimes. Experimental manipulation of the severity of the penalty had no effect on public ratings of the seriousness of specific crimes (Roberts 1988). For example, public ratings of the seriousness of a crime such as impaired driving were not influenced by the magnitude of the maximum penalty possible for a conviction (thereby undermining one of the arguments traditionally advanced against lowering the maximum penalties to more reasonable levels of severity).

Summary

The portrait of public opinion that emerges from this body of research is that public views of the sentencing process are generally unaffected by policy changes. If neither the punitive reforms in America nor the proportionality-based, restraint-inspired Canadian reforms have affected public attitudes towards the courts, it seems unlikely the latest proposals in the United Kingdom will improve British confidence in the courts. Public views of the seriousness of specific offences do not seem to be affected by the severity of actual or theoretical sentences. The solutions to changing public opinion in this critical area must lie elsewhere.

At this point I turn to the specific proposals advanced by the Sentencing Review Report, and the extent to which they are likely to promote public confidence in sentencing.

Home Office Sentencing Review proposals and the views of the public

What are the consequences for the recent sentencing proposals advanced by the Home Office Sentencing Review? First, it seems unlikely that the Review's proposals are going to have an important impact on public confidence in the courts, simply because no reform has had much success in this regard. In addition, the Review's proposals are not simplistic and cannot be easily conveyed to the public. The shift to a more record-driven sentencing process is accomplished by modifying the principles of sentencing. This involves transforming the concept of proportionate sentencing (see Home Office 2001: 13–14).

The Home Office report suggests that in addition to the gulf between the practice of the courts and the sentencing preferences of the public, there is also a philosophical divide with respect to the principles of sentencing. If this is the case, making sentencing harsher will have only a limited effect on public confidence. Modifying the structure of sentencing will be necessary to instil greater confidence in the courts, and the report suggests that this should be accomplished by increasing the importance of the criminal record. Is this likely?

Appendix 5 of the report presents results from opinion surveys and suggests that public opinion is squarely behind utilitarian sentencing: 'The general public are very clear about what they want sentencing to achieve: a reduction in crime' (Home Office 2001: 108). The source of this conclusion is a public survey in which respondents were asked to indicate their support for one of seven purposes of sentencing. Results revealed that the option of 'changing the offender's behaviour' attracted the highest percentage of respondents.

Two difficulties arise with the Review's interpretation of these data. First, proportional sentencing was not one of the sentencing purposes which respondents were asked to consider; the options of 'punish' and 'express society's disapproval' cannot be used as adequate surrogates for proportionality-based sentencing. Second, public opinion research in a number of jurisdictions has demonstrated that although all sentencing purposes appeal to members of the public, the just deserts principle of proportionality emerges as being most important.

Public support for different sentencing aims

For example, Walker, Hough and Lewis (1988) report the findings from a British Crime Survey in which respondents were asked to identify the principal aim of sentencing. Incapacitation was cited by 29 per cent of the sample, and individual deterrence by one-third. However, the just deserts response alternative attracted significantly more support: it was identified by 41 per cent of respondents (Walker, Hough and Lewis 1988: table 10.2; see also Hough, Lewis and Walker 1988: table 11.5). This suggests that incapacitation is an important but not *the* most important consideration for the public.

Gerber and Engelhardt-Greer (1996) asked respondents to identify the most important sentencing purpose and found much stronger public support for retribution (51 per cent) than for rehabilitation (21 per cent), incapacitation or deterrence (both of which attracted the support of 13 per cent of the sample). In the most recent test of public support for competing sentencing aims, Darley, Carlsmith and Robinson (2000) examined the sentencing preferences of subjects and concluded that 'the rated likelihood of recidivism ... *did not contribute significantly to the severity of the sentences assigned*' (emphasis added) and further: 'severity of the sentence assigned was determined by the respondents' perceptions of the seriousness of the offence and the degree of moral outrage the offence provoked, those variables highlighted by a just deserts stance on sentencing' (p. 676). This finding replicates a number of earlier studies that reached the same conclusion: when asked directly, the public appear very concerned about recidivism, but their actual sentencing preferences are in reality guided more by desert considerations[12] (e.g. Roberts and Gebotys 1987; Warr, Meier and Erickson 1983).[13]

Relative importance of sentencing factors

The other branch of support for the Sentencing Review's position that the public wish to see a greater role assigned to an offender's criminal record comes from responses to a survey cited in the Review's report in which members of the public were asked to identify the 'factors that should have a great deal of influence on a sentence' (Home Office 2001: appendix, figure 4). Clearly, criminal history is an important consideration for the public: an offender's previous convictions headed the list of factors which included items such as the age of the offender and the cost of the sentence to the taxpayer. However, the just deserts option of 'crime seriousness' was not offered to respondents. When respondents are asked to consider sentencing factors that include crime seriousness *and* criminal record, the former proves to be much more important than the latter.

For example, in the study conducted for the Sentencing Advisory Panel by Russell and Morgan (2001), British respondents were asked to consider a range of aggravating factors for the offence of domestic burglary, including the fact that the offender was 'persistent'. The three sentencing factors that attracted most support from the public were all related to crime seriousness and unrelated to the offender's criminal history: the extent of force used, the degree of injury to the victim, the extent of the trauma to the victim and the damage to the home (i.e. whether it had been vandalised). Indeed, persistence was absent from the group of factors perceived by the public to warrant the greatest degree of aggravation (see Russell and Morgan 2001). This finding is consistent with earlier research. In the only other exploration of public opinion regarding the relative importance of sentencing factors, the extent of the offender's record was less important to the public than other factors such as the extent of harm to the victim, a factor relating to the seriousness of the crime (Roberts 1988: table 21).

The question, then, is not whether the public favour harsher sentencing for recidivists than first offenders (they undoubtedly do support such a policy), but whether the shift to a record-driven sentencing system with its concomitant loss of proportionality (see von Hirsch 2002) is likely to increase public confidence in the sentencing process.

Of course, at the end of the day, even if the public do favour a model of sentencing which accords greater weight to an offender's previous convictions than the seriousness of the crime, their support is founded upon a belief that such a model is likely to achieve significant reductions in crime or reconviction rates. If a reformulated sentencing system does not achieve these reductions, levels of public confidence are likely to sink still further.

To summarise, there is little reason to believe that increasing the importance of an offender's criminal record at the expense of the desert principle of proportionality is going to achieve higher levels of public confidence in the sentencing process.

Responding to the crisis in public confidence

What can be done to address the crisis in public confidence? The Home Office Review report identifies a number of important steps to improve levels of public knowledge of, and subsequently confidence, in the courts. The time is certainly ripe to undertake a major initiative in this direction; such a step has been advocated by researchers (e.g. Hough 1996). In the remainder of this chapter, I can only sketch some ideas with respect to what is the most important element of the problem. The research evidence that has accumulated from several countries suggests that increasing public knowledge about sentencing is critical. It is curious that although criminal justice expenditures in western nations are substantial, almost nothing is spent on public legal education with respect to sentencing and parole.

Any hope of promoting public confidence in the sentencing process lies in dissipating, or at least addressing, public misconceptions about sentencing and setting in train mechanisms to address public concern and widespread media coverage of high-profile cases. The Sentencing

Review Report makes some innovative and timely recommendations in this regard. (For a description of the original research on this point conducted by the Sentencing Review, see Appendix 5 of the Report.)

In light of the highly restricted access to sentencing decisions and sentencing statistics, distorted media coverage of sentencing and the inherently complex nature of the process, it is unlikely that the public will ever have a very accurate understanding of sentencing. The best that can be hoped is that people will have a more realistic appreciation of the sentencing process, and this may involve conveying a limited number of important messages, of which the following are examples:

- that attrition in the criminal justice system means that there are clear limits on the ability of the sentencing process to affect aggregate crime rates;

- that relative to other western nations, sentencers in England and Wales are not particularly lenient;

- that sentences of imprisonment do generally adhere to proportionality requirements which are central to public conceptions of sentencing;

- that sentences of imprisonment are affected by parole not exclusively for the benefit of the offender but because graduated release offers better hopes for preventing further offending;

- that community punishments can carry meaningful consequences for the offender;

- that violation of community punishments results in a vigorous response from the courts.

The challenge of course is to devise a mechanism by which objective statements about sentencing can be effectively conveyed to a mass audience.

As well, there is a clear need to create a mechanism to explain atypical sentences to the public. The Sentencing Advisory Panel has identified the promotion of public confidence as one of its activities, and perhaps there is the possibility of greater public legal education in the area by means of the Panel's website and related publications. Another possibility is the creation of an information service attached to the Crown Prosecution Service. Is it possible that the CPS can provide information about a case once the statutory period of appeal of conviction or sentence has elapsed? A more aggressive attempt to publicise and disseminate reasons for sentences may help diffuse some public anger in cases in which important mitigating factors resulted in a sentence that had the appearance of leniency.

Sentencing guidelines

The Home Office Review of sentencing has recommended the creation of sentencing guidelines for England and Wales. Promulgation of such guidelines would undoubtedly increase the clarity of sentencing practices and help the public reach an informed opinion about whether a particular sentence is within the appropriate range. Guidelines should also promote confidence in the consistency of sentencing in England and Wales. The danger associated with such a step is that it may lead to public pressure to make the guidelines harsher; this has been the experience in some of the state-wide American guideline systems.

Truth in sentencing

The concept of truth in sentencing has acquired a reputation for punitiveness as a result of American legislation which creates 'flat time' sentences of imprisonment, or which requires offenders to serve almost all the sentence in custody. However, there is a more benign form of truth in sentencing which argues that public confidence would be promoted by making the language (and structure) of sentencing more honest. Two examples will suffice for the purposes of illustration. Almost all offenders convicted of murder in England and Wales will be released within 20 years. The label 'life imprisonment' creates an unrealistic expectation among the public of detention until death, a reality for only a very small number of the most notorious cases. If the sentence were described as a 'life sentence' and the parole provisions spelled out more clearly to the public, penal practice may not seem so inconsistent with community views.[14]

Several of the Home Office report's recommendations will result in the sentencing process becoming more transparent and hence comprehensible to the public. For example, the current confusing collection of different court orders will be replaced by a single 'community punishment order'. This has the potential to create a viable and comprehensive alternative to incarceration for the less serious cases which now result in the custody of the offender.

There is also a need to address features of the sentencing framework which create false public expectations. The statutory maxima, for example, are so far from the sentences imposed in courts that they raise false expectations among members of the public. The result is that almost any sentence imposed will appear derisory in light of the theoretical maximum. A review (and revision) of the maximum penalty structure along the lines of that which was proposed by the Advisory Council on the Penal System (in 1978) may well have significant benefits in terms of public. Neither of these proposals is about making sentencing tougher, but rather about introducing greater clarity or transparency into the sentencing process.

Educating policy-makers and criminal justice professionals

Finally, as the Home Office Sentencing Review Report notes,[15] any response to the crisis in public confidence should also address the other part of the equation. Educating the public is only part of the solution; it is also necessary to ensure that policy-makers, politicians and indeed judges too have access to the scholarly literature on public opinion and sentencing. A continued reliance on single questions from opinion polls will just confirm the stereotype that the public are more punitive than the courts. The limited literature on the issue suggests that policy-makers have distorted views of the true nature of public opinion, and ascribe more punitive attitudes to the public than is in fact the case. For example, McGarrell and Sandys (1996) found that Indiana legislators overestimated the extent of public support for capital punishment.[16]

A wealth of research on public attitudes to crime and punishment has by now accumulated in many jurisdictions, yet how much of this research has permeated the political consciousness? A pessimistic response would be that the literature has not moved beyond the confines of scholarly journals and academic conferences. Perhaps, then, the time has also come for academics to attempt to convey the results of their research directly to policy-makers, who may not have the time to comb through professional journals in order to ascertain the true tenor of public attitudes towards sentencing.

Notes

1 George Sumner took a different view of the law–opinion relationship, arguing that 'Stateways cannot change folkways', and that 'Acts of legislation come out of the mores' (1906: 55). Sumner argued that legislation is an *effect*, rather than a *cause* of public opinion.
2 The poll to which the minister referred was in fact an unrepresentative, unscientific newspaper 'survey', in which interested readers were asked to express their views on the issue.

3 See Ashworth and Hough (1996).

4 For commentary on the substantive changes proposed by the Review, see Roberts (2002b) and von Hirsch (2002).

5 There are in fact no fewer than ten references to public opinion or public confidence in sentencing in the Home Secretary's relatively brief speech.

6 The interpretation that judges responded to public opinion has other weaknesses too. Why, for example, would judges become more punitive towards *adult* offenders, when the murder was committed by *juveniles*? Is it plausible that a sufficient number of judges would simultaneously become sensitive to the views of the public to create the pattern captured in the graph? Finally, is it not reasonable to suggest that judges might revert to previous practices once the public outcry diminished? No such pattern has been observed.

7 It might be expected that elected judges are more susceptible to community opinion. However, the American research on this question has produced equivocal results, with some researchers finding that elected judges were influenced by shifts in public opinion (e.g. Glick and Pruet 1985).

8 It is also true that the polls on sentence severity fail to capture the subtleties of public attitudes towards punishment, and tend to misrepresent the public as being more punitive than they really are when confronted with specific cases or when provided with sufficient information (and time) to come to an informed judgement (see Ashworth and Hough 1996; Cullen *et al.* 2000; Roberts and Stalans 1997; Zamble and Kalm 1990; Zander and Henderson 1993). For the purposes of this chapter, I am simply using these polls to document the existence of a crisis of confidence in the sentencing process.

9 It should be pointed out that sentencing is far from the only issue which confuses the public. A recent poll conducted on behalf of the Cancer Research Campaign in the UK found that more than half the respondents subscribed to a number of myths about cancer; most male respondents, for example, believed that cancer was contagious. Surveys of Americans on other important social issues generate similar results. Delli Carpini and Keeter (1992) summarise the results from a political survey by noting that 'even when confronted with an issue of obvious significance [the Gulf War] and interest to most citizens, the amount of information collected and held by many of them is relatively small' (p. 30).

10 Kury and Ferdinand (1999) demonstrate that these trends with respect to public opinion are not restricted to the public in common law jurisdictions.

11 Unlike some mandatory sentencing provisions in other jurisdictions, there is an 'escape clause'. The court may impose a lesser sentence if it finds that there are particular circumstances which would make a three-year sentence unjust.

12 Some of these surveys involved non-British samples of respondents. However, there is no evidence that public support for sentencing purposes varies greatly between western nations.

13 These researchers approached the issue of public support from another direction: they examined correlations between the severity of public sentences and measures of the various sentencing purposes. The most powerful predictor of sentence severity in both studies was the seriousness of the offence, supporting the position that the just deserts sentencing philosophy underlies public sentencing preferences. The advantage of this method is that the public's sentencing model is derived from their actual sentencing decisions, rather than from a question which may reflect mere familiarity with different purposes, or may reflect the nature of options presented to respondents.

14 The Sentencing Review's public opinion research found strong support for the principle of truth in sentencing (see Home Office 2001: 113).

15 See Home Office (2001: 10).

16 For example, McGarrell and Sandys (1996); Riley and Rose (1980). This research is summarised in Roberts (1992: 157–8).

References

Advisory Council on the Penal System (1978) *Sentences of Imprisonment – A Review of Maximum Penalties. Report of the Advisory Council on the Penal System.* London: HMSO.

Andenaes, J. (1971) 'The Moral or Educative Influence of Criminal Law', *Journal of Social Issues*, 27, 17–31.

Ashworth, A. and Hough, M. (1996) 'Sentencing and the Climate of Public Opinion', *Criminal Law Review*, November, 776–87.

Auld, Lord Justice (2001) *Review of the Criminal Courts of England and Wales.* London: Stationery Office.

Banks, C., Maloney, E. and H. Willcock (1975) 'Public Attitudes to Crime and the Penal System', *British Journal of Criminology*, 15, 228–40.

Beckett, K. (1997) 'Political Preoccupation with Crime Leads, Not Follows, Public Opinion', *Overcrowded Times*, 85, 1–9.

Bessette, J. (1997) 'In Pursuit of Criminal Justice', *The Public Interest*, 129, 61–92.

Blunkett, D. (2001) *Speech by the Home Secretary on Sentencing Reform.* National Probation Service Conference, 5 July 2001. (Available from Home Office website.)

British Crime Survey (1998) Data tables available from the author.

Burke, D. (2000) *Press Release: Australians Support NT Laws.* 8 March.

Cavadino, M. and Dignan, J. (1992) *The Penal System: An Introduction*, 2nd edn. London: Sage.

Cullen, F., Fisher, B. and Applegate, B. (2000) 'Public Opinion about Punishment and Corrections', in Tonry, M. (ed.), *Crime and Justice: A Review of Research.* Chicago: University of Chicago Press.

Darley, J., Carlsmith, K. and Robinson, P. (2000) 'Incapacitation and Just Deserts as Motives for Punishment', *Law and Human Behavior*, 24, 659–83.

Delli Carpini, M. and Keeter, S. (1992) 'The Public's Knowledge of Politics', in Kennamer, D. (ed.), *Public Opinion, the Press and Public Policy*. Westport, CT: Praeger.

Dicey, A.V. (1914/1962). *Lectures on the Relation between Law and Public Opinion in England during the Nineteenth Century*. 2nd edn. London: Macmillan.

Dowds, L. (1994) *The Long-Eyed View of Law and Order: A Decade of British Social Attitudes Survey Results*. London: Home Office.

Freiberg, A. (2001) *Sentencing Review 2001*. Melbourne: Department of Justice.

Gerber, J. and Engelhardt-Greer, S. (1996) 'Just and Painful: Attitudes Toward Sentencing Criminals', in Flanagan, T. and Longmire, D. (eds), *Americans View Crime and Justice*. Thousand Oaks, CA: Sage.

Glick, H. and Pruet, G. (1985) 'Crime, Public Opinion and Trial Courts: An Analysis of Sentencing Policy', *Justice Quarterly*, 2, 319–43.

Home Office (1998) *Prison Statistics. England and Wales 1998*. London: Home Office.

Home Office (2001) *Making Punishments Work. Report of a Review of the Sentencing Framework for England and Wales*. London: Home Office.

Hough, M. (1996) 'People Talking About Punishment', *Howard Journal of Criminal Justice*, 35, 191–214.

Hough, M. and Moxon, D. (1988) 'Dealing with Offenders: Popular Opinion and the Views of Victims in England and Wales', in: Walker, N. and Hough, M. (eds), *Public Attitudes toward Sentencing*, Cambridge Studies in Criminology. Aldershot: Gower.

Hough, M. and Roberts, J.V. (1998) *Attitudes to Punishment: Findings from the British Crime Survey*, Home Office Research Study No. 179. London: Home Office.

Hough, M. and Roberts, J.V. (1999) 'Sentencing Trends in Britain: Public Knowledge and Public Opinion', *Punishment and Society*, 1, 7–22.

Hough, M. and Roberts, J.V. (2002) 'Public Knowledge and Public Opinion of Sentencing: Findings from Five Jurisdictions, in Hutton, N. and Tata, C. (eds), *Sentencing and Society: International Perspectives*. Ashgate (in press).

Hough, M., Lewis, H. and Walker, N. (1988) 'Factors Associated with "Punitiveness" in England and Wales', in Walker, N. and Hough, M. (eds), *Public Attitudes to Sentencing. Surveys from Five Countries*. Aldershot: Gower.

Kury, H. and Ferdinand, T. (1999) 'Public Opinion and Punitivity', *International Journal of Law and Psychiatry*, 22, 373–92.

Lord Bingham (1997) *The Sentence of the Court*, Police Foundation Lecture, July 1997. London: Police Foundation.

Lovegrove, A. (1998) 'Judicial Sentencing Policy, Criminological Expertise and Public Opinion', *Australian and New Zealand Journal of Criminology*, 31, 287–313.

McGarrell, E. and Sandys, M. (1996) 'The Misperception of Public Opinion toward Capital Punishment', *American Behavioral Scientist*, 39, 500–13.

Maguire, K. and Pastore, A. (eds) (1999) *Sourcebook of Criminal Justice Statistics*. Washington, DC: Bureau of Justice Statistics.

Mattinson, J. and Mirrlees-Black, C. (1998) 'Attitudes to Crime and Criminal Justice: Findings from the 1998 British Crime Survey', *Research Findings*, No. 111.

Pastore, A. and Maguire, K. (2000) *Sourcebook of Criminal Justice Statistics – 1999*. Washington, DC: Department of Justice.

R. v. Sargeant (1974) 60 Cr. App. R. 74.

Riley, P. and Rose, V. (1980) 'Public vs. Elite Opinion on Correctional Reform: Implications for Social Policy', *Journal of Criminal Justice*, 8, 345–56.

Roberts, J.V. (1988) *Public Opinion and Sentencing: The Surveys of the Canadian Sentencing Commission*. Ottawa: Department of Justice Canada.

Roberts, J.V. (1992) 'Public Opinion, Crime and Criminal Justice', in Tonry, M. (ed.), *Crime and Justice. A Review of Research*, Vol. 16. Chicago: University of Chicago Press.

Roberts, J.V. (2002a) 'Public Opinion and Mandatory Sentences of Imprisonment: A Review of International Findings', unpublished manuscript. Department of Criminology, University of Ottawa.

Roberts, J.V. (2002b) 'Alchemy in Sentencing: An Analysis of Sentencing Reform Proposals in England and Wales', *Punishment and Society*, in press.

Roberts, J.V. and Cole, D. (eds) (1999) *Making Sense of Sentencing*. Toronto: University of Toronto Press.

Roberts, J.V. and Doob, A.N. (1989) 'Sentencing and Public Opinion: Taking False Shadows for True Substances', *Osgoode Hall Law Journal*, 27, 491–515.

Roberts, J.V. and Gebotys, R. (1987). 'The Purposes of Sentencing: Public Support for Competing Aims', *Behavioural Sciences and the Law*, 7, 387–402.

Roberts, J.V. and Stalans, L. (1997) *Public Opinion, Crime, and Criminal Justice*. Boulder, CO: Westview Press.

Roberts, J.V., Doob, A.N. and Marinos, V. (2000) *Judicial Attitudes Towards Conditional Sentences of Imprisonment: Results of a National Survey*. Ottawa: Department of Justice Canada.

Roberts, J.V., Stalans, L.S., Indermaur, D. and Hough, M . (2002) *Penal Populism and Public Opinion. Lessons from Five Countries*. New York: Oxford University Press.

Russell, N. and Morgan, R. (2001) *Sentencing of Domestic Burglary*. Sentencing Advisory Panel. (Available at www.sentencing-advisory-panel.gov.uk.)

Silvey, J. (1961) 'The Criminal Law and Public Opinion', *Criminal Law Review*, 349–58.

Sumner, G. (1906). *Folkways: A Study in Sociological Importance of Usages, Manners, Customs, Mores, Morals*. New York: Ginn.

Tomaino, J. (1997) 'Guess Who's Coming to Dinner? A Preliminary Model for the Satisfaction of Public Opinion as a Legitimate Aim in Sentencing', *Crime, Law and Social Change*, 27, 109–19.

Tonry, M. (1996) *Sentencing Matters*. New York: Oxford University Press.

von Hirsch, A. (2002) 'Record-Driven Sentencing: Reflections on the Halliday Report's Proposed Treatment of Prior Convictions', *Punishment and Society*, in press.

Walker, N. (1985) *Sentencing: Theory, Law and Practice.* London: Butterworths.

Walker, N. and Marsh, C. (1988) 'Does the Severity of Sentences Affect Public Disapproval? An Experiment in England', in Walker, N. and Hough, M. (eds), *Public Attitudes toward Sentencing,* Cambridge Studies in Criminology. Aldershot: Gower.

Walker, N., Hough, M. and Lewis, H. (1988) 'Tolerance of Leniency and Severity in England and Wales', in Walker, N. and Hough, M. (eds), *Public Attitudes to Sentencing. Surveys from Five Countries.* Aldershot: Gower.

Warr, M. (1995) 'Public Opinion on Crime and Punishment', *Public Opinion Quarterly,* 59, 296–310.

Warr, M., Meier, R. and Erickson, M. (1983) 'Norms, Theories of Punishment and Publicly Preferred Penalties for Crimes', *Sociological Quarterly,* 24, 75–91.

Wilkins, L. (1974) 'Directions for Corrections', *Proceedings of the American Philosophical Society,* 118, 235–47.

Zamble, E. and Kalm, K. (1990) 'General and Specific Measures of Public Attitudes toward Sentencing', *Canadian Journal of Behavioural Science,* 22, 327–37.

Zander, M. and Henderson, P. (1993) *Crown Court Study. Royal Commission on Criminal Justice,* Research Study No. 19.

Zdenkowski, G. (2000) 'Limiting Sentencing Discretion: Has There Been a Paradigm Shift?', *Current Issues in Criminal Justice,* 12, 58–73.

Chapter 3

Relations between the lay and professional judiciary: now and Auld

Rod Morgan

Setting the scene

The bench of Bristol Magistrates' Court, like the bench of most major cities in England and Wales, includes a full-time district judge. However, unlike other English cities the appointment of a judge in Bristol is of recent origin, was fiercely resisted and is said initially to have involved some discreditable discourtesy. The appointment resulted not from a recommendation from the local Lord Chancellor's Advisory Committee but from the Magistrates' Court Service Inspectorate (MCSI). Senior lay magistrates locally resented the proposition, but it was successfully pressed on them by the Lord Chancellor's Department (LCD). In his early days in Bristol the professional incumbent, an experienced stipendiary who had previously worked in London, was reputedly given cases to deal with which his lay colleagues considered to be undemanding and probably beneath his dignity – vehicle parking infractions and the like. That is, the lay magistrates appear to have delivered a studied insult and asserted their determination not to relinquish to the judge those more serious cases which we must assume they saw his arrival as intending to cream off.

It seems probable that this spat was prominent in Lord Justice Auld's mind when he wrote, regarding local benches successfully delaying the appointment of a district judge where the MCSI and LCD think it desirable: 'such parochialism demeans the otherwise worthy contribution magistrates make to the running of the criminal justice system, and it should no longer hold sway' (Auld 2001: chapter 4, para. 89). He recommended that in future 'the Lord Chancellor should be more ready to take the initiative to assign a District Judge to an area where, having consulted as appropriate, he is of the view that local justice in the area requires it' (ibid.).

This saga, and scathing criticism, is probably a suitable starting point from which to address the question of relations between lay and professional members of the judiciary. I will do so in the light of my own research (Morgan and Russell 2000)[1] and the recommendations of the Auld Report. I propose considering two questions. First, how do lay and professional members currently work with and relate one to the other? Secondly, how plausible, in the light of their current working relations, are Auld's proposals? I will not argue the case for and against lay involvement in judicial decision making: I have done that elsewhere (Morgan and Russell 2000: chapter 1).

Lay magistrates and district judges: roles, performance and relationships

Let me first sketch the factual background. The magistrates' courts currently deal with approximately 96 per cent of all criminal cases. Within the magistrates' courts approximately 91 per cent of appearances are heard by lay magistrates as opposed to district judges (Morgan and Russell 2000: chapter 8). There are currently about 30,500 lay magistrates in England and Wales, approximately 100 full-time district judges (formerly called stipendiary magistrates) and a further 150 part-time district judges. Almost half the full-time district judges sit in London where, until 1964, all summary cases were dealt with by stipendiaries. Most full-time district judge appointments are to the major cities and metropolitan centres, though they assist elsewhere when local requests for assistance are made and the assistance is considered appropriate (ibid.: chapter 1). Lay magistrates sit on average 41 times a year (a full half-day session) – though sizeable minorities sit much more or less frequently – whereas district judges typically sit for 350 sessions a year. A good many district judges hold other judicial appointments: they are part-time recorders or tribunal chairmen (ibid.: chapter 2), a characteristic on which Auld comments and to which I will return.

On the basis of a substantial survey of other jurisdictions in Europe and Common Law systems elsewhere we concluded that the English and Welsh criminal court system relies on lay decision-making – regarding matters of fact and sentencing by lay magistrates in summary cases, and regarding matters of fact by jurors in contested Crown Court cases – to a greater extent than any other criminal court system in the world. However, it is an error to believe that England and Wales, and other Common Law jurisdictions originally modelled on the English system, are unique in involving lay magistrate-like decision-makers. It is, for example, a key feature of the German-Scandinavian tradition and it was a prominent feature of the Soviet system. It is found in many countries and most commonly involves lay persons sitting alongside full-time legally-qualified judges in criminal cases of moderate or high seriousness (ibid.: chapter 7; Doran and Glenn 2000).

Auld makes three major recommendations with implications for the role of lay magistrates and their relationship with the professional judiciary (a term which I was persuaded not to use in my research report on the grounds that it might be interpreted as derogatory, meaning that lay magistrates are unprofessional):

- that the magistrates' courts and the Crown Court be vertically integrated to form a unified criminal court system comprising three divisions, the Magistrates' Division, the District Division and the Crown Division (Auld 2001: chapter 7);

- that the tribunal in the new District Division comprise, in contested cases, a professional judge as chairman and two lay magistrates and should deal with cases of medium seriousness, that is those likely to incur penalties of more than six months and no more than two years imprisonment (ibid.);

- that the jurisdiction of the summary courts, the Magistrates' Division, remain as it is and the balance of lay magistrates and district judges hearing cases within the Division remain broadly as at present and have cases allocated to them much as at present (ibid.: chapter 4).

The latter recommendation sounds like a ringing endorsement of the status quo in the summary courts and suggests that existing practice is satisfactory and should pretty well continue as now. In reaching that conclusion Auld makes a good many references to the findings from my own research, the data collected for which included large surveys of public and regular court user knowledge and opinion in addition to observational and documentary analysis of what lay and stipendiary magistrates actually do. We concluded our report as follows:

Our findings are not entirely consistent nor are their implications entirely clear. It is nevertheless possible to anticipate likely public reactions to certain suggestions for change, were they to be widely canvassed. The office of Justice of the Peace is ancient. It represents an important tradition of voluntary public service for which, despite some recruitment difficulties in some parts of the country, thousands of candidates continue to come forward, prepared to give up a great deal of their time for no financial reward. In no other jurisdiction of which we are aware does the criminal court system depend so heavily on voluntary unpaid effort. At no stage during our fieldwork ... has it been suggested to us that in most respects the magistrates' courts do not work well or fail to command general confidence. Successive governments, moreover, have favoured the encouragement of active citizens or of an active community. The lay magistracy, whatever its imperfections, is a manifestation of those concepts. We doubt that any suggestion that the role of Justice of the Peace in the magistrates' courts be eliminated or greatly diminished would be widely understood or supported. (Morgan and Russell 2000: para. 8.8).

Auld accepted that view. However, he also noted the other part of our final paragraph:

It is also evident, however, that the public does not have strong feelings about the precise role of lay magistrates in the magistrates' courts. They think that summary offences, particularly if not contested, are suitable to be dealt with by a single magistrate. They equally consider that more serious decisions should be taken not by single persons but by panels. Cost considerations, as well as tradition, suggest that that could only be done, in the short term at least, by continuing to make extensive use of lay magistrates. Criminal justice practitioners, though appreciative that most lay magistrates deliver a quality service, have greater confidence in professional judges. Successive governments have introduced initiatives to make the criminal courts more efficient, not least to reduce the time that cases take to complete. Stipendiary magistrates, not surprisingly, are more efficient and inquisitorial in their approach. However, this has to be balanced against the potential increase in cost to the Prison Service of their decisions.

These wider considerations suggest that the nature and balance of the contribution made by lay and stipendiary magistrates could be altered so as better to satisfy these different considerations without prejudicing the integrity of a system founded on strong traditions and widely supported. (ibid.)

This latter conclusion Auld describes as delphic (Auld 2001: chapter 4, para. 6) – a description with which I am content. In conducting our research we decided from the outset that it was not our place to make recommendations as to the future of the magistrates' courts. We interpreted our task as one of providing as full an account of existing practice as possible. Armed with our data, it would then be possible for practitioners – and it should be remembered that in late 1999 many lay magistrates widely believed that the government intended to diminish their role – to debate in an informed fashion the logic and supporting evidence for any proposed changes. Nevertheless, being aware that some measure of change was likely, we thought it appropriate to indicate in broad terms the likely tolerance of the public and practitioners of changes in one general direction or another. Our 'delphic' conclusion was intended to suggest that radical change would likely encounter stiff opposition on various grounds, but there was substantial room for manoeuvre regarding the make-up of the tribunal hearing different types of appearances and cases.

Our conclusion was based on a number of findings of which I should briefly remind readers. First, we noted that most district judges rarely, if ever, sit in mixed panels with their lay colleagues. It happens in some parts of the country very occasionally, usually as a training exercise or in the youth court. Routine practice, however, is that district judges normally sit alone and lay magistrates ideally sit as threesomes, though a considerable minority of sessions are presided over by twosomes. Moreover, since the cases allocated to lay magistrates and district judges heavily overlap – though judges tend to deal with 'heavy business' and seldom hear guilty plea summary motoring cases in the absence of defendants, fine enforcement cases and so on – it is possible systematically to compare their performance and decision-making. The principal differences are:

- district judges are substantially quicker at dealing with court business than their lay colleagues (we estimated 30 per cent more appearances cases in equivalent time);

- district judges challenge applications from both the defence and prosecution both more often and more effectively than lay magistrates – fewer applications for adjournments are made to them, and those that are made are more likely to be refused – and thus their increased use would almost certainly reduce by a significant margin delay and the number of court appearances;

- in like-for-like cases district judges make substantially greater proportionate use of custody – roughly twice as much – as do their lay colleagues, both pre-trial and at sentence.

These differences in performance between lay magistrates and district judges are matched by differences in the manner in which the two groups are perceived:

- District judges have the edge over lay magistrates when it comes to having the confidence of regular court users (CPS caseworkers, solicitors and barristers, police and probation officers, etc.). Both groups command high levels of general confidence and lay magistrates are marginally more likely to be thought to show courtesy to court members and concern for distressed participants, but district judges are generally considered more consistent and confident in their decision-making, questioning appropriately, giving clear reasons for decisions and generally exhibiting command over proceedings.

- The public, though generally ill-informed about the identity of the two groups of magistrates (three-quarters of people are unaware that there are two types of magistrates), are open – once matters have been explained to them – to the idea that certain decisions (remand decisions, minor offences, etc.) can appropriately be dealt with by a single magistrate as opposed to a panel, and in most people's judgment that means desirably, though not necessarily, those cases being dealt with by a district judge.

Finally, it is not clear, when all cost considerations are taken into account, that employing district judges to replace lay magistrates would be more expensive. This is an issue to which I will return.

To summarise, therefore, the overwhelming majority of business in the magistrates' courts is dealt with by lay magistrates, though in major metropolitan centres (London, Birmingham, Manchester, Liverpool, Nottingham and other major cities and a few county areas) a growing proportion of business – tending towards the heavy end of the spectrum – is dealt with by a steadily growing band of district judges who, since early 2001, have been organised nationally under a Senior District Judge. This means that district judges can now be deployed wherever they may temporarily be needed without a special commissioning process. They sit almost entirely separately and they behave differently. Thus though district judges, like lay magistrates, have assigned to them a legally qualified court clerk, they seldom, unlike lay magistrates, consult them. Relationships between district judges and their lay colleagues are generally amicable, particularly in areas where their appointment has been longstanding. But it is more accurate to say that in most areas there is little or no relationship between the two types of magistrate. They are remote from each other. That is, aside from the odd training event, district judges are not well known to most of their lay colleagues: they do not sit with each other and they seldom attend meetings together. They are selected by different means, trained separately and they come from different backgrounds, the district judges being solicitors or barristers who, to be eligible for full-time appointment, must first have sat as part-time district judges and been positively appraised in that role by their peers.

Lay magistrates and district judges merely occupy the same courthouses, getting on with their respective caseloads. Moreover, most full-time district judges spend a fair proportion of their time sitting in courts other than their own – helping out elsewhere whenever the national office receives a request for assistance that is considered appropriate.

What is clear is that there is a widespread feeling among lay magistrates, exhibited in acute form by the Bristol saga, that the appointment of additional district judges represents an aspect of the increasingly centralised administration and governmental managerialism of the criminal court system and serves to marginalise their own position. According to this perspective the increase in the number of district judges is of a piece with: the amalgamation in recent years of petty sessional divisions and their grouping under joint clerkships; the closing of many local courthouses; the appointment of court area chief executives, many of them administrators rather than former justices' clerks; and the granting to justices' clerks powers formerly the prerogative of magistrates.

Auld's Magistrates' Division: endorsement of the status quo?

Before discussing Auld's proposed vertical integration of the criminal courts and creation of a middle tier, the District Division, we should first consider how firm is his apparent endorsement of the status quo in the Magistrates' Division? Or, just as importantly, how likely is it that the adoption of Auld's principal recommendations will shore up the status quo in the magistrates' courts? I think it likely that there will be a further steady increase in the number of district judges. I reach this conclusion on five grounds.

First is the Auld recommendation we have already noted: namely, that in future 'the Lord Chancellor should be more ready to take the initiative to assign a District Judge to an area where, having consulted as appropriate, he is of the view that local justice in the area requires it' (Auld 2001: chapter 4, para. 89). That is, the initiative should not be left to the localities but taken on by the centre. I think this recommendation will be seized on and additional district judges appointed, particularly in areas where there is evidence of delay, where the lay magistrates prove to be less than flexible and where there are difficulties recruiting suitable lay magistrates: these conditions are most likely to arise in the metropolitan centres.

Secondly, we should note that though Auld sees no case for altering the present balance of lay magistrates and district judges he nevertheless maintains that 'the position may be different' if his recommendation that there be a unified court with an intermediate tier is adopted. There would then be only a compelling case for retaining 'a sizeable lay magistracy' (ibid.: para. 42) – how sizeable Auld does not say, though he notes that having many more district judges would 'require a major programme of change' and would take time. I think it is clear that in order to pave the way for his District Division Auld favours substantially increasing the number of district judges who he observes often sit also as recorders and that appointment as a district judge is 'emerging as the first step on a judicial rung that may lead to a permanent appointment as a Circuit Judge and, possibly, beyond' (ibid.: para. 88). The vertical integration of the criminal courts implies the further development of judicial careers, both of which I expect to be encouraged.

It is for this reason that I conclude, thirdly, that lay magistrates should not feel greatly reassured by Auld's recommendation that there be no extension of justices' clerks' case management jurisdiction (ibid.: chapter 4, para. 58). What is being safeguarded is less the prerogative of lay magistrates and more the developing role of the professional judiciary. Note, for example, that Auld concludes that district judges have no need of a legally qualified clerk to sit with them in court (ibid.: para. 53) – an anomalous, indeed luxurious, current provision to which we drew attention in our research report (Morgan and Russell 2000: para. 6.6.1; see also Sanders 2001: 37) – and that it will be for district judges, not lay magistrates or justices' clerks, to determine the appropriate venue for the hearing of either-way cases in the event of the defence and prosecution disagreeing (Auld 2001: chapter 7, para. 40).

Fourthly, though public opinion might be invoked to protect the position of the lay magistracy – our survey found, for example, that the lay magistracy is generally considered by the public to better represent the community than the professional judiciary and be more sympathetic to defendants' circumstances (Morgan and Russell 2000: 79) – Auld has a magisterially dismissive view of public opinion: he does not consider it can or should be a major determinant in shaping policy. 'Public confidence is not', in his opinion, 'an end in itself; it is or should be an outcome of a fair and efficient system. The proper approach is to make the system fair and efficient and, if public ignorance stands in the way of public confidence, take steps adequately to demonstrate to the public that it is so' (Auld 2001: chapter 4, para. 32).

This view arises from Auld's perception that the public is both ignorant and confused. His conclusion is informed by data we and others (Sanders 2001) collected and reported on during the Auld review. We found:

- that whereas most people have heard of magistrates;

- most people, three-quarters, are unaware that there are two types of magistrates;

- most people do not know how often magistrates sit in court and though a clear majority know that all criminal cases currently begin in the magistrates' courts only a bare majority know that most lay magistrates are not legally trained and that there is no jury in magistrates' court cases (Morgan and Russell 2000: chapter 5).

Which is to say, public ignorance of the system is fairly extensive.

Auld suggests that we were 'baffled' by some of the conflicts we found in some of the expressions of public opinion we collected (Auld 2001: chapter 4, para. 29). And he is more than a little scornful of the fact that, having revealed how extensive public ignorance is, we and others nevertheless attach significance to public opinion regarding what might be done. He quotes our saying that 'it would be a mistake to construe lack of public knowledge with lack of opinion or public indifference' (Morgan and Russell 2000: para. 8.7, quoted in Auld 2001: chapter 4, para. 31) regarding the future organisation of the criminal court system. He implies that there is something illogical or irrational in our stance.

I do not think there is any contradiction in our position here. There are a good many public policy issues about which most of us have only a dim idea of the facts – the likely implications of adopting the Euro, or the probable consequences of making certain financial and contractual arrangements for the redevelopment of the London Underground, for example. But that does not mean that most of us will not rapidly form a view of what is important or what should be done when matters are explained to us. Were public knowledge the necessary condition for political participation, the case for democracy would be difficult to sustain. There is no reason why most people should be closely conversant with the facts of many public policy arrangements most of the time: but this is no reason for not consulting them about changes which, ultimately, are likely, occasionally, to affect every household. It is the essence of participatory democratic theory that giving people the opportunity to participate in decision-making beyond the vote in periodic elections enhances their capacity for responsible citizenship (Pateman 1970). In our survey of public opinion we explained to respondents, having first established what they did or did not know, the existence and nature of the two types of magistrates before asking them which cases should best be heard by different tribunals. We were not 'baffled' by our results. Indeed, I did not personally find our results surprising. We simply acknowledged that surveys of public opinion, ours included, seldom provide clear, unambiguous indications of what should be done. But they do reveal the values to which people subscribe and may indicate the limits of public tolerance to change. The problem with Auld's stance is that it appears to assume that the judges, and the politicians they advise, are the best and sole arbiters of what system is fair and efficient and the public must then be persuaded that what the judges have decided is ideal. We doubted whether any proposals greatly to reduce the role of lay magistrates would likely be accepted and I think that Auld's proposals greatly to reduce the role of the jury will similarly encounter resistance, particularly if presented in a manner suggesting that public opinion on the issue is of little value because it is ignorant. Nevertheless, we indicated (see above) that the state of public opinion is such that the public would likely tolerate greater use of single judges hearing the more straightforward and less serious types of appearances and cases in the summary courts.

Fifthly, Auld's handling of the question of costs should be noted. One joke currently doing the rounds in Whitehall is that the only figures in the Auld Report are the paragraph numbers. The joke reflects the reality. The Treasury will clearly insist that figures – the numbers of cases likely to follow different pathways, the cost implications of those numbers, etc. – be applied to all of Auld's key propositions. But though Auld occasionally mentions costs and possible savings in passing he avoids numerical estimation of any sort. Ironically, however, he is prepared to suggest that our attempt to estimate the cost implications of employing more district judges in place of lay magistrates is at best incomplete and at worst flawed. We (Morgan and Russell 2000: chapter 6) found the following:

- Estimates of the direct costs to the LCD alone of using the two types of magistrate show, not surprisingly, that lay magistrates are far cheaper – a lay justice we estimated costs £495 p.a. compared to £90,000 for a stipendiary, which translates to £3.59 compared to £20.96 per case.

- However, when overheads are loaded into the equation, the difference is far smaller – £52.10 compared to £61.78 per appearance.

- If opportunity costs are added – a controversial issue in which fairly courageous assumptions have to be made – we estimated that lay magistrates are more expensive – £70.80 compared to £61.78 per court appearance.

- Further, if the cost consequences of current differential decision-making are added, the calculations pull in different directions. Employing more district judges will lead to fewer court appearances as a result of their more robust examination of applications: this would save money. However, district judges' greater use of custody would lead to greater expenditure for the criminal justice system overall.

Auld, who declined to assist with the costing of his own proposals, nevertheless chose to cross-examine ours. He thought, *contra* the Magistrates' Association, that we were correct to include an estimation of opportunity as well as direct costs, but he judged that our calculations were 'necessarily somewhat theoretical and speculative and . . . open to criticism in a number of respects' (Auld 2001: chapter 4, para. 7). Of our conclusion that more district judges would be likely to add to the number of custodial decisions and thus costs, he says:

Save as a cynical measure of expediency, it would be wrong to consider whether to change the present sharing of summary jurisdiction on the basis that District Judges are too hard or that magistrates are too soft in their decisions as to custody. (Auld 2001: chapter 4, para. 8)

In fact, just to set the record straight, we at no stage argued that policy should be decided on the basis of costs, any costs: we simply attempted to estimate the likely cost consequences of different policy scenarios. Nevertheless I cannot forbear to note that having adopted his lofty posture in this regard, Auld goes on to argue, either explicitly or implicitly, that whatever the savings or additional costs of having more district judges, they are merited by the benefits of having district judges. Thus, with respect to their greater use of custody:

> As it happens, I believe that District Judges are more likely to follow national practice and sentencing policy guide-lines in this respect than magistrates, with their individual traditions and training, and history of disparate sentencing. (ibid.: chapter 4, para. 8)

That is, if there is a difference in the remand and sentencing decisions of lay and stipendiary magistrates, then the lay magistrates are, in Auld's opinion, too soft. Of course he is correct to say that there is evidence of disparate sentencing between magistrates' benches. What he does not say is that we do not have evidence of disparate sentencing between judges because the judges, unlike the lay magistracy, have over the years blocked almost all attempts by researchers systematically to look at how consistent judges' sentencing is (Ashworth 1998): their practice may be just as disparate. Further, as I emphasise below, Auld chooses effectively to ignore for other purposes the disparity represented by lay magistrates and district judges' decision-making which his proposals will likely perpetuate. But my principal point is to note Auld's assumption that if there are differences in policy, then the judges are correct. Thus, conversely, if district judges grant fewer applications for adjournments than their lay colleagues, the savings are apparently to be welcomed: Auld does not challenge the estimated savings under this heading. Indeed it is apparently not cynical for him to suggest that in our own research we almost certainly under-estimated the savings that would accrue from having additional district judges. He correctly points out, for example, that we failed to estimate – we did not do so because, as we fully acknowledged in our report, we could find no firm basis on which to do it – the reduced knock-on costs of having fewer court appearances for the police, the legal aid budget, the CPS, etc. (Auld 2001: chapter 4, para. 9). I think that the fact that savings may arise from making greater use of district judges will inevitably encourage their greater use.

The five approaches outlined above – as much between as on the lines of the Auld Report – seem to me to suggest less commitment to the current balance of lay magistrates and district judges in the Magistrates' Division than at first appears. If I am correct, and the tendency towards employing additional district judges is acted on, it will have implications for the relationship between the two groups. In our large-scale survey of lay and stipendiary magistrates we found, not surprisingly, that whereas the stipendiaries could overwhelmingly think of several reasons for having more stipendiaries – faster, more efficient, better able to deal with legally complicated cases, and so on – the majority of lay magistrates could cite no reasons at all. Conversely, whereas one or two stipendiaries conceded that there were arguments against having more stipendiaries – that it is unfair to have one person sitting in judgment, for example – the majority of lay magistrates subscribed to several negative arguments. The two groups do not see eye to eye on the possible futures of their respective contribution and since one group comprises unpaid volunteers, this is a factor to be heeded: lay magistrates might widely withdraw their unpaid labour were they to see their own status being diminished and their role reduced. Which brings us to Auld's big idea.

The District Division: the implications of Auld's big idea

Auld's proposed middle-tier court – the District Division – would hear either-way cases likely to lead, in the event of conviction, to a sentence of more than six months' and no more than two years' imprisonment. Uncontested cases would be sentenced by a district judge (though Auld suggests it could be a judge of any level, depending on the character of the case) sitting alone. Contested cases would be heard by a mixed tribunal normally comprising a district judge in the chair sitting with two lay magistrates. This proposed mixed tribunal of lay and professional members conforms broadly to what in our own survey we found to be the Germano-Scandinavian model, though the arrangement is found in several jurisdictions outside that European region (see Morgan and Russell 2000: 103–104). Auld proposes an arrangement as follows. Lay magistrates sitting with a district judge in the District Division will jointly determine guilt or innocence, but not sentence. As Auld summarises it:

Trial by such a 'mixed' tribunal would have a number of the characteristics and safeguards provided by trial in the Crown Court. A professional judge would make all the rulings and orders at the pre-trial stage, conduct any necessary case management and rule on bail. In the trial itself, the professional judge would also deal with all questions of law, procedure and evidence, hearing arguments on them and making rulings, where necessary in the absence of the magistrates.

For all other purposes, however, the mixed bench would constitute a single tribunal. It would hear all the evidence together and, at the close of the trial, the judge and magistrates would retire together to consider the question of guilt or innocence. Clearly the judge would take the leading role in guiding the discussion in areas in which the law, or the application of the law to the facts, is in any way uncertain. But he would not need to give the magistrates the sort of elaborate directions Crown Court judges give to juries, since they come to the task with the benefit of their experience and training in structured decision taking in the magistrates' court. Trials in the District Division should thus be considerably shorter than trial by judge and jury, since the magistrate members would be familiar with the practices, procedures and language of the court, together with much of the day-to-day law required. At the close of their deliberations, the judge and magistrates would make their decision, by majority if necessary, each having an equal vote. On their return to the courtroom, the judge would give the reasoned decision of the court. (Auld 2001: chapter 7, paras 29–30)

These proposals are broadly along the lines canvassed by some commentators (see, for example, Sanders 2001: 38). Sentence, however, would be for the judge alone. The magistrates would play no part. Why? Auld offers two reasons:

- Lay magistrates would, he contends, lack the necessary competence and experience: sentencing at this level of seriousness would be very different from sentencing in the summary court and would become more complicated still were the recommendations of the Halliday Report (2001) implemented (Auld 2001: chapter 7, para. 31).

- It would not be practical to involve lay magistrates: following trial most cases would have to be adjourned for sentence and 'it would often be difficult to reconstitute the same panel for the purpose of passing sentence' (ibid.).

These objections are not well grounded – if lay magistrates can be found willing to hear lengthy contested cases then it should not be impossible to reconvene them briefly to determine sentence – and will likely be regarded as insulting by many lay magistrates. But it seems to me that they also constitute a smokescreen for avoiding possibly the greatest objection to the involvement of lay magistrates in sentencing in the proposed District Division. I refer to a consideration which has nothing to do with practicality or lay magistrates' competence. Namely that to concede panel sentencing in the proposed District Division would throw into starker relief and call into question lone sentencing in the Magistrates' and Crown Divisions, something which it is apparent from our surveys of the public and of lay magistrates is widely considered objectionable in serious criminal proceedings, though I should emphasise that we canvassed opinion on this point only with regard to decisions in the magistrates' courts (Morgan and Russell 2000: chapter 5).

Auld, interestingly, when briefly discussing general aims, objectives or principles chooses entirely to avoid what some observers (principally Sanders 2001) consider to be a point of principle in decision-making, namely that whereas it is appropriate (on grounds of cost, efficiency, etc.) for lone decision-makers to decide matters with modest consequences, decisions with more serious consequences should ideally be made by panels. This is arguably a safeguard akin to that found in most criminal court systems, requiring more serious cases to be dealt with according to more testing procedures (jury trial, for example) and heard by more highly qualified and experienced judges. Auld, despite having the matter repeatedly drawn to his attention (see Morgan and Russell 2000: para. 2.9; Sanders 2001: 42–3) ignores the fact that it is a matter almost entirely of chance whether a defendant appearing in a magistrates' court in which a district judge regularly sits has his case heard by a panel of lay magistrates or a lone district judge, and further, that that chance factor is likely to make it more or less probable that there will be certain decision-making outcomes. This is as serious an example of decision-making disparity (or what is often called 'postcode justice') as that between lay benches to which Auld drew attention (see above). The present arrangement has recently been described by a minister as 'odd' and 'arbitrary'(Bradley 2001). Yet Auld ignores it and in so far as he recommends that lay magistrates and district judges continue to sit separately in the magistrates' courts, and continue to have allocated to them cases as at present, he proposes to perpetuate the anomaly (though it could be argued that his proposals for the institution of a national framework for the training of magistrates, in which district judges should be involved, may serve to reduce the decision-making differences between lay magistrates and district judges – Auld 2001: chapter 4, para. 100).

Regarding lone sentencing by judges in the Crown Court Auld maintains that he received no proposals for change. This also is odd because the case for panel decision-making in the Crown Court is clearly set out in one submission from a commentator extensively cited by Auld (Sanders 2001: 39) and in recent years, during the course of undertaking successive research projects, I have repeatedly heard barristers argue the shortcomings of lone decision-making and the likely benefits of panel decision-making in the Crown Court. What is clear is that the fact that district judges currently tend to hear, in conformity with the recommendations of the Venne Report (1996) – which Auld endorses – 'heavy' business means that what I will call the 'panel principle' is inverted in the magistrates' courts, and will, *ceteris paribus*, become more so to the extent that additional district judges are appointed. That is, more minor cases tend disproportionately to be heard by panels and more serious cases by lone judges.

As regards lay magistrates sitting with district judges in the District Division, there are two issues to be considered. Which lay magistrates are likely to do it? And how will they do it?

I think some lay magistrates will welcome the opportunity to try contested cases alongside district judges in the District Division and will find time to do it. However, I think some of their colleagues, also with time to do it, will decline to be involved on the grounds that their professionalism and experience is demeaned by their exclusion from certain legal procedures and sentencing. I suspect that many more lay magistrates, however, will not be involved because their involvement will prove impractical. That is, they will not have time to undertake District Division sittings in addition to their Magistrates' Division work or they will not be able to devote the extended periods that District Division trials will involve. There is a real dilemma to be faced here: the trade-off between expertise and experience and equality between professional and lay judges.

Auld points out that an objection to mixed panels is that they will be dominated by professional judges (Auld 2001: chapter 7, para. 24). This is an issue about which there is a great deal of anecdotal but virtually no hard evidence both with regard to practice in the Crown Court (where mixed panels hear appeals from magistrates' courts decisions) and overseas. In Germany, where lay persons – a sort of equivalent of lay magistrates – sit alongside professional judges in serious cases, the lay participants are reportedly known as 'decorative flower pots', the implication being that they are mere window dressing. There is some contrary evidence from Denmark and Finland (Godzinsky and Ervasti 1999). Doran and Glenn, summarising the evidence from other jurisdictions, argue that 'the very presence of the lay members may in itself influence the stance adopted by the professional' (2000: 44). Whatever the case, I doubt whether these foreign examples should be used as indicators of the likely pattern here. English and Welsh magistrates are much more highly trained and experienced than their Scandinavian and German counterparts. They sit frequently and separately from professional judges – which their continental equivalents do not. I doubt that they will greatly defer to the opinions of district judges when deciding guilt or innocence. Auld agrees with this view (2001: chapter 7, para. 24).

Nevertheless a key concern must be which magistrates choose to sit in the District Court and whether it should be a choice or an obligation. And this question is related to the latest data, collected in our own research, on the social composition of the lay magistracy, their sitting patterns and what Auld recommends be done to change both factors. We found that the present lay magistracy is:

- gender balanced;

- ethnically representative of the population at national level, though generally not locally,

- overwhelmingly drawn (65–80 per cent compared to 20–25 per cent of the population generally) from professional/managerial occupations;

- disproportionately (two-fifths) retired from full-time employment (Morgan and Russell 2000: chapter 2).

This is a very different pattern from district judges in particular and the professional judiciary in general, they being mostly male and white and, in the case of district judges, generally younger (full-time district judges are typically appointed in their early 40s).

Auld is unhappy about the present make-up of the lay magistracy and devotes a good deal of space in his report to their recruitment, selection and use. He would like them to be more ethnically representative of local populations and drawn from a wider spectrum of occupations. He thinks advertising and recruitment could be done more professionally. He also thinks that court listing and magistrates' sitting patterns could be more flexible to suit the needs of different occupational groups (Auld 2001: chapter 4 paras 59–86). There is a real tension, however, between the demand that the lay magistracy be socially more representative and that they be professionally trained and become sufficiently experienced so as to be able to match the forensic power of the professional judiciary. Auld thinks that the opportunity to try more serious cases in the District Division would add to the attractions of being a magistrate (ibid.: para. 73). He may well be correct, but wishing to be a magistrate is one thing, being an effective independent voice is quite another. I suggest that to be an effective independent voice magistrates could scarcely train and sit less often than they already do and that the burdens of the office mean, as we stated it in our report and as Auld carefully noted, that:

> If the duties of lay magistrates are relatively onerous as well as being unpaid, it is not surprising that the composition of benches consists overwhelmingly of persons with the time and personal resources to bear that burden. (Morgan and Russell 2000: para. 2.2.4, quoted in Auld 2001: chapter 4, para. 61)

In making his proposal for mixed tribunals I do not think that Sanders gave sufficient attention to this dilemma and I fear that adding prolonged District Division sittings to their duties will mean, all other things being equal, that the magistrates who sit on contested cases in the District Division will be even more disproportionately retired and middle-class incumbents than the lay magistracy generally. The other danger is that because such magistrates already sit the most (20 per cent of magistrates currently sit more frequently than weekly), they will be the most 'case hardened' and thus insufficiently different from their professional colleagues. My hypothesis is that the acquittal rate in the proposed District Division will be very substantially lower than that resulting from jury trials. The best, albeit modest, safeguard against this outcome would be to insist that all magistrates had, as part of their duties, to undertake a minimum number of sittings in the District Division so that the duty was the obligation of all and not the choice of a minority. That may not be practical, however.

Will district judges relish sitting with lay magistrates in the District Division? I doubt it. But I think it will be good for them. Whether the exchange of this arrangement for the loss of a very large number of jury trials will represent progress is a controversy from which I will stand back, together with the question of whether sentencing in very serious cases should be a matter for lone judges – a question which scarcely anyone is currently prepared to put on the agenda.

Finally, it seems clear that if either the principal recommendations of the Auld or the Halliday Reports (Home Office 2001) are adopted, the lay magistracy stand on the threshold of critical change. Important choices have to be made. It appears that many lay magistrates are currently taking the stance that sentence review proceedings, as recommended by Halliday (ibid.: chapter 7), lie outside their role and they would not wish to be involved. My own view is that if the government adopts either Halliday or Auld, which of course they may not – the immediate cost implications of both Reports are very considerable – and lay magistrates mostly decide not to involve themselves in sentence review or District Court proceedings, they run the risk of further encouraging a trend already underway and which they mostly deprecate – the relegation of lay magistrates to hearing minor cases a significant proportion of which could arguably be dealt with administratively, while the professional judiciary, sitting alone, take over the hearing of more serious, contested business. If participatory democracy has value and meaning, it surely encompasses lay participation in judicial decision-making: existing lay magistrates in England and Wales should not lightly prejudice the future of their own office.

Notes

1 The research on which this paper was ultimately based was conducted by myself and Neil Russell of Research Services of Great Britain, commissioned jointly by the Home Office and the Lord Chancellor's Department. All the data and findings regarding the operation of the magistrates' courts in England and Wales referred to in this text have been fully published in the report on that research (Morgan and Russell 2000).

References

Ashworth, A. (1998) *The Criminal Justice Process: An Evaluative Study*. Oxford: Oxford University Press.

Auld Report (2001) *Report of the Review of the Criminal Courts of England and Wales*. London: HMSO.

Bradley, K. (2001) Unpublished address to the AGM of the Kings College Centre for Criminal Justice Studies, 21 November.

Doran, S. and Glenn, R. (2000) *Lay Involvement in Adjudication*, Research Report No. 11, Review of Criminal Justice System in Northern Ireland. Belfast: Criminal Justice Review Group.

Godzinsky, V.-M. de and Ervasti, K. (1999) *Laymen as Judges*. Helsinki: National Research Institute of Legal Policy.

Home Office (2001) *Making Punishments Work: Report of a Review of the Sentencing Framework for England and Wales* (the Halliday Report), London: Home Office.

Morgan, R. and Russell, N. (2000) *The Judiciary in the Magistrates' Courts*, London: Home Office/LCD.

Pateman, C. (1970) *Participation and Democratic Theory*. London: Cambridge University Press.

Sanders, A. (2001) *Community Justice: Modernising the Magistracy in England and Wales*. London: IPPR.

Venne Report (1996) *The Role of the Stipendiary Magistracy*. London: HMSO.

Chapter 4

Taking account of race, ethnicity and religion

David Faulkner

Context and background

Whether sentencing policy should take account of differences in race, ethnicity or religion, and, if so, how are issues which need to be addressed in the context of the Halliday Report. However, that subject needs to be set in the context of the wider debate which has been taking place since the period of large-scale immigration from the Commonwealth during the 1950s and 1960s about the significance of race and ethnicity, and more recently religion, for the nature of British society and the institutions of the British state. That debate produced the Race Relations Acts of 1968 and 1976, which prohibited direct or indirect discrimination in employment or in the provision of services, and it began to have a major impact on law enforcement and criminal justice as a consequence of the racial violence in London and other cities in 1981. The Scarman Report on those incidents (Scarman 1981) had a significant influence on police practice and on the structure, if not always the spirit, of police relationships with local communities.

Various other attempts were made to improve the situation of minority groups during the next 15 years, including their treatment by the criminal justice system, but a sense of disadvantage and injustice remained. Examples in criminal justice included initiatives in the recruitment and training of staff, and ethnic monitoring of staff and the provision of some services. The Conservative government resisted any extension of the Race Relations Act to the criminal justice services, but section 95 of the Criminal Justice Act 1991 introduced a requirement for the Secretary of State to publish information which would help those engaged in the administration of justice to perform their 'duty to avoid discrimination ... on the ground of race or sex or any other improper ground'.

Soon after its arrival in office in 1997, the Labour government asked Sir William Macpherson to hold a public inquiry (Macpherson 1999) into the death of Stephen Lawrence, who had been murdered in South London four years previously, in order in particular to identify the lessons to be learned for the investigation and prosecution of racially motivated crimes. The report was damning in its criticism of the Metropolitan Police, and made 70 recommendations relating to police practice and accountability in the recording and investigation of racist crimes, the treatment of victims and witnesses, the prosecution of racist offences, and the recruitment, training and retention of staff. The government immediately published its own Action Plan for implementing the report, and continues to produce an annual report on progress.

Expecting a stronger commitment to issues of race and ethnicity from the newly elected government, the Runnymede Trust set up in 1998 a Commission on the Future of Multi-Ethnic Britain. The Commission's task was to 'analyse the current state of multi-ethnic Britain, and to propose ways of countering racial discrimination and disadvantage and of making Britain a confident and vibrant multicultural society at ease with its rich diversity'. Its report, published in October 2000 (CFMEB 2000), was in three parts – a vision for Britain; chapters dealing with various social issues and services, including the police and the wider criminal justice system; and strategies for change including political leadership, legislation and organisational reform.

The debate on race and ethnicity has been for many years focused on the need to prevent discrimination, mainly in the supply of goods and services (as in the Race Relations Acts of 1968 and 1976); to improve understanding, for example through appointments, training and ethnic monitoring; and to a lesser extent to encourage assimilation. Perhaps the main impact of the reports of the Stephen Lawrence Inquiry and the Commission on the Future of Multi-Ethnic Britain came from their recognition of the need to move on from that agenda to one of promoting equality and valuing diversity. That change of emphasis is reflected in the Race Relations (Amendment) Act 2000, which places on public authorities, including for the first time the criminal justice services, a positive duty not only to prevent discrimination but also to promote racial equality.

The debate took a new dimension after the terrorist attacks in the United States on 11 September 2001. Religion, and especially Islam, became a new focus of attention. In its emergency legislation on terrorism, Parliament extended the existing provisions relating to public order and racially aggravated offences to cover religion as well as race, although more far-reaching and controversial proposals were defeated in the House of Lords. A wider public debate took place at that time, during the first half of December 2001, about the need for a common sense of citizenship, or of moral and cultural values, which would unite the country across racial, ethnic and religious boundaries, and the extent to which the country could afford to tolerate, or should positively welcome, a diversity of cultures.

Nature of the debate

Race, ethnicity and religion are difficult subjects to discuss in any context, and sentencing is a more difficult context than most. The need to avoid discrimination and promote equal opportunitites is (almost) universally accepted in employment and the provision of services, and in respect of race it has for most purposes been a statutory requirement for over 30 years. Most public and voluntary organisations (and many in the private sector) have statements or policies on equal opportunities, and try to include black and Asian members among their staff and their boards and committees. As already described, the Race Relations (Amendment) Act 2000 went further and imposed on public authorities a duty not just to avoid discrimination but also to promote racial equality. The Act applies to the criminal justice services, but not the judiciary who are not seen organisationally as a 'service' or as providing a service to the public. To impose such an obligation on the judiciary would be seen as an encroachment on its independence, and probably a constitutional innovation.

Even so, many white people find it difficult to have an open discussion on matters of race, ethnicity or religion, either in public or in private, often for fear of giving offence, provoking criticism or revealing ignorance, or because it 'only leads to trouble'. They will sometimes try to ridicule any opinions different from their own by characterising them as 'political correctness'. In criminal justice, as in other areas of public policy or academic study, the subject is all too often avoided, sometimes deliberately for reasons such as those described, but sometimes because people – from whatever background – are not sure if they have anything useful to say, or because they feel intimidated. Members of minority groups may also be reluctant to broach the subject because they do not want to be stereotyped as representing a separate group, still less treated as representing minorities generally – with many of whom they may have little in common – in a situation where white people still think of themselves as 'us' and of minorities without differentiation as 'them'.

Attempts to promote serious public discussion still produce hostile reactions, as was seen from the reports of the Stephen Lawrence inquiry and the Commission on the Future of Multi-Ethnic Britain. Certain newspapers, and some representatives of the Police Federation, sought to discredit the Stephen Lawrence inquiry as having exposed the public to increased danger because the police were no longer 'allowed' to enforce the law and as a sinister attempt to undermine their authority. The same newspapers and some individual commentators similarly portrayed the Commission on the Future of Multi-Ethnic Britain as trying to destroy the notion of British identity and the social or moral values on which British society is thought to be based, often by attributing to the report statements – for example that the term 'British' is racist – which it did not contain. The government gave its full support to the report of the Stephen Lawrence inquiry, but quickly distanced itself from the Commission when it thought it might itself be subjected to criticism.

The problems of communication and understanding, and especially as they affect national identity and loyalty, are beginning to acquire a new religious dimension as a result of the events of 11 September.

Minorities' experience of criminal justice

Specifically in the area of criminal justice, it can be said that:

- Members of minority groups are more likely than white people to be victims of crime and more likely to be in fear of crime.

- The police are less likely to identify a suspect if the victim is black.

- Black people are six times more likely than whites to be stopped by the police.

- Black people are more likely than white people or members of other groups to be dealt with by arrest rather than summons and by prosecution rather than a caution, and to be remanded in custody rather than given bail.

- Black people are more likely than whites to be charged with offences which lead to trial at the Crown Court rather than the magistrates' court; to elect for trial at the Crown Court where they have a choice; and to plead 'not guilty'. They are less likely to be the subject of a pre-sentence report. All these factors expose them to the possibility of a more severe sentence in the event of conviction; they are, however, more likely than white people to be acquitted.

- The Crown Prosecution Service discontinues a higher proportion of cases against black defendants on evidential grounds.

- Members of ethnic minorities, but especially black people, are over-represented in the prison population. Black people account for 14 per cent of males and 22 per cent of females in prison, although they only comprise about 2 per cent of the general population. In total almost one prisoner in four is from a minority group.

- Disparities between the treatment of minorities and of white people are less marked among those of South Asian and Chinese origin.

- Minority groups are under-represented among the staff of most criminal justice services, especially in senior posts. Numbers are gradually increasing, especially in the magistracy, the Probation Service and the practising legal profession, but they are still very low among senior officers or the higher judiciary.

- Members of minority groups are less satisfied than white people with their treatment after reporting an offence or incident to the police.

- Users from minority groups rated services poorly in relation to their recognition of different needs of minority group members; these include the courts and the police (in addition to local councils and the immigration service) (Faulkner 2001).

These comparisons are for the most part based on the actual numbers of white and black or Asian people involved in the incidents, actions or situations concerned, and the disparity between those proportions and the proportions in the population as a whole. The disparity is often less if the comparison is made with the population of a particular geographical area, or of a particular age group, in which minority groups are themselves disproportionately represented. Similar disparities are to be found in other areas of activity, for example education, and the Commission on the Future of Multi-Ethnic Britain found evidence that within criminal justice the experience of the Irish was very similar to the experience of black people (CFMEB 2000).

It is difficult to say conclusively how far this information constitutes evidence of prejudice or discrimination, or how far it at all it reflects higher rates of offending among black (or Irish) people. The evidence is uncertain, complex and open to different interpretations – bias in the system, greater criminality among black people, and a range of social, economic, cultural and historical factors which may affect both (Smith 1997). However that may be, surveys have shown that black people especially have less confidence than white people in the criminal justice process, and many of them feel a deep sense of unfairness about the way in which black people are treated. That sense seems, however, to be directed more towards the system as a whole than towards sentencing in particular.

Discrimination in sentencing

The main evidence that there may be racial discrimination in sentencing is the disproportionate number of black people in the prison population relative to their number in the population as a whole – seven times what might be expected for men and even more for women. The difference cannot, however, be explained by asserting simply that black people commit more or more serious crime, or that sentencing involves some element of racial prejudice.

Crude figures for arrests and conviction may at first sight suggest that black people commit proportionately more crime than white or Asian people. But figures of arrests and convictions are not a reliable or consistent indication of the number of offences that are actually committed. Nor do comparisons based on total populations take account of factors that are associated with higher levels of criminality, such as age, social and family background or economic circumstances, regardless of racial or ethnic background. The Social Exclusion Unit (1998) has recognised that members of ethnic minority groups are more likely than the rest of the population to live in poor areas, be unemployed, have low incomes, live in poor housing, have poor health and be victims of crime. Higher rates of criminality are only to be expected. It seems a reasonable conclusion that black people cannot be shown to commit more crime than white people from similar social or economic backgrounds (although Asian people may commit less).

Questions to be answered include the following:

- When allowance has been made for differences in social and economic background and other relevant factors, are there still reasons to suspect discrimination in sentencing?

65

- If so, is there a case for building more safeguards into the sentencing structure, and what would they be?

- If not, or if no definite answer can be given, can a case be made for safeguards on more general grounds such as improving transparency and public confidence in the system?

Roger Hood's research (1992), conducted at three Crown Court centres in the West Midlands in 1989–90, is still the most authoritative and comprehensive study of the effect of race or ethnic origin on sentencing outcomes. The study showed that some element of discrimination appeared to exist, especially at one court centre, although many of the differences in the sentences imposed on different groups of offenders could be explained by the greater number of black defendants who appeared for sentence and by the nature and circumstances of the offences of which they were convicted. Nacro and others would argue that although the sentences may not themselves reflect any conscious or unconscious prejudice against black people, they are the outcome of decisions taken at earlier stages in the process, as indicated above, and that those decisions may in their turn reflect some unconscious stereotyping and are likely to have a disparate impact on members of different racial groups. An example given at the Cropwood Round Table Conference for which this paper was originally prepared was of the practice at a magistrates' court where defendants surrendering to bail were generally offered advice on legal representation, but advice was not offered to black defendants because 'they are so laid back and don't care'.

Such situations were not covered by Roger Hood's study, nor did it consider magistrates' courts. In any event, the study is now nearly ten years old, and much attention has been given to the subject in the meantime, including an extensive programme of judicial studies and magistrates' training. A fresh study, on a larger scale, might produce different results, but in the meantime it is not possible to say that convincing evidence of discrimination actually exists.

A case might still be made, on general grounds of racial justice or public confidence, for procedural or evidential requirements which could be seen as providing safeguards against the possibility of discrimination, even if it has not been proved to exist, or as helping to promote equality. For example, at a Home Office conference shortly before the introduction of the Bill which became the Criminal Justice Act 1991, it was argued that recommendations in social inquiry (now pre-sentence) reports could be influenced by assessments of a person's social background and circumstances. If those were racially correlated, the person's race could potentially affect the range of sentences for which they could be considered, so resulting in indirect discrimination. Some participants argued that the provisions of the Race Relations Act 1976 should be extended to the criminal justice services, but the outcome was section 95 of the Act, as already mentioned.

Few people, and certainly no one in government or the judiciary, would be likely to support any proposal that would amount to positive discrimination in sentencing, or one that was focused explicitly on minorities or particular racial, ethnic or religious groups. Many judges and magistrates incline instinctively to the view that justice should be 'colour blind', and resent any interference with their discretion or any implication that they might be unknowingly preju- diced. Governments and political parties are acutely aware of the 'white backlash' which might follow what could be presented as an attempt to give special privileges to minority groups. More widely acceptable measures might be to establish certain features of a person's background as mitigating factors, or introduce procedural require- ments to take certain considerations into account. Examples might be evidence of disadvantage due to racial discrimination, or cultural or religious attitudes to family loyalties, marriage or sexual relationships. But this approach would still be controversial; it is difficult to see clearly what features or considerations the courts could legitimately take into account (social or economic disadvantage is not an excuse for crime); the process would be likely to be seen as time-consuming and burdensome, and probably provocative; and there could be no certain- ty that it would achieve the intended results. It could be argued that if the courts are determined to avoid discrimination or to promote equality, they have no need for extra requirements; and that if they are not, they will find ways of circumventing those requirements or making them ineffective.

The government's intentions and the Halliday Report

Early in 2001, the Labour government set out its own intentions for reforming the sentencing framework in the White Paper *Criminal Justice: The Way Ahead* (Home Office 2001a); the means of giving effect to those intentions (with some subtle reinterpretation) are the subject of the Halliday Report (Home Office 2001b).

The government seemed at the time of the White Paper to intend that:

- sentencing should focus more on the offender than on the offence, with a strong focus on the assessment of risk;

- community sentences should be rigorously enforced, with severe and automatic penalties for breach;

- offenders should be given training and education to help them not to reoffend; but

- those who do reoffend should receive progressively longer sentences of imprisonment, probably with some restriction on the court's discretion; and

- there would be special sentences of extended imprisonment for those assessed as dangerous, and for those considered to be suffering from 'severe and dangerous personality disorder'.

Halliday develops these intentions, adding to them four especially significant recommendations. These are in effect that:

- the principle of proportionality or 'just deserts' should be retained, but modified to take account of the offender's previous record as well as the seriousness of the current offence;

- prison sentences of under 12 months should be reformed to reduce where possible the time spent in custody and to include supervision after release;

- courts should have a capacity to review and in suitable cases to modify the sentence in the light of the progress being made; and

- a more coherent and comprehensive set of sentencing guidelines should be developed, under the auspices of a suitable (probably judicial) authority.

The Halliday Report has very little to say about race, ethnicity or religion. It recommends an extension of section 95 of the Criminal Justice Act 1991 to include a duty for the Secretary of State to publish information about the effectiveness of sentences and about any differences of approach between different courts, and this information could (though the Report does not say so) include material about any differential impact on minority groups. It is understandable, against the background described in this chapter, that the Report should have stopped short of recommending statutory provisions which would, for example, make a person's race, ethnicity or religion a factor to be taken specifically into account in a sentencing decision. But nor does the Report contain any discussion of its recommendations' potential impact in terms of differential outcomes for racial, ethnic or religious groups, or of the means by which such outcomes could be identified and if necessary corrected.

The Report's silence on this subject attracted criticism from some of those who commented on the recommendations on the grounds that it was irresponsible to ignore a matter of such public importance and controversy. It would certainly be irresponsible for the government or Parliament to ignore it when framing the resulting legislation, or when putting the legislation into effect. The subject is also one which a more wide ranging inquiry, for example a departmental committee, might be expected to examine in some detail. But it did not feature prominently in the evidence which was put to the review, and the government was unlikely to welcome a speculative discussion (of the kind put forward in this paper) which did not lead to any specific recommendations. These are matters which a civil servant, to a greater extent than a departmental committee, would have to take into account. To the extent that the criticism is justified, it is more a criticism of the form of the review than of the report which it produced.

It is perhaps significant that the government rejected out of hand a recommendation in Sir Robin Auld's parallel report on the criminal courts (Auld 2001) that provision should be made to ensure that some representation of racial minorities can be provided on juries hearing cases where there is a racial aspect.

There is nothing, either in the White Paper or the Halliday Report, which could be criticised as discriminatory in itself. But the concerns which were expressed at the time of the 1991 Act, and the evidence from the United States and Australia that rigid structures for sentencing can result in a disproportionate increase in the number of black or aboriginal people in the prison population,[1] suggests that special scrutiny is needed of some of the proposals, and of the way in which those that are implemented operate in practice. Examples include any differential impact resulting from:

- the use (especially any automatic use) of an offender's previous record to increase sentence;

- the reform of sentences under 12 months, and the resulting balance between the use of custody or supervision;

- procedures for the assessment of risk, or of suitability for programmes under community rehabilitation or punishment orders, together with the content of the programmes themselves;

- the enforcement of community sentences;

- the outcomes of sentencing reviews;

- the design of any pilot or development projects, and the rigour and integrity of their evaluation;

- the nature and especially the rigidity of the new sentencing guidelines;

- the composition, authority and legitimacy of the body which makes the guidelines and supervises their application.

One of the most difficult judgments to be made in reforming the sentencing framework is whether a reduction in the discretion available to the court would actually benefit black offenders, or those from other minority groups, by reducing the opportunities for stereotyped judgments. Another is whether the increased severity of sentencing – which in today's political circumstances is usually the objective – will be focused on offences which are disproportionately committed by members of minority groups, with the result that they are increasingly criminalised and form an increasing proportion of the prison population, and if so whether that matters. If increased severity can be justified on the basis of well-substantiated empirical evidence that it will protect society as a whole, any disproportionate effect on minority groups may be relatively unimportant. If not, and the evidence on this point is still very uncertain, then the result could be injustice and a source of legitimate grievance.

Towards a policy on diversity and sentencing

Conviction and sentence are the outcome, and climax, of a process which begins with the investigation of an offence and continues through the procedures for detection, prosecution and trial. Their legitimacy and integrity depend on the integrity of those procedures, and the outcome is supremely important, both for individual defendants and their victims, and for society as a whole. Any serious suspicion of discrimination would be intolerable in a liberal democracy or any civilised society. Avoidance of discrimination and respect for diversity are necessary conditions on which the justice of the sentencing process depends. Members of minority groups may be especially vulnerable to injustice, but the country as a whole has an equal interest, and white people stand to benefit to an equal extent. Against the background of hesitation and awkwardness described earlier in this chapter, it is important to recognise, and emphasise, that the whole country's interests are involved. Nor can measures to ensure justice in sentencing be confined to sentencing as such: they need to be taken across the criminal justice system as a whole.

Policies to prevent discrimination and to promote respect for diversity in sentencing need to have three aspects – measures relating to the criminal justice system and process as a whole; measures relating to the principles of sentencing generally; and measures set in the particular context of the government's proposals for sentencing reform following the Halliday Report.

Measures relating to the system and process as a whole would include:

- systematic monitoring of the various processes, including sentencing and other judicial decisions, together with periodical reviews of the adequacy and integrity of the monitoring process itself;

- extended training, and especially judicial training, to include a requirement for judges and magistrates to share their experience with colleagues, together with follow-up studies of the impact of training on practice;

- continued efforts to improve recruitment, retention and promotion in the relevant services, taking the Stephen Lawrence inquiry report, the Home Office Action Plan and the subsequent annual reports as starting points, but focusing especially on the composition of the higher judiciary at all levels – and including the establishment of an independent appointments commission as now argued by most interested organisations outside government;

- a comprehensive programme of research, to begin by updating and extending Roger Hood's study of race and sentencing and to include interviews with sentencers;

- a rigorous discipline, and perhaps a statutory requirement, for the thorough analysis of the effects – and side effects – of new legislation, and a commitment to reconsider policies that impact disproportionately on members of ethnic minority groups;

- open and effective communication between services, courts and their local communities.

Principles to be embodied in legislation should include:

- proportionality of the sentence in relation to the seriousness of the offence and the culpability of the offender, to be seen as setting an upper limit to the degree of punishment to be imposed;

- parsimony, in the sense that the sentence should be no more severe than is necessary in the circumstances of the case;

- recognised provision for compassion or mercy, so that less severe sentences can be imposed in suitable cases;

- judicial discretion, structured by guidelines and due process, but not restricted by automatic or mandatory sentences;

- if any form of extended sentence is needed for the protection of the public, such sentences should be subject to special procedures and review, with the reasons for the sentence and the expectations associated with it to be explained in open court.

The critical issues affecting discrimination and diversity which arise directly from the Halliday Report are those considered in Chapter 8 of the report 'The Shape of the Framework: Legislation and Guidelines', and in particular:

- how the guidelines are constructed, the purposes they are intended to serve, how far they go into detail, how far they are discretionary or mandatory and the degree of flexibility which they leave to the courts;

- the composition, character, authority and accountability of the body which draws up the guidelines;

- how the courts observe the guidelines in practice, and how rigorously and comprehensively their practice is monitored and evaluated.

All these issues are the subject of consultations which were still taking place at the time of writing. They raise issues of constitutional, legal and practical importance, affecting for example the guideline-making body's relationship with the Court of Appeal, government and Parliament, which are beyond the scope of this chapter. But for our immediate purposes:

- the guideline-making body should include people from a range of racial, ethnic and religious backgrounds;

- it should be required to consult widely, taking advice from all relevant interests and all sections of society;

- it should have access to and be required to consider relevant research and statistics;

- it should have the capacity to commission its own research and statistical analysis;

- in framing guidelines it should have a duty to do so in ways which will avoid and prevent discrimination and to promote racial equality;

- it should have a duty not only to frame guidelines but also to monitor and evaluate their application and impact, with specific reference to any disproportion or disparity;

- it should have a similar duty in respect of sentencing practice generally, with a view to amending or issuing new guidelines if they are needed;

- its terms of reference should allow it to propose primary legislation as well as to formulate guidelines;

- it should have a duty to address questions of discrimination and racial equality in its annual report, and powers to issue *ad hoc* or thematic reports as occasion demands.

The government's intentions on the detail of the Halliday Report were still uncertain at the time of writing, partly because it was not clear how far the present Home Secretary would share his predecessors' views and expectations when he established the review, and partly because of the delay in carrying forward the proposals which had been brought about by the events of 11 September and the change of priorities towards legislation on terrorism. Whether or not the Halliday Report is implemented as fully or as urgently as had previously been expected, there is a strong case for establishing, or re-establishing, the principles of sentencing in statutory form – with the implications for race, ethnicity and religion in mind, but with justice for all those involved in or affected by the sentencing process as the objective.

Notes

1 In 2000, the Australian government was criticised in a statement to the United Nations Committee on Racial Discrimination for the discriminatory effects on the aboriginal population of its policy of increasing sentences for persistent offenders (see also Freiberg 2001). In the United States, the effect

of guidelines and mandatory sentences has been significantly to increase the proportion of black offenders in prison: 60 per cent of the federal prison population is black. The situation is, however, complex: for a summary, see Reitz (2001).

References

Auld Report (2001) *Report of the Review of the Criminal Courts of England and Wales*. London: HMSO.

Commission on the Future of Multi-Ethnic Britain (2000) *The Future of Multi-Ethnic Britain*. London: Profile Books.

Faulkner, D. (2001) *Crime, State and Citizen: A Field Full of Folk*. Winchester: Waterside Press.

Freiberg, A. (2001) 'Three Strikes and You're Out – It's Not Cricket: Colonization and Resistance in Australian Sentencing', in Tonry, M. and Frase, R. (eds), *Sentencing and Sanctions in Western Countries*. Oxford: Oxford University Press.

Home Office (2001a) *Criminal Justice: The Way Ahead*, Cm 5074. London: Stationery Office.

Home Office (2001b) *Making Punishments Work: Report of a Review of the Sentencing Framework for England and Wales*, the Halliday Report. London: Home Office.

Hood, R. (1992) *Race and Sentencing*. Oxford: Clarendon Press.

Macpherson of Cluny, Sir W. (1999) *The Stephen Lawrence Inquiry*, Cm 4262. London: Stationery Office.

Reitz, K. (2001) 'The Disassembly and Reassembly of U.S. Sentencing Practices', in Tonry, M. and Frase, R. (eds), *Sentencing and Sanctions in Western Countries*. Oxford: Oxford University Press.

Scarman (1981) *The Brixton Disorders 10–12 April 1981*, Report of the Inquiry by the Rt Hon. Lord Scarman OBE, Cmnd 8427. London: HMSO.

Smith, D. (1997) 'Ethnic Origins, Crime and Criminal Justice', in Maguire, M., Morgan, R. and Reiner, R. (eds), *The Oxford Handbook of Criminal Justice*. Oxford: Oxford University Press.

Social Exclusion Unit (1998) *Bringing People Together: A National Strategy for Neighbourhood Renewal*, Cm 4045. London: Stationery Office.

Chapter 5

Setting sentencing policy through guidelines

Michael Tonry

Slumbering quietly, for the moment, in the Halliday Report's Chapter 8 is a disarmingly understated but central proposal that, if adopted and taken seriously, would radically change English sentencing policies and practices. (Here and hereafter, with apologies to the Welsh, 'England' and 'English' are meant to refer to England and Wales.) The proposal is for the creation of a sentencing commission charged to establish guidelines that, at least, would provide presumptive starting points for judicial considerations of sentences in individual cases.

The proposal is central because the report's recommendations for community, 'custody-plus' and custody sentences, and its policy proposals concerning criminal histories and assessments of offenders' needs and risks of reoffending, are all premised on the existence of guidelines much more detailed and comprehensive than now exist. Somebody must create them.

The proposal is disarming because it receives little discussion, and is presented almost as if it raised primarily technical issues. Chapter 8 indicates that guidelines will be needed if the report's core policy proposals are to be implemented, and that a sentencing commission under that or another name will be required to develop them. Several models are set out that differ in the extent of control and participation they afford the judiciary. The possibility is mentioned that the Sentencing Advisory Panel could play an important role.

The proposal is radical, however, because the guidelines required to support implementation of the report's main substantive sentencing policy recommendations must be of a scope, complexity and specificity several orders of magnitude beyond those of the existing case law guidelines enunciated by the Court of Appeal. They must address all offences, not just a handful of the most serious, and in particular must address high-volume offences of low and moderate severity for which no guidelines now exist. If the Halliday Report's recommendations concerning the centrality of proportionality as a guide and a limit on severity of punishment are to be respected, the guidelines must express sentencing standards comprehensively and not simply offence by offence. Guidelines must be coherent and principled not only within a single type of offence such as sexual assault or robbery but across all offences. Finally, if Halliday's recommendation that each successive offence receive an additional increment of punishment is to be pursued, the guidelines must indicate precise starting points for a wide range of offences and amounts of increased punishment associated with some successive number of 'recent and relevant' prior offences. Considered judgments of 'recency' and 'relevance' are likely to vary between offences and hence themselves require careful and contingent formulation

The Halliday Report indicates that guidelines are 'an essential part of the new framework' (Home Office 2001: vi). The guidelines would set standards for sentencing in the magistrates' and higher courts and would encompass all offences. The guidelines would 'specify graded levels of seriousness of offence, presumptive "entry points" of sentence severity in relation to each level of severity, how severity of sentence should increase in relation to numbers and types of prior conviction, and other possible grounds for aggravation and mitigation' (Home Office 2001: vii).

That's a tall order. England has no experience with comprehensive sentencing guidelines. The existing guideline judgments issued by the Court of Appeal 'remain clustered around the serious offences that attract substantial prison sentences' and do not address the high-volume offences, 'notably burglary, theft, deception, and handling stolen goods', that constitute the courts' volume business (Ashworth 2001: 75). In addition, as Martin Wasik, chairman of the Sentencing Advisory Panel, points out, 'There is little or no research evidence of their effectiveness in enhancing consistency' (Wasik 2001: 3).

English policy-makers have not before had to wrestle with top-down formulation of comprehensive, detailed sentencing policies. Parliamentary consideration of proposed changes to criminal and sentencing statutes is top-down but is necessarily pitched at high levels of abstraction and generality. The work of the Court of Appeal is squarely within the Common Law tradition of iterative development and refinement of doctrine as cases arise. It can be detailed but is not comprehensive across offences and is generally not comprehensive within a single offence. The work of the Sentencing Advisory Panel is potentially comprehensive within single offences but, because it is meant to elaborate and support the Court of Appeal's Common Law methodology, not across offences.

The magistrates' courts since the 1960s have been working with voluntary guidelines for some, initially motoring, offences, but as of 2000, according to Andrew Ashworth (2000: 55):

> It appears that magistrates in many areas have been using these [guidelines'] starting points, but in some areas the guidelines have been 'adapted to local conditions' and in a few areas the guidelines are not adopted . . . Important as the guidelines may be in offering practical guidance where Parliament and the Court of Appeal are silent, they have no authority whatsoever. They cannot bind magistrates in law, and justices' clerks are aware of this.

Likewise, England has little experience with 'independent bodies' or 'independent judicial bodies' charged to set sentencing policy. Halliday uses both phrases, possibly for reasons not specified to avoid unwanted connotations of the term 'sentencing commission'. There is considerable US experience with sentencing commissions and for simplicity I use that term. The Sentencing Advisory Panel established under sections 80–1 of the Crime and Disorder Act 1998 is the closest England has come to a sentencing commission. Its authority, however, is limited to the provision of recommendations to the Court of Appeal about guidelines for 'particular categories of offences'.

This chapter draws on US and, to a lesser extent, Dutch experience with guidelines to raise issues that are variously explicit and implicit in Halliday's proposals. More sentencing commissions have failed than have succeeded, and lessons can be drawn from the failures. Developing guidelines of the scope and ambition Halliday envisages will raise immensely difficult issues on which the enterprise will likely founder unless they are foreseen and avoided. Some guideline systems have won widespread judicial support, successfully altered sentencing patterns, reduced sentencing disparities in general and particularly in relation to race, ethnicity, and gender, and provided a tool for managing probation and prison populations. Lessons have been learned about circumstances that do and don't conduce to those achievements.

The policy and empirical literature on sentencing guidelines is surprisingly thin and that on sentencing commissions is even thinner.

There is a substantial legal literature on doctrinal issues but I ignore this. My *Sentencing Matters* (1996) canvasses the US policy and empirical literatures through 1995 and is the only entire book on the subject. A smattering of articles on empirical research and evaluations can be found in legal and social science periodicals. There is likewise only one entire book on sentencing commissions (von Hirsch, Knapp and Tonry 1986) and a handful of articles (e.g. von Hirsch 1986; Tonry 1991). There is only one soup-to-nuts insider's book-length account of a commission's guideline development work (Parent 1988) and there are two book-length outsider's accounts (of the federal (Stith and Cabranes 1998) and unimplemented New York (Griset 1991) efforts). Two of my edited books (Tonry and Hatlestad 1997; Tonry 2001) contain policy histories on guideline development and implementation in particular American states. I draw on those works in this chapter but also necessarily draw heavily on personal experience and knowledge. US experience identifies the nature of the involvement of the judiciary as the single most important element in whether sentencing commissions succeed or fail. If judges dominate the commission's work, it will fail. If judges actively or passively resist guidelines, they will fail. If judges cooperate in and endorse the commission's work, and accept the legitimacy of the resulting guidelines, the overall venture may succeed.

The main body of this chapter consists of three sections. The first canvasses issues concerning the nature, composition, leadership and functions of a sentencing commission. Such commissions have existed in the United States for a quarter of a century and things have been learned about when, why and how they succeed and fail. The evidence perforce is mostly anecdotal. There are significant differences in the legal and political culture between England and the US; American experience might not be transferable. But it might be, so there is value in looking to it.

The second section addresses issues that must be confronted and resolved in adopting presumptive sentencing guidelines. These include ranking of offences by severity, the effects of guilty pleas and criminal records, the handling of aggravating and mitigating circumstances, the need for impact projections concerning resource availability and disparate racial/ethnic and gender effects of policy choices, and the allowable extent and justifications for departures from guidelines. Some of these issues appear simple but for some people raise very difficult problems in constitutional and political theory. An example is the question whether offences should be ranked by the commission on the basis of an assessment of their comparative intrinsic (or typical) seriousness, or whether deference must be paid to seriousness rankings implicit in maximum authorised sentences set out in statutes. To most people who consider that question, the answer is obvious. Alas, though, different people perceive different answers to be obvious. This short chapter cannot examine such questions in detail but attempts to identify the major issues that are likely to arise and the principle alternative ways of thinking about them.

The third section concludes by considering whether the influence of the English judiciary presents an insuperable obstacle to the achievement of Halliday's goals, and if not how judicial involvement in the policy process, and cooperation in implementation, might be achieved. The conclusion also considers whether, in light of the high risk of failure an English sentencing commission will face, the effort is worthwhile. The answer is yes.

Commissions

Halliday's Report sets out four commission models: Option A (the Court of Appeal sitting in a special capacity), Option B1 (an independent body with strong judicial leadership, appointed by the Lord Chancellor, and composed solely of judges and magistrates), Option B2 (an independent body with strong judicial leadership, appointed by the Lord Chancellor, and composed of judges 'as well as professionals and academics'), and Option C (an independent body appointed by the Lord Chancellor, but without reserving its leadership to the judiciary, 'and having a more even set of members') (Home Office 2001: 55–6). Implicitly, as often is the case when three options are presented, Halliday favours the middle proposals (Options B1 and B2).

For reasons provided below, I believe the choice should be between Option C, and an additional variant, Option D (an independent body, appointed partly by the Lord Chancellor and partly by the government, without reserving leadership to the judiciary, and having a minority or bare majority of judicial members). If US experience is generalisable to England, commissions based on Options A, B1 and B2 are foreordained to failure and those based on C and D have some likelihood, under favourable conditions, of success.

Halliday's implicit preference for Options B1 and B2 appears to be based on beliefs that cooperation and support from English judges is essential to a successful sentencing law overhaul, and that they will not cooperate if they are not in charge. No doubt there is truth in this. English senior judges are influential, politically powerful and jealous

79

of their prerogatives, and they did through public opposition and statutory interpretation undermine and nullify key provisions of the Criminal Justice Act 1991 (Ashworth 2001). However, US experience instructs that commissions composed solely of judges or dominated by them are unlikely to devise guidelines of sufficient rigour and specificity to get the Halliday Report's jobs done. For proposals as comprehensive and ambitious as Halliday's, it is preferable from a strategic policy perspective to make a serious effort and fail than to take half-hearted measures that are categorically unlikely to achieve Halliday's aims. A judicially run and dominated commission is unlikely to adopt guidelines of sufficient ambition to effect major changes in sentencing practice. A commission in which judges play important roles, and in which judicial members support the policies adopted, is capable of adopting ambitious policies and winning judicial support for them. So, at least, the US experience suggests.

The creation and operation of a successful sentencing commission is not easy. More than half of the sentencing commissions in the United States have failed. Some failures were absolute. Commissions in Maine, Connecticut and New Mexico, for example, decided that their mission was a fruitless one and produced reports opposing the adoption of guidelines. Others, such as in New York (Griset 1991), South Carolina, and in the first instance Pennsylvania (Martin 1984), developed guideline proposals that were rejected by legislatures. Still others, notably Wisconsin, Tennessee, Louisiana and Florida, developed guidelines that were implemented but within a few years the legislature abolished the commission and, usually, the guidelines (Tonry 1991; Reitz 2001a).

Other commissions that survived in literal terms are seen by many as substantive failures. At one extreme, Pennsylvania's commission adopted presumptive guidelines that were approved (technically, not disapproved) by the legislature but were eviscerated by appellate courts that construed appellate review standards so deferentially to trial judges that the 'presumptive' guidelines are effectively voluntary (Reitz 2001a). At the other extreme, the US Sentencing Commission promulgated guidelines of such complexity and severity that they are generally characterised as a good idea gone bad (e.g. Doob 1995).

Table 6.1 in Reitz (2001a) shows the experiences of American sentencing commissions. The most successful commissions (Minnesota, Washington, Oregon and North Carolina) were adequately funded and staffed, and undertook ambitious statistical analyses of past sentencing practices in order to inform policy-making, provide a basis for making impact projections and provide a baseline for evaluation of the operation of the guidelines. In other words, unlike commissions described above whose failures generally resulted in part from inadequate funding or technical skill, these commissions had adequate resources of appropriate kinds.

And all four commissions were charged to develop *presumptive* sentencing guidelines. Statutes instructed courts in all five jurisdictions that sentencing judges must provide 'substantial and compelling' justifications for imposing sentences other than as indicated by applicable guidelines. The appellate courts in Washington, Oregon and Minnesota construed those words in slightly different ways but more or less consistently with their plain meanings. However, in one polar case, the federal appellate courts enforced the guidelines with such vigour that the guidelines are widely reviled and widely (hypocritically and surreptitiously) circumvented (Tonry 1996: chapters 2 and 3; Stith and Cabranes 1998). At the opposite pole, Pennsylvania's guidelines were reduced to nought by appellate courts that decided not to enforce them (Reitz 1997). This is evocative of the Court of Appeal's wilful undermining in *Cunningham* (1993) 14 Crim. App. R. (S) 444 of the provision in subsection 2(2)(a) of the Criminal Justice Act 1991 that provided that prison sentence lengths should be '... commensurate with the seriousness of the offence'. The Court of Appeal rewrote those plain words by construing them to mean '... commensurate with the punishment and deterrence that the seriousness of the offence requires'. This stands on its head both the stated aim of the White Paper that preceded the 1991 Act and all conventional understandings of 'commensurability' and 'proportionality' as terms of art in relation to punishment (Ashworth 2001: 78).

Before discussing key issues about commissions that must be decided before one could be established in England, it may be helpful to recall Judge Frankel's original proposal. The subtitle of his book *Criminal Sentences – Law without Order* (1971) derived from his perception that sentencing in US federal courts was 'lawless,' by which he meant that sentencers were unguided by legal rules or presumptions when making decisions about offenders' liberty. He contrasted this unfavourably with tort and contract law for which legal doctrine provided such guidance as to both liability and damages.

His proposed solution, the implementation of presumptive sentencing guidelines adopted by a specialised administrative agency, was based on several arguments. One was that setting comprehensive sentencing policies would best be done by a dedicated agency that could accumulate specialised expertise and an institutional memory. Legislatures were seen as less able to do this job because attention spans are short and staff turnover is high. A second was that acknowledgment of the importance of democratic accountability could be achieved either actively by requiring legislative approval of proposed guidelines or passively by providing that proposed guidelines be presented to the legislature and take effect after a designated period unless rejected. A third was that a specialised agency with members appointed for fixed terms would be somewhat more insulated than are legislatures from short-term passions and concerns for political expediency. A fourth was that persons might be appointed as commissioners who had specialised expertise and who collectively embodied the perspectives of a cross section of interested agencies and disciplines. A fifth was that an ongoing staff under stable leadership could perform important collateral functions including data collection, performance monitoring, training, development of proposed amendments and impact projections.

All of these aims have been realised by the handful of successful commissions in Minnesota, Washington, Oregon and North Carolina, and many of them have been achieved by Delaware's hybrid Sentencing Accountability Commission (Tonry 1996: chapters 2 and 3; Reitz 2001a, 2001b). In most of these states, for example, commissions are regularly called upon to develop impact projections of proposed statutory changes. The resulting projections are taken seriously, staff are regarded as credible and analyses often result in refinement or abandonment of proposed statutory amendments (Boerner and Lieb 2001; Wright 2002).

Commissions don't, can't and in democratic theory probably shouldn't provide complete insulation from populist and other short-term political pressures. They have, however, provided buffers that have kept policies steadier and have spared states like Minnesota, Washington, North Carolina and Delaware some of the more extreme forms of contemporary three-strikes, truth-in-sentencing and mandatory minimum sentence laws. Minnesota and North Carolina also managed to constrain prison population growth at levels well below the national average.

That short overview is meant to demonstrate that commissions can, but often do not, achieve the goals that Judge Frankel had in mind, and that the Halliday Report appears to envisage. It's not easy though. The following propositions set out some of what's been learned from US experience.

First, avoid judicial dominance. Most commissions dominated by judges have failed to develop successful guidelines systems. Some of the systems developed by judges, most famously in Maryland and Florida, were defensive efforts to forestall other sentencing changes that might more fundamentally constrained judicial discretion (Carrow 1984). Many of the systems designed by judges have resulted in 'voluntary' guidelines. The evaluation literature in the US has not documented a single instance where voluntary guidelines have successfully changed sentencing patterns in a jurisdiction (Tonry 1996: chapter 2).

Some of the successful commissions have been chaired by judges (e.g. Thomas Ross in North Carolina, Douglas Amdahl in Minnesota). All have included influential judges among their members. All have been independent agencies, usually in the executive branch of government. Strikingly, most of the judges who have played key roles in developing successful guidelines systems were trial judges at the time (though most were subsequently promoted to higher judicial posts).

Why is the record of judicial involvement in guideline development so dismal? Maybe because judges by training and ideology are especially committed to the desirability of judicial discretion and reluctant to establish sentencing rules that seriously constrain that discretion. Or maybe because judges and most practising lawyers are used to focusing on one case at a time, they are less accustomed to thinking in broad policy terms than are legislators, executive branch officials and policy analysts. Whatever the reason, sentencing policy is too important a subject to be left (solely) to the judges.

One argument for judicial domination of development of sentencing guidelines warrants special mention and unequivocal refutation. This is the notion that development of sentencing standards is somehow an unconstitutional violation of judicial independence. In 25 years working on sentencing policy issues in the US, I have never heard an American judge make that argument. No one there questions the authority of legislatures to define the elements of crimes, set mandatory or minimum penalties, specify sentencing criteria and create rebuttable and irrebuttable presumptions about appropriate dispositions. In any case, in England as in America, there is no doubt that legislators have constitutional authority to enact sentencing laws of general application (Ashworth 2000: 44–8). As Lord Bingham (1996: 25) wrote concerning statute-mandated minimum sentences:

> There is room for rational argument whether it is desirable to restrict the judges' sentencing discretion in the way described or not. As parliament can prescribe a maximum penalty without infringing the constitutional independence of the judges, so it can prescribe a minimum. This is, in the widest sense, a political

question – a question of what is beneficial for the polity – not a constitutional question.

Whether the commission should be placed in the judicial or the executive branches involves assessments of English constitutional law that are beyond my competence. The US federal sentencing commission is an independent rule-making body in the judicial branch. If this is doable in England, there is no reason why that model should not be adopted here. If, however, 'in the judicial branch' entails only actions by the Court of Appeal or a senior judge, the commission should be located in the executive branch.

Second, only a minority or bare majority of the members should be judges. The commission should be independent of the Court of Appeal and able to make decisions by majority vote (though ideally unanimously after vigorous debate and compromise) of members who include a majority or large minority of non-judges. Interests and values in addition to those held dear by judges are germane to the formulation of wise and workable sentencing policies. If decision processes do not give influential voice to proponents of those other issues and values, they are likely to be ignored or undervalued. This is partly a gloss on the first point. There need to be enough non-judicial members to assure that deliberations and decisions take serious account of non-judicial views.

There are other reasons why many or most members should be non-judges. These can be illustrated starkly by reference to Option A (the Court of Appeal under another name). First, other professionals, including lower court judges, magistrates, prosecutors, probation officers, prison officials, defence lawyers and academics, possess relevant specialised knowledge. Many would argue that the views of ex-offenders, victims, former offenders and treatment providers should be represented. Second, guidelines must be sold not only to judges but also to prosecutors, defence lawyers, magistrates and probation officials. Each in significant ways can influence case dispositions before or after trial, or both. In the States, members of commissions, including judges, were often seen and used as points of contact with and ambassadors to their respective constituencies. This is important to the adoption/approval/non-rejection of proposed guidelines but also to their successful implementation. A respected, credible prosecutor or probation officer may be much better placed to sell a commission's proposals to their colleagues than can a commission composed solely of judges.

Ideas about transparency and accountability are also relevant. Detailed sentencing guidelines are sufficiently law-like that their development should occur in the open, involve wide consultation and incorporate the views of a wide range of people. They are in effect a form of delegated legislation. The independence of individual judges setting sentences in individual cases within constraints of applicable law should be sacrosanct, but this does not mean that judges alone should set sentencing policy.

Third, the chair probably should be a judge, though this is not essential. This point acknowledges the centrality of judges to sentencing and sentencing politics in England. Judges are the professional group whose acceptance of a new guidelines scheme will be most important to its success, and the ____ commission's credibility in the eyes of judges is therefore vital. Having a judge as chair and having the commission informally called the commission after its chair are both likely to be symbolically important to judges.

Considerably more important, though, is that the chair be a politically powerful figure who is committed to the guidelines idea and prepared to expend personal political capital to win their adoption and assure their successful implementation. This could be a judge but need not. In Minnesota, the American jurisdiction generally said to have had the most successful commission and guidelines, the key figure (though not the chair) was Judge Douglas Amdahl, at the outset of the commission's work a trial judge and eventually chief justice of the Minnesota Supreme Court. In North Carolina, the chair and key figure was Judge Thomas Ross, at the outset a trial judge and later director of the Administrative Office of the North Carolina Courts. In Delaware, the key figure and sometime chair was Judge Richard Gebelein; he had also previously been state Attorney General. In Washington, the key figure (though not the chair) was Norm Maleng, the elected County Attorney of King County (Seattle). In Oregon, the key figure (though again not the chair) was the elected Oregon Attorney General Hardy Myers.

For England, there may be a trade-off here to be considered. The ideal chair would be a politically powerful senior judge who cared deeply about guidelines and was prepared to spend political capital to achieve a workable, principled guidelines system. Credibility in the eyes of the judiciary and effectiveness could be achieved in one person. If, however, a judicial chair could not be found who fitted that description, a non-judicial chair would be preferable. A commission chaired by a judge who is, on balance, apathetic, unenthusiastic or hostile to guidelines will not likely accomplish much of value. If a choice must be made between having a judge as chair and having an effective chair, effectiveness should take precedence. A toothless set of guidelines, like Pennsylvania's or several states' judicially adopted voluntary guidelines, is worse than no guidelines at all.

Fourth, the commission's key functions should be the development and successful implementation of presumptive sentencing guidelines for all offences. A sentencing commission is a specialised administrative agency and it needs the resources of a successful administrative agency. In the short term, this includes experienced administrative and research staff and sufficient money to complete a two-year guideline development process. The process perforce will include widespread consultation concerning particular subjects and successive iterations of draft guidelines; a combination of original data collection and analysis of existing data sets to provide baseline data for policy purposes, for forecasting and for the evaluation of operation and effects of the guidelines; and development of capacities for training judges and other practitioners at the outset and providing ongoing training and technical assistance after implementation.

In the medium and long terms, the commission will need resources for ongoing monitoring and training, for evaluation and for continuing refinement of the guidelines. Both to inform policy-making and take advantage of the uniquely rich data sets commissions typically create, ongoing work should include an active programme of intramural and extramural research.

Fifth, the guidelines should be presented to Parliament and automatically take effect six months after the presentation date unless rejected in full by vote of Parliament. Parliament cannot, of course, bind subsequent parliaments but the principle should be established that guidelines should be rejected in full or not at all. The rationales for a commission include its development of specialised expertise and its capacity to develop a coherent set of interlocking guidelines. Piecemeal review and acceptance or rejection would be inconsistent with the notion that the commission's special expertise should be respected and deferred to, and would inevitably result in anomalies when some particular provisions were rejected and others, premised on them, were not. Requiring acceptance (through inaction) or rejection (by vote) would place pressure on the commission to develop defensible guidelines as the success of the whole would be defeated if a single controversial provision imperilled promulgation of the guidelines as a whole. The guidelines should be promulgated through inaction rather than after an affirmative vote because that gives presumptive weight to the commission's decisions and makes it more likely they will be approved.

Why Parliament rather than the Court of Appeal, or the Lord Chancellor, as the final arbiter? First, the judiciary is neither the only constituency nor the only bureaucracy that has an interest in sentencing policy. Giving the judiciary the final word would in effect be to provide for the adoption of guidelines only to the extent and in the form the judiciary approves. Second, the commission might decide on policy grounds that more constraint is needed than judges favour, and there would be a fox-in-the-hen-house quality to a provision that let the judges decide whether the commission's judgment about the need for constraint was correct. The judiciary could, of course, like any other constituency, make its views known to Parliament during the six-month review period.

Sixth, the commission, with the possible exception of the chair, should be part-time. This ukase may appear odd, and is based on only one case. No state sentencing commission had full-time members except, rarely, the chair. The federal Sentencing Reform Act of 1984 initially provided for a seven-member full-time commission. This proved so disastrous that the legislation was amended in the early 1990s to provide for part-time commissioners. The statute required that three commission members be judges. Throughout the commission's life, all judicial members have chosen to continue hearing cases, so they have in effect been part-time. The remaining four initial members were full-time and several proved themselves meddling nuisances who organised cliques, interfered in the staff's day-to-day work and tried to establish independent political bases for themselves. The positions were well-paid (at the level of a federal Court of Appeals judge) and the duties were far from full-time. The staff must be full-time, but the commissioners need only attend regular meetings and do interim reading.

Seventh, the Lord Chancellor should appoint judicial members and the Home Secretary should appoint non-judicial members. Bifurcated appointment powers make sense on a number of grounds. For formal and substantive reasons, the Lord Chancellor is in an especially good position to select judicial members. There is, however, no reason to impute comparative advantage to the Lord Chancellor concerning appointment of prosecutors, probation and prison officials, academics or other non-judicial members. The Home Secretary through the Home

Office staff interacts professionally and regularly with these groups and has much more extensive experience and networking on which to draw. Moreover, there is reason to be apprehensive that many judges are sceptical about the desirability and workability of meaningful guidelines (that apprehension would be warranted in every jurisdiction in which I've ever worked). There is also reason to apprehend that a judicial appointment authority might not select people known to be enthusiastic supporters of guidelines or known to be less than completely sympathetic to judicial sensibilities or preferences.

Hybrid appointment schemes were common in the US. All appointments to the seven-member US Sentencing Commission were made by the US President with the advice and consent of the US Senate. Three of the seven members, however, had to be judges selected from a longer list of nominees put forward by the Chief Justice of the US Supreme Court. Elsewhere, details varied from state to state but the most typical model called for the state governor to make some appointments, the state legislature to make some and the state supreme court to make some.

In the end, the success of a system of guidelines depends on the technical knowledge, policy sophistication, political acumen and leadership of the body that creates it. More commissions have gone wrong than right, and no set of structural arrangements can assure success. However, experience suggests choices among structural alternatives that can make success more and less likely. The gravamen of this section is that the leadership and membership of a sentencing commission are absolutely essential to the success of any guidelines-drafting effort. Get these seriously wrong and the venture cannot succeed.

Guidelines

Getting the commission's membership right is necessary but not sufficient for getting guidelines right. Answers to a small number of crucial questions can be got wrong and they can doom or at least unnecessarily complicate the entire enterprise. I can't in the length allowed for this chapter discuss all the major issues, or any at length, but touch on the most important.

First, the commission needs to agree on a governing rationale or purpose. Sentencing guidelines succeed when and because they make normative and policy sense. More overtly in the US but inevitably also in England, judicial and other practitioners choose whether and how to comply with statutes, rules and guidelines (in this paragraph I'll use the word rules to mean all of these). Rules that practitioners consider to be unwise, unfeasible or unjust will seldom be enforced with vigour or integrity. This is why many mandatory minimum sentencing laws are so often inconsistently and unjustly applied. Conversely, if practitioners understand the logic and underlying principles of a rule, they are more likely to apply it consistently and fairly even if they disagree with it. This is the experience in the US states with successful guidelines systems. A commission's first order of business consequently should be to work on and provisionally adopt an agreed rationale and set of purposes.

Setting the general purposes of sentencing is easy. Few people would disagree that primary purposes include crime prevention and reduction, the affirmation of widely held public moral values and the imposition of deserved punishments. Others might add something about victims; I believe high priority should be given to addressing victims' needs but that this raises social welfare or civil law rather than criminal law issues. Whether, however, victims' issues are or are not among the general purposes of sentencing, reasonable people can quickly reach agreement about purposes when stated at this level of abstraction.

Agreeing a rationale is considerably harder, as the early references to *Cunningham* illustrate. Reasonable people have divergent but powerful intuitions about just punishment. The draftsmen of the 1991 Act, and the scholars on whose work they drew and relied, meant for the 1991 Act to be premised on desert rationales and accordingly meant and understood the term 'commensurate' when applied to punishment to mean 'commensurate [or proportionate] to the gravity of the offence'. This presumably seemed straightforward or obvious to them. To the judges who decided *Cunningham* it must have seemed equally straightforward and obvious that judges must take account of what they (much more than any other relevant professional group) see as an inexorable need for deterrence.

I drew the preceding paragraph's contrast a bit tendentiously, but for emphasis. The point is that, whatever the deterrence literature may show, many judges believe themselves to be in the marginal deterrence business. Ignoring this, the 1991 Act experience shows, foreseeably can lead to judicial resistance. Recognising this, however, emphasises the importance of persuading judges that policies are sound, legitimate and principled. If the commission itself cannot reach and then justify choices in such matters, the guidelines will be incoherent or unpersuasive. Neither adjective gives grounds for confidence that sentencing judges will enthusiastically accept and apply guidelines.

US experience indicates that people of good will working together as members of sentencing commissions can reach and then explain decisions about rationales, and accordingly can explain and justify decisions based on those rationales. This is a major part of the Washington, Oregon and North Carolina stories, in which judges were initially reluctant participants in the development of guidelines but eventually became active proponents and helped convince the judiciary at large that guidelines were sound in principle and wise in policy. Most US commissions adopted some form of desert or limiting retributivism as their governing rationale. The US commission refused to adopt a rationale and many observers attribute the federal guidelines' incoherence, excessive severity and lack of credibility to this decision and its consequences (Stith and Cabranes 1998).

Reaching agreement about rationales is not easy. Omnibus purposes of 'retribution, deterrence, incapacitation, rehabilitation, and moral education' are too broad and all-inclusive to serve as a policy premise. Relatively pure retributive or utilitarian rationales are unlikely to win broad-based support. A hybrid that takes serious account of ideas about desert and yet allows flexibility to acknowledge competing widely accepted values is the most likely to win widespread support.

The Halliday Report opts for 'limiting retributivism' (Home Office 2001: appendix 8) but of a vague sort. In the abstract, most versions of limiting retributivism offer three major claims. Offenders cannot justly be punished more severely than their current offence deserves. Offenders should never be punished more severely than the minimum they deserve unless there are good articulated reasons for doing so. Within those bounds, other considerations may justify the imposition of different sentences on offenders convicted of comparable crimes.

Whatever decision the commission initially makes, however, should be provisional. Consideration of particular issues (for example, taking account of prior offences or sentencing for concurrent offences) may indicate that no policy response that commands wide support is consistent with the initial rationale. Sometimes the solution will be to defer a decision and think about it some more. Sometimes the solution will be to revisit a provisional rationale that, the commission may decide, needs refinement or qualification.

Second, the guidelines adopted should cover at least all serious offences. Whether 'serious offences' should be understood roughly to mean indictable and either way offences, or should be defined *de novo* is a decision for the commission to take. It is, however, at minimum important that guidelines cover all categories of offences which are prosecuted in considerable numbers and for which substantial prison sentences (say, exceeding one week) are imposed.

The key point is that guidelines should include all regularly recurring offences for which prison can be imposed, including burglary, theft, receiving stolen goods, garden variety assaults and minor drug crimes. Wide breadth of coverage is substantively important. The Halliday proposals if adopted will effect a major change in sentencing policies and practices and the guidelines' main aim is to facilitate their implementation. Equally importantly, wide coverage forces policymakers to consider options in light of other choices. If, for example, stranger rape is punishable with a four-year prison sentence, can a four-year sentence be justified for a third-time low-value, commercial burglar? Or, if a decision is made to increase stranger rape sentences from a four-year to an eight-year mean sentence, for what other offences should sentences be reduced, and by how much, to implement the rape sentencing decisions within existing resources? Development of comprehensive guidelines forces attention to such questions.

Third, the commission should develop its own ranking of offence severity. This obscure but important point raises fundamental questions of constitutional and political theory for some people. The problem is that comprehensive guidelines require classification of offences into a manageable number of categories on the basis of their seriousness. Almost all people, regardless of the punishment theory or rationale they espouse, share powerful intuitions about proportionality: more serious crimes deserve severer penalties than less serious crimes (the 'proportionality principle') and comparably serious crimes deserve comparably serious penalties (the 'equality principle'). In order to devise comprehensive guidelines, some method must be used to identify comparably severe offences that can be put into particular offence seriousness categories.

The difficulty is that in no jurisdiction does legislation provide sufficient guidance for the necessary sorting. In some US jurisdictions, for example, that adopted versions of the Model Penal Code, felonies are divided into three classifications each subject to specified maximum authorised sentences. There are several ways in which such a system is insufficient to guide sentencing commissions. First, three is too few categories. Most commissions developed six to twelve categories of offence seriousness, and accordingly had to make their own decisions on how to allocate offences to categories. One might argue that they should have respected legislative offence classes and done no more than partition those into subclasses. None did this, however, because of beliefs that the legislative classes were over-broad and insufficiently discriminating. Second, with only three offence classes, offences were described generically and commissions decided that various sub-categories of offence warranted different seriousness rank. For example, robbery permutations with and without guns, with and without victim injury, with and without high property loss might all fall in different guideline severity categories. Third, some legislative classifications were simply seen as unsound, the products of a moment's moral panic or political expediency. These decisions were not controversial or seen (by most people) to raise constitutional issues, because US guidelines are invariably put before the legislature for active or passive consideration.

In England, I suspect, this issue may be more controversial than in the US. Offences are not classified in English law except implicitly by reference to maximum authorised sentences, and very broadly in terms of whether indictable, summary or triable either way. From this it might be inferred that Parliament has classified all offences (all subject to maximum sentence X or X plus or minus Y per cent are deemed in one class, etc.). Almost undoubtedly, such an inferred classification system will be incoherent and full of anomalies. This is not surprising since criminal penalty legislation tends to be adopted piecemeal, and seldom to be reconsidered, so over time the whole is a product of a wide range of different times, personalities and cultural norms about punishment.

The commission must largely ignore any inferred parliamentary classification scheme and devise its own. If the guidelines are facially incoherent or arbitrary, and classify together offences that in day-to-day understanding are of substantially different seriousness, they will lack credibility altogether. They will necessarily prescribe comparable sentences for offences that are generally seen as substantially different in their seriousness. This violates the equality principle and, since judges no more than other people wish to act unjustly, foreseeably will foster unjust sentences, circumvention of the guidelines and stark disparities between like-situated offenders who did and did not benefit from circumvention. Guidelines that lack surface credibility will not be taken seriously.

The answer for England is that the commission must classify offence seriousness in its own way. This has in practice seldom proved difficult. Research in many countries and US sentencing commission experience show that western peoples, at least, have widely shared beliefs about offence seriousness. Concern about respect for parliamentary sovereignty can be addressed by requiring that the proposed guidelines be placed before Parliament for passive or active consideration, but subject to a proviso that the guidelines must be accepted or rejected in their entirety.

Fourth, the commission should be required to carry out and publish impact projections for its final proposed set of guidelines. Provision of state resources to operate corrections systems should reflect policy decisions about levels and priorities of public expenditure. The commission should by statute be instructed to try to develop guidelines whose application when implemented will, in light of stated and reasonable assumptions about case flows and compliance patterns, be consonant with existing and planned probation and prisons capacities (both physical and human). Should the commission decide that increased public investment is necessary, the report to Parliament accompanying the proposed guidelines should justify such decisions.

This proposal is simple good government. There are no free lunches. Public investments should be the product of deliberate public policy choices. A resource constraint policy forces realism on policy-makers: if severer penalties are wanted for offence X, there must either be facilities available to deliver those penalties or decisions must be made to reduce penalties for other offences or increase public investment. The commission could not appropriate funds but its report to Parliament should include why public investment should be increased and by how much.

Fifth, the commission should be required to carry out and publish projections of the likely effects of proposed guidelines on racial, ethnic and gender disparities. Members of some minority groups in England are grossly disproportionately over-represented among prison inmates. No major study of sentencing disparities has been completed since Roger Hood's study (1992) of sentencing of whites, Afro-Caribbeans and Asians in Midlands courts. His conclusion, that offence and criminal record differences explain much of the apparent disparity but that case processing variables explain some and some remain unexplained, remains the final authoratative word on the subject. Racial, ethnic and gender disparities are *prima facie* undesirable. A sentencing commission should accordingly be fully apprised of the ramifications of its policy choices for the sentencing of members of different social groups.

We know that some policies affect some groups more than others. For example, a sentence discount on the basis that a defendant is a primary care provider to minor children would benefit women more than men. Or a decision in the United States to lengthen prison terms

93

for violent offences would disparately affect black defendants since we know that violence rates are higher among black Americans than among whites (for understandable social-structural and SES reasons).

This proposal speaks to the commission's final report, but its logic argues for use of disparate impact analyses at every stage of its decision processes. The resulting data showing how a particular policy will exacerbate or ameliorate disparities affecting a particular group will not determine policy choices but will assure that the commission is informed of their implications. Imagine for example that members of an ethnic minority group, the Eloi, were believed on the basis of self-report and police data to commit sexual offences at twice the general population rate. A proposal to double average prison sentence lengths for sexual offences would increase the Eloi fraction of prisoners and create or worsen disparities. Conceivably that knowledge would lead to reconsideration or refinement of the proposed policy. Or not. Credible data would probably show that most Eloi sexual offences were intra-group, which would mean that punishing Eloi offenders more severely might better protect potential Eloi victims. This might by many be seen as justification for the adoption of a policy known to be likely to increase prison population disparities.

The Eloi hypothetical arises in every legal system. Some groups have higher violence rates than others and decisions to punish violent offences more severely do foreseeably worsen imprisonment dispari-ties. This occurs in the US in relation to black offenders. Black offending rates for robbery, rape and homicide are substantially higher than for whites and recent moves to increase penalties for violent crimes foreseeably worsen black/white prison disparities. Rape and homicide are primarily intra-group and black rapists and murderers accordingly mostly victimise black victims. Not taking violent crimes by black offenders seriously can also be seen as not taking crimes against black victims seriously and as a result few policy-makers have opposed penalty increases on disparate racial impact grounds. (Were I involved in making such policies, I would see worsening racial disparities as an evil to be avoided to the extent possible and would reduce penalties across the board so that disparities would not worsen and offences against minority victims would still be seen to be taken seriously.)

There are offences for which disparate impact analyses might affect policy choices. Drug trafficking and minor street offences are examples. If members of particular groups are disproportionately involved in drug trafficking, decisions to increase penalties or law enforcement vigour for drug crimes will disproportionately burden those groups.

Conversely, decisions to lessen penalties or moderate enforcement will benefit those groups. This might be thought of as a harm reduction strategy focused on social exclusion/inclusion that paralleled harm reduction strategies targeting public health.

Sixth the commission should adopt a policy that no number of offences in the same seriousness category can be sentenced in aggregate to a sentence more severe than the most severe sentence authorised in guidelines for the next most serious offence category. This concerns the question how to set a just sentence when several offences are being considered simultaneously. England has got this right, under the label of the 'totality principle' and the US has got it wrong. The Halliday Report would preserve the totality principle, described thus: '[W]hen several offences are sentenced together, the combined effect should be more severe than would have been justified by the most serious offence, but not so severe as to be outside the range for that offence' (Home Office 2001: 13). If a defendant were being sentenced for 20 household burglaries, or for one burglary and 19 shopliftings, the aggregate sentence could not exceed that which would otherwise be justified for a serious burglary. Or another example, if the range of appropriate sentences for shoplifting is 0–12 months, and that for armed robbery is 2–5 years, on a strong version of the totality principle the aggregate sentence could not exceed 12 months and on a weak version 24 months. If a 25-month sentence were imposed, the result would be a shoplifting punishment more severe than an armed robbery punishment, violating both proportionality concerns and commonly held intuitions about offence severity. The leading common law analysts who have considered the problem have endorsed the totality principle (Lovegrove 1989; Ashworth 2000: 226–30) and Swedish practice embodies it (Jareborg 1998).

The Americans and the Dutch have got it wrong. Both countries have fallen prey to a formal retributive logic that every offence deserves punishment. In the extreme US case, one draft of US Sentencing Commission guidelines was premised on the notion that every increment of penal harm or culpability deserved a measurable increment of punishment (Robinson 1987). This works for violent offences which can be scaled generically but not for property offences. If, for example, the penalty for a theft of $1,000 warrants three months' imprisonment, how much does a $500 million dollar securities fraud warrant? Linear extension of the idea that $1,000 deserves three months would generate impossibly long sentences. The proposed solution: depending on the amount involved, for large numbers take the square or cube root of the property value and use the resulting number in a linear logic. That was not credible, and was rejected for the normal US policy of having no policy at all. Judges may exercise unguided discretion in deciding whether sentences for multiple offences must be served concurrently or consecutively.

Dutch prosecution guidelines for sentence recommendations do a little better but in an unprincipled way (Tak 2001; Schurer and van Loon 2001). The numerical guidelines give designated point values to every crime and to every regularly recurring feature of crimes. When multiple crimes are under consideration, the full point score for all crimes is calculated. However, if the resulting total exceeds a certain level, it is discounted by 50 per cent and above another level by 75 per cent. This produces realistic sentence recommendations but an underlying principled rationale is hard to articulate.

I may be belabouring the point a bit since Halliday proposed retaining the totality principle. I do so because a logic that every prior offence warrants an increment of additional punishment for each successive offence, often associated with Jack Straw when Home Secretary, has been gaining currency. This is not exactly the same subject but is parallel ('Each current offence warrants an additional increment of punishment') and raises similar issues of principle. It would be a pity if a sentencing commission failed to preserve such a widely admired policy as the totality principle.

Seventh, the commission should adopt a policy strictly limiting the extent to which the punishment for a current offence can be increased on account of prior convictions. One possible policy might provide that no number of prior offences of the same or lower seriousness as the current offence can justify a prison sentence more than 50 per cent longer than could be imposed under applicable guidelines, and that no number of prior offences of a higher seriousness category can justify a prison sentence more than 75 per cent longer. This proposal is based on similar premises as the totality principle: deserved punishments should be proportionate to the culpability expressed by the primary current offence.

Many people have an intuition that offenders who have previously been convicted of a crime should be dealt with more harshly, all else equal, than offenders who have not been previously convicted. Different arguments can be offered for why that should be so – because previous convictions offer bases for stronger predictions of subsequent offending, because a person who has offended previously is somehow more culpable than a first offender, because first offenders receive a benefit-of-the-doubt discount that they lose when sentenced subsequently, or because subsequent offending is a manifestation of defiance against the state or the court. Whatever the reason, however, respect for proportionality concerns should dictate that the primary determinant of a just sentence be the offence for which it is imposed. The Halliday Report's recommendation that sentences be based on the current offence and any 'recent and relevant prior' convictions is defensible on principle only if qualified in a way such as I have proposed.

England does not have a restrictive principle for sentence increments on account of prior crimes that parallels the totality principle for multiple concurrent crimes. US systems of guidelines, even those that explicitly adopted a just deserts or modified just deserts rationale, have got this grievously wrong. In many guideline grids, authorised sentences for people with prior convictions are two, three, or four times longer than for first offences. This is especially ironic in jurisdictions like Minnesota, Oregon and Washington that devoted close attention to the establishment of offence severity scales and to the extent to which penalties should increase *for first offenders* for each increase in offence severity. Although those relations were worked out with care, the effects on sentence of prior convictions were dealt with only crudely. The implicit principle is that deserved punishment varies more with the number of prior offences than with the seriousness of the current crime, and that can't be correct.

In England, having got the totality principle right, a sentencing commission might well be able to get a parallel principle right for addressing the relevance of prior 'recent and relevant' convictions.

A sentencing commission must address many other questions than these.

Guilty pleas. How should guilty pleas be handled, and should it matter when in the process a guilty plea is made? English law comfortably accommodates the progressive loss of mitigation doctrine by which sentence discounts up to a third are given to defendants depending on whether and when they plead guilty. Guidelines development would afford opportunity to reconsider that doctrine. It is hard to justify in principle since it provides a powerful incentive to innocent persons to plead guilty and waive their right to trial; it increases by 50 per cent the penalty a wrongly convicted defendant will receive after trial. For all defendants it provides a penalty for asserting the basic human right to demand a trial. The rationale for guilty plea discounts is that without them most defendants would plead not guilty and the courts would grind to a halt. The empirical evidence in support of this belief is weak.

Sentence discounts raise another troubling problem. In practice they exacerbate sentence disparities adversely affecting Afro-Caribbean defendants. Roger Hood's research (1992) showed that Afro-Caribbean defendants plead guilty less often and later than did white defendants, which means that on average they received harsher sentences on this basis. There is good evidence in England and other countries that young men from many minority groups feel discriminated against by the police and for this reason often are alienated from the criminal justice system (Tonry 1997: chapter 1). The result is that people who may have good grounds for their alienation are nonetheless penalised for it.

Development of guidelines provides an opportunity to reconsider the mitigation doctrine and possibly to reduce racial disparities in sentencing.

Guidelines format. What form should the guidelines take: should they be expressed as a numerical grid for all offences, as separate grids for specific types of offences, as a series of statute-like statements? All these formats are in use somewhere and things are known about their properties, strengths and weaknesses.

Guidelines specificity. How detailed should guidelines be? They can range from broad to narrow. The US federal guidelines are highly detailed, divide offences into 43 severity levels and assign specific weights to a long list of aggravating circumstances. The Pennsylvania guidelines list only statutory offence definitions and all aggravating and mitigating factors are weighted as the judge in his or her discretion believes appropriate. Minnesota's guidelines fall in between.

Almost any factor (for example, gun use or possession; gratuitous infliction of injury; racist motive; victim vulnerability) can be handled in one of three ways: as an element that determines offence severity, as a designated aggravating or mitigating circumstance, or as justification for a judicial decision to depart from the applicable guidelines. Take gun use as an example. The offence classifications could sub-partition violent crimes to rank those involving guns at higher severity levels. Or, the offence definitions used in the offence rankings could be restricted to elements of offences as defined in statutes, but rules on aggravation and mitigating circumstances could designate gun use as an approved aggravator. Or, the approved aggravating and mitigating circumstances might be silent on guns but judges might indicate gun use as a reason for departing from the otherwise applicable guideline.

Criminal history. Halliday strongly and repeatedly asserts that past criminal records should play a role in setting sentences for current offences: ' ... severity of sentence should increase when an offender has sufficiently recent and relevant previous convictions' (Home Office 2001: iii, recommendation 3). Obvious subjects for rule-making include tests for 'recency' and 'relevancy' and for under what circumstances 'sufficiency' is present. These questions, however, are merely the beginning of those that criminal history raises.

Here are some others. Should there be one 'recency' test? For example, that all convictions in the preceding five years (or five years at liberty?) count, or should the answer vary depending on the nature of the current or the prior offence? Should relevancy be general (all prior convictions within the recency period) or particular (for current violent crimes, only prior violent crimes count)? Should all relevant and recent prior convictions be given the same weight, or should some, for example violent or sexual crimes, be given greater weight? And so on. Existing US systems of guidelines provide examples in operation of all these possibilities.

A well-led and sensibly constituted commission will have to make these and other essential policy decisions. Doing so successfully will require that commission members come to the task with open minds and prepared to look to relevant data, experience elsewhere, the products of impact projections and the likely reactions of practitioners.

Conclusions

Judges are part of the sentencing policy problem and must be part of the solution. They are part of the problem by definition. They make many of the crucial decisions and for any change in policy to work requires a change in their decisions. They are also part of the problem ideologically in England and in most countries. Judges tend to believe that sentencing is a craft that cannot except very crudely be subjected to rules, that judges have special understanding of sentencing, and accordingly that the best sentencing systems will be those that give large discretions to judges. Put bluntly, judges' centrality in the process and their common belief in their need for discretion mean that they often are fierce and effective opponents of proposed changes in sentencing policy or practice. If the weight of judicial opinion is strongly opposed to a sentencing policy innovation, they will kill it. They may through public opposition prevent its adoption. If it is adopted, they have the power to stop it through non-compliance or through imaginative appellate decision-making.

Judges must be part of the solution. No system of guidelines can succeed unless prevailing judicial sentiment is kindly disposed. In modern jargon, this is an issue of legitimacy. If judges do not see guidelines as principled and sensible and a reasonable accommodation of competing values and goals, they will be seen as an illegitimate intrusion on judicial discretion and as a source of unjust outcomes.

How can judges be won over? First, the commission must be seen by judges to be credible. Halliday proposes doing this by giving judges 'ownership' of the commission. He would give judges a dominant or exclusive voice in its work, give the Lord Chancellor the power of appointment, give the judiciary a majority of seats on the commission and locate the commission in the judiciary.

This for reasons urged above goes too far. The bases for scepticism that a judicial-dominated commission would produce a bold sentencing policy innovation are just too strong. The better course is to be conscious of the centrality of the judiciary, to select powerful and influential judicial members and to make sure judges are active in policy discussion and development.

Second, the commission must always be concerned about practical matters of implementation, about the processes by which new policies must be carried out if they are to succeed. Partly this is a matter of credibility. If a proposed policy is likely to be seen by judges as unworkable, or raises serious foreseeable implementation problems, one way or another the commission must adapt accordingly – change the policy or put forward a feasible solution to the implementation impediment.

Third, very substantial thought and resources must be invested in educating the judiciary and all affected practitioners about the guidelines development process and about the guidelines ultimately adopted and the reasons why they were adopted. The goal, put differently, is to persuade judges and others that the proposed guidelines are a Good Thing.

There are grounds for pessimism that the English judiciary may be so indisposed to the development of guidelines that meaningfully restrain sentencing judges' discretion that the chances of success are too low to justify the effort. As a newcomer to Britain I lack sufficient knowledge to take a view.

If that pessimism is warranted, a fallback question is whether commission-developed guidelines really are a necessary element of the Halliday proposals. The answer is unclear. Existing legislation on community and confinement penalties could be repealed and replaced with legislation establishing the proposed community, custody-plus and custody sentences, without the creation of either a commission or guidelines. So could Halliday's proposals for continuing judicial oversight of the implementation of penalties. So could many specific recommendations concerning the nature and management of community penalties including intermediate sanctions.

The final question is whether the risks justify the effort of creating a sentencing commission and charging it to develop guidelines. The answer on balance is yes, but more because of the need to bring the Rule of Law more fully to English sentencing than to achieve implementation of the Halliday proposals.

On the affirmative side, the Halliday Report provides an opportunity to bring the Rule of Law to English sentencing. Sentencing is about the state's deprivation of individuals' liberty or property because they have reliably been adjudged to have violated key behavioural standards. At present, though English law observes a wide variety of evidentiary, procedural and processual standards aimed at assuring justice in adjudication, it contains few such standards aimed at assuring justice in punishment. Most conspicuously, save for the Court of Appeal guideline judgments whose scope is narrow and whose influence is uncertain, and statutory provisions setting maximum (and a few minimum) sentences, English law contains no rules governing the nature and amounts of punishment. Sentencing in England in 2002, like the US sentencing described by Judge Marvin Frankel in 1972, is lawless.

The creation of a sentencing commission and the development of guidelines will facilitate the achievement of Halliday's proposals. And guidelines if successful will make English sentencing more consistent, transparent and predictable; will reduce the scale of racial, ethnic and gender disparities; will provide a tool for the management and control of state resources devoted to the punishment of offenders; and will make judges more accountable for their decisions about citizens' liberties.

On the negative side, guidelines, even where they have been successful, are not an unqualified blessing. In particular they sometimes create injustice by failing to acknowledge meaningful differences between cases. Justice in sentencing requires that like cases be treated alike and that meaningfully different cases be treated differently. Completely individualised, indeterminate sentencing aimed to treat different cases differently, and, whether it did this successfully or not, often was seen (and demonstrated) to fail to treat like case alike. Sentencing guidelines, truth-in-sentencing laws and mandatory minimums all aim to treat like cases alike but often fail to treat meaningfully different cases differently. Getting the balance right is difficult and every system is imperfect. Whether guidelines or other determinate sentencing systems are desirable for a particular jurisdiction depends on the nature of its sentencing patterns. In a country like the US, in which sentences are measured in years, decades and lifetimes, an unwarranted disparity may cost a citizen years of his or her life. Pursuit of the goal of treating like cases alike may be sufficiently important to risk excessive rigidity and a loss in ability to treat different cases differently. In a country like Sweden in which most sentences are measured in days and weeks and only a tiny fraction are for a year or longer, the dangers of unwarranted disparity will typically be slight and only a small price need be paid to maximise the capacity to individualise sentences and treat different cases differently.

By European standards, England locks up a large fraction of its people and for relatively long terms. In these respects it looks more like the US than Sweden. The risks of unwarranted sentencing disparities are far greater in England than in Sweden, and for serious crimes lengths of sentences in England approach those in the US. As a result, England is a jurisdiction in which the dangers to liberty represented by too great judicial discretion are substantial. In a balancing of harms, the risks of unwarranted disparity in England sufficiently outweigh those of unwarranted uniformity to make guidelines worth attempting.

References

Ashworth, A. (2000) *Sentencing and Criminal Justice*, 3rd edn. London: Butterworths.

Ashworth, A. (2001) 'The Decline of English Sentencing and Other Stories', in Tonry, M. and Frase, R.S. (eds), *Sentencing and Sanctions in Western Countries*. New York: Oxford University Press.

Bingham, Sir T. (1996) 'The Courts and the Constitution', *Kings College Law Journal*, 7, 12–26.

Boerner, D. and Lieb, R. (2001) 'Sentencing Reform in the Other Washington', in Tonry, M. (ed.), *Crime and Justice – A Review of Research*, vol. 28. Chicago: University of Chicago Press.

Carrow, D. (1984) 'Judicial Sentencing Guidelines: Hazards of the Middle Ground', *Judicature*, 68, 161–71.

Doob, A. (1995) 'The United States Sentencing Commission: If You Don't Know Where You Are Going, You Might Not Get There', in Clarkson, C. and Morgan, R. (eds), *The Politics of Sentencing Reform*. Oxford: Clarendon.

Faulkner, D. (2001) *What Is the Boundary between Legislation and Guidelines in Sentencing? What Role Should Parliament Have?* Paper prepared for QMW Public Policy Seminar on Policy and Practice for Sentencing, 23 October.

Frankel, M. (1972) *Criminal Sentences: Law without Order*. New York: Hill & Wang.

Griset, P. (1991) *Determinate Sentencing: The Promise and the Reality of Retributive Sentencing*. Albany, NY: SUNY Press.

Home Office (2001) *Making Punishments Work*, Report of a Review of the Sentencing Framework for England and Wales (July 2001). London: Home Office Communication Directorate.

Hood, R. (1992) *Race and Sentencing*. Oxford: Oxford University Press.

Jareborg, N. (1998) 'Why Bulk Discounts in Multiple Offence Sentencing?', in Ashworth, A. and Wasik, M. (eds), *Fundamentals of Sentencing Theory: Essays in Honour of Andrew von Hirsch*. Oxford: Oxford University Press.

Lovegrove, A. (1989) *Judicial Decision-Making, Sentencing Policy, and Numerical Guidelines*. New York: Springer-Verlag.

Martin, S. (1984) 'Interests and Politics in Sentencing Reform: The Development of Sentencing Guidelines in Pennsylvania and Minnesota', *Villanova Law Review*, 29, 21–113.

Parent, D. (1988) *Structuring Sentencing Discretion: The Evolution of Minnesota's Sentencing Guidelines*. Stoneham, MA: Butterworths.

Reitz, K. (1997) 'Sentencing Guidelines Systems and Sentencing Appeals', *Northwestern Law Review*, 91, 1441–506.

Reitz, K. (2001a) 'The Status of Sentencing Guidelines Reforms in the United States', in Tonry, M. (ed.), *Penal Reform in Overcrowded Times*. New York: Oxford University Press.

Reitz, K. (2001b) 'The Disassembly and Reassembly of US Sentencing Practices', in Tonry, M. and Frase, R.S. (eds), *Sentencing and Sanctions in Western Countries*. New York: Oxford University Press.

Robinson, P. (1987) *Dissenting View of Commissioner Paul H. Robinson on Promulgation of Sentencing Guidelines by the US Sentencing Commission*. Washington, DC: US Sentencing Commission.

Schurer, G. and van Loon, R. (2001) 'The Netherlands Adopts Numerical Prosecution Guidelines', in Tonry, M. (ed.), *Penal Reform in Overcrowded Times*. New York: Oxford University Press.

Stith, K. and Cabranes, J. (1998) *Fear of Judging: Sentencing Guidelines in the Federal Courts*. Chicago: University of Chicago Press.

Tak, P. (2001) 'Sentencing and Punishment in the Netherlands', in Tonry, M. and Frase, R.S. (eds), *Sentencing and Sanctions in Western Countries*. New York: Oxford University Press.

Tonry, M. (1991) 'The Politics and Processes of Sentencing Commissions', *Crime and Delinquency*, 37, 307–29.

Tonry, M. (1996) *Sentencing Matters*. New York: Oxford University Press.

Tonry, M. (ed.) (1997) *Ethnicity, Crime, and Immigration: Comparative and Cross-national Perspectives*. Chicago: University of Chicago Press.

Tonry, M. (2001) 'Punishment Policies and Patterns in Western Countries', in Tonry, M. and Frase, R.S. (eds), *Sentencing and Sanctions in Western Countries*. New York: Oxford University Press.

Tonry, M. and Hatlestad, K. (eds) (1997) *Sentencing Reform in Overcrowded Times*. New York: Oxford University Press.

von Hirsch, A. (1986). 'The Enabling Legislation', in von Hirsch, A., Knap, K.A. and Tonry, M. (eds), *Sentencing Commissions and Their Guidelines*. Boston: Northeastern University Press.

von Hirsch, A., Knapp, K.A. and Tonry, M. (eds) (1986) *Sentencing Commissions and Their Guidelines*. Boston: Northeastern University Press.

Wasik, M. (2001) *How Should Guidelines Be Produced? How Should They Be Monitored?* Paper prepared for QMW Public Policy Seminar on Policy and Practice for Sentencing, 23 October.

Wright, R. (2002) 'Counting the Cost of Sentencing in North Carolina, 1980–2000', in Tonry, M. (ed.), *Crime and Justice – A Review of Research*, vol. 29. Chicago: University of Chicago Press.

Chapter 6

The uses of imprisonment

Alison Liebling[1]

Introduction

> The Prison Service has to live with ... prisoners during their time
> in prison. The rest of the country lives with them afterwards. We
> cannot afford to lock them up and forget them. We must ensure
> that the Service makes proper use of the time which a prisoner
> spends in prison, and the best use of the money available for
> keeping him or her there. The aim must be to reduce the likelihood
> of prisoners re-offending after release. (Woolf Report 1991)

> Home Office Aim 4 – HM Prison Service Aim: 'Effective execution
> of the sentences of the courts so as to reduce reoffending and
> protect the public'. (Prison Service 2001)

The purpose of the Halliday Review (Home Office 2001) was to
formulate a new correctional vision which would enhance public
understanding and confidence and improve the efficiency and effectiveness of sentences. There is a critique in the report of short prison
sentences (less than 12 months), as well as a critical review of the
apparent meaninglessness of the second half of prison sentences. There
is (paradoxically) a recommendation for a new sentence of anywhere
between two weeks and three months, with a period of supervision to
follow, during which time offenders who breach their more stringent
supervision conditions would be swiftly returned to custody (Home
Office 2001: 20). This new sentence of custody-plus, that is custody
followed by work carried out in the community, aims to reduce
reoffending. The imprisonment part of this sentence would be 'for

punitive purposes' (Home Office 2001: 20) and would be followed by 'a programme under supervision in the community aimed at tackling offending behaviour'. Imprisonment is the threat which makes compliance with community penalties more likely.

For those small number of offenders 'for whom post custody supervision is not needed' a sentence of 'plain custody' of up to three months would be available. There are also tentative proposals for intermittent custody, weekend custody and a 'suspended sentence plus', to be made possible by a review of the current estate and the development of 'community prisons' that would lend themselves to that sort of sanction. Halliday suggests that these proposals might increase the prison population by an additional 6,000 places.

This chapter provides a brief review of constructive uses of imprisonment, and then considers these possibilities in the light of some of the Halliday proposals. The chapter is incomplete as it has not taken account of the just published Resettlement Thematic Review (HMCIP 2001), a forthcoming report on resettlement by the Social Exclusion Unit, nor the impending publication from a review of local prison work with the short term offender. There is an impending review by the National Audit Office of all prison-based programmes and activities, including drugs, work and education. There are two other caveats, which I shall mention briefly below. The first is related to prison population size, and the second is a note of caution on any assumption that prisons can be positive.

Caveat I: The current prison population in England and Wales

Four milestones were reached by the Prison Service of England and Wales in November 2001: over 68,000 prisoners; 19,000 prisoners doubled up in cells built for one; 4,900 life sentence prisoners; and over 4,000 women (personal comment). Local prisons are in crisis and are 'creaking at the seams'. This over-use of prison is linked to an unjustifiable promotion of the idea that 'prisons can work' alongside a loss of confidence in *delivery* within criminal justice generally. The idea of prison as an 'unavoidable last resort' has been lost.

The prison population in England and Wales on 2 November 2001 was 68,181, an increase of 3,995 on the corresponding Friday of 2000. This figure includes 53,582 adult males; 10,576 male young offenders (aged 15–21 inclusive); 3,452 adult females; and 581 young females. There are around 13,000 prisoners on remand. The operational capacity of the estate is 71,510 (67,247 male places and 4,263 female places).[2] There are an additional 1,636 offenders under Home Detention

Figure 6.1   Prison population 1988-2001

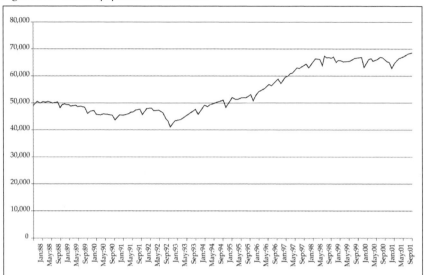

Curfew.[3] The imprisonment rate in England and Wales is 124 per 100,000 general population, the second highest among western European countries. The growth witnessed from 1993 to 2001 has been phenomenal, and has continued despite a downturn in recorded crime rates (Home Office 2000). Most of the rise is accounted for by an increase in custody rates. Drug offenders constitute the fastest growing group (particularly on the female side) and account for just over a quarter (26 per cent) of the overall increase in sentenced prisoners since 1993 (burglars account for 21 per cent; violent offenders for 18 per cent; theft and handling 11 per cent and sex offenders 9 per cent). Figures also show that offenders convicted of lesser property offences (theft and handling) accounted for 42 per cent of those sentenced to three months or less (9,590 receptions) in 2000 (personal comment). There has been an apparent lowering of the custody threshold: that is, a change in the sentencing climate.

The decade 1990–2001 saw a steadily *reducing* prison population followed by the rapidly increasing population described above. As Lord Woolf remarked 'ten years on' from his report into the disturbances at Strangeways, the last decade has seen the lowest as well as the highest prison population for over a century (see Figure 6.1). In considering the uses of imprisonment, this background 'noise' is important. There was a slight slow down in the rate of increase in the size of the prison population over 1999 and 2000, but the increase has stepped up again in 2001, is likely to continue and may grow again in anticipation of impending legislation. Current projections suggest that the population may reach 83,500 by 2008 (Gray and Elkins 2001).[4] The female population in England and Wales has increased by more than the male population. These recent massive increases in prison population size (that is, a strategy of collective incapacitation) means we are imprisoning relatively low-risk (low-cost) offenders, which reduces the cost-effectiveness of prison. Interventions tend to work better with 'medium/high risk' offenders (Losel 1995; Friendship *et al.* forthcoming). The consideration of positive uses of imprisonment to follow is predicated on an assumption that a reduction in prison use overall would enhance the cost-effectiveness of prison.

Caveat II: Problems with the use of imprisonment

Prisons are, and must be, places of legal suffering. (Gallo and Ruggiero 1991: 273).

> ... It breaks up families. It is hard for prisoners to retain or subsequently to secure law-abiding jobs. Imprisonment can lessen people's sense of responsibility for their actions and reduce their self-respect, both of which are fundamental to law abiding citizenship. Some, often the young and less experienced, acquire in prisons a wider knowledge of criminal activity. Imprisonment is costly for the individual, for the prisoners's family and for the community. (Home Office White Paper 1991: para. 1.16)

Dostoyevsky commented, after four years in a Siberian prison, that his time in prison had awoken within him a deep optimism about the future of mankind, because, if man could survive the horrors of prison life, he must be a 'creature who could withstand anything'. Quite apart from this kind of suffering, there is evidence that the prison might contribute to the cycle of crime:

> When the bonds linking youth to society – whether through family or school – are weakened, the probability of delinquency is increased. (Sampson and Laub 1993: 247)

Sampson and Laub's 1993 study of crime and deviance over the life course shows that prison reduces opportunities to achieve relational and economic stability which in turn reduce reoffending. Their theory of informal social control demonstrates how social bonds (in particular employment and marriage) may inhibit offending. Imprisonment weakens these (initially weak) bonds which are difficult to re-establish and which constitute a significant source of legitimate or law-abiding behaviour. Imprisonment thereby becomes part of the cycle of the social process of delinquency. The quality or strength of social ties are crucial in determining the life course of individuals over time. They outweighed differences between groups in early childhood experiences.

> ... the stronger the adult ties to work and family, the less crime and deviance occurred among both delinquents and controls.
> (Sampson and Laub 1993: 248)

Although early offending behaviour precedes imprisonment, Sampson and Laub show that those offenders with 'the most to lose' had the best chance of positive 'recovery' or change. Imprisonment in youth and early adulthood had a negative effect on later job and relationship stability, which were 'negatively related to continued involvement in crime over the life course' (ibid.). This was related to length of incarceration and could not be explained by individual differences such as previous criminal history, excessive drinking, etc. These indirect but powerful 'criminogenic' effects of imprisonment on life course transitions are significant:

> ... the effect of confinement may be indirect and operative in a developmental, cumulative process that reproduces itself over time. (ibid.: 168)

I am particularly sceptical about the short-term use of imprisonment. What is the rationale for very short prison terms? To make probation work? To punish? To deter? To protect? To reform? The prison is obviously better at punishment than at its other roles (see Tables 6.1 and 6.2). A total of 57.5 per cent of prisoners in a recent survey of prison life reported that their time in prison felt like a punishment. Note the interesting differences (from Liebling and Arnold 2001).

Short terms of imprisonment cannot be said to protect, except in so far as they break into an increasing spiral of offending and change its course. Prisons are not very successful at reform or rehabilitation (see Table 6.2: 27 per cent of prisoners agree or strongly agree that they are being helped to lead a law-abiding life on release; see also Home Office

Table 6.1   Prisoner evaluations of aspects of their treatment in five prisons (2001): Punishment

Question	Belmarsh %	Holme House %	Risley %	Doncaster %	Wandsworth %
4. My time here seems very much like punishment.					
– Strongly agree/agree	83.1	46.8	53.4	49.1	61.7

Table 6.2   Prisoner evaluations of aspects of their treatment in five prisons (2001): Rehabilitation

Question	Belmarsh %	Holme House %	Risley %	Doncaster %	Wandsworth %
6. I am being helped to lead a law abiding life on release.					
– Strongly agree/agree	13.2	29.8	29.8	35.1	21.6

1999; Lloyd *et al.* 1994; and below, on reconviction rates), although I shall return to look at some of the evidence for apparent progress in this area later in the chapter.

On the other hand, we are increasingly reliant on the prison for the achievement of certain policy and political objectives. There are increasing expectations of the prison. Particular establishments are trying very hard at a local level to break into the cycle of crime. So, to the main business of this chapter. What positive work can be achieved using the prison? Can prisons live up to these expectations? What is the prison 'good at' and how should it be used? This chapter explores briefly some of the positive uses of imprisonment and some of the evidence about 'what works', drawing on some of what is most currently available.[5] It describes the nature of various types of positive prison regimes, including the therapeutic regime at Grendon, and other attempts to innovate and introduce positive regimes which address offending behaviour. I shall then consider the evidence on short custodial regimes and consider the Halliday proposals in the light of what we currently know about prison.

Using the prison to reduce reoffending

The narrowest approach to the question of prison use is to ask whether specific programmes offered in prison actually reduce reoffending. There are broader ways of approaching this question – for example, to focus on particular types of regimes rather than discrete programmes and to look more widely at 'effectiveness'. These issues will be addressed later in the chapter. First, it is important to establish how reliable reoffending studies are. Most rely on reconviction rates as their measure of effectiveness.[6] Below I offer some figures and a familiar note of caution.

Reconviction rates as a measure of effectiveness

Of all prisoners discharged in 1995, 58 per cent were reconvicted for a standard list offence within two years of leaving prison (Kershaw *et al.* 1999). For prisoners released in 1995, 33 per cent returned to prison. The reconviction rate for adult males was 53 per cent (with a 30 per cent return to prison rate within two years); for male young offenders the rate was 77 per cent (with a 52 per cent return to prison rate); it was 47 per cent for females (with a 21 per cent return to prison rate). In general, reconviction rates increase with the number of previous convictions and the number of previous sentences served. There are serious difficulties inherent in using reconviction rates as a measure of whether or not 'prison works'. They are not neutral, technical 'facts'. The term reconviction as used in research studies can mean arrest, the receipt of a sentence, the receipt of a prison sentence, a parole violation, or offence seriousness. The exact relationship between reconviction and reoffending is not known. The British Crime Survey estimates that for every 100 crimes committed, only 2 result in a criminal conviction. Reconviction rates then are only a proxy measure of offending; they may reflect increasing use of custody, police and prosecution practice; different follow-up periods are used in different studies or may be appropriate for different types of offences; there are technical difficulties (such as missing data); the statistics are collected with different aims in mind and they may mask important differences between probation centres and areas or individual prisons. In the UK the term reconviction is typically defined as 'the conviction for any offence during follow-up' (Newcomen, personal comment). Reconviction rates are generally lower for offenders given longer sentences (this reflects the age and other differences in the characteristics of these offenders). For offenders serving sentences of up to 12 months the reconviction rate is 58 per cent; for offenders serving 4–10 years the rate is 26 per cent (Lloyd *et al.* 1994). What this illustrates is the finding that the most *serious* offenders are not necessarily the most *frequent* offenders. For a small number of more serious offenders serving longer terms, the Prison Service has arguably started to intervene, moderately successfully, if reconviction rates can be trusted (see appendix 6.1 to this chapter). It is the shorter sentence persistent offender the prison has more trouble with.

I want to look at the 'what works' debate generally and at the kinds of programmes currently offered in prison. These programmes are currently offered mainly to prisoners serving medium to long-term sentences. However, there are prospects for these programmes to be started in custody and continued in the community (a model I support). First, what is the evidence that 'programmes' work?

The what works debate revisited

> ... it is simply untrue that 'nothing works' when it comes to treatment with offenders: intervention, particularly cognitive-behavioural intervention, can have an impact on a range of target behaviours, including criminal behaviours. (Hollin and Howells 1996: 4)

Martinson's conclusion ('with few and isolated exceptions, the rehabilitative efforts that have been reported so far have had no appreciable effect on recidivism', Martinson 1974) was based on an evaluation of 231 outcome studies carried out between 1945 and 1967. The review essay is actually full of mixed results as most of those interested in this field now know. His pessimistic thinking happened to coincide with 'just deserts' and other thinking of the time, but the article was rebuffed by Palmer in a 1975 article, 'Martinson Revisited'. In Palmer's opinion:

> In fact, almost every method turned out to be associated with some combination of positive results, inconclusive or ambiguous results, and negative results (meaning no significant differences between treatment and control groups). All his review suggests is that different things work with different groups and to different degrees, under different conditions – this could be seen as offering promising leads. It suggests the need for more research effort and more sophisticated techniques. 'Martinson's standard was whether any technique worked universally – a search for the impossible'. (See Palmer, 1975: especially pp. 138–9)

Palmer also suggested that policy-makers tended to seek utopian results – the sort of words used by academic researchers like 'complexity' and 'steady scientific progress' made policy-makers 'cringe'. According to his critics, failure to implement programmes effectively was not taken into account in Martinson's evaluation, nor in many of the negative evaluations which followed. Sociological critiques of the rehabilitative aspirations of institutions have been blamed for the failure of institutions to take up or properly implement 'promising programmes' identified in research (Hollin and Howells 1996: 10–11). Few of the studies evaluated by Martinson were methodologically 'robust'. Of the 34 that were, 16 showed positive treatment results. The 'nothing works' doctrine was never then fully supported by the evidence. It was also less influential on practice (as practitioners prefer to 'do something constructive' and are influenced by results with individuals) than often supposed (Vanstone 2000).

More recent critical reviews of the Martinson 'nothing works' evaluation study have proliferated. Thorough reviews of research and practice in understanding and working with offenders and the successful development of the 'meta-analysis' approach have led to a realignment of the 'nothing works' thesis. Meta-analyses find that theoretically well-founded cognitive-behavioural and multimodal types of treatment have positive effects. These studies also suggest that interventions should focus on criminogenic needs; and they should be properly managed, with clear aims and objectives (McGuire and Priestly 1995). Distinctions should be drawn between clinical and criminogenic outcomes. Research shows that more intensive intervention programmes should be targeted at 'high-risk' offenders; they should be structured, focused, and should include a cognitive component (addressing attitudes, values and beliefs), and should, wherever possible, be conducted in the community. Staff ownership and training is crucial, and an element of family work can be effective. Process studies are fundamental to outcome evaluations, as problems of implementation make outcome studies weak (Losel 1995).

More recent reviews of 'what works' in reducing reoffending identify eight common criminogenic factors. These are dynamic factors which can be addressed in prison (and which form the basis of the Canadian Needs Identification and Analysis system). They are: poor educational skills; poor employment skills; poor or absent marital/family relationships; having criminal friends and associates; substance abuse; poor community functioning (financial problems, poor accommodation, lack of support); personal and emotional factors (cognitive deficits, impulsivity, aggression, lack of empathy); and antisocial attitudes (Willmot 2000). Interventions which do not target these factors seem to be ineffective (and can be counterproductive). Willmot's review suggests that enhancing employability using workshop supervisors in detailed performance feedback and support, literacy and numeracy programmes, and offering parenting skills and fostering meaningful family contact are effective strategies which impact on reoffending. Many of these kinds of programmes are currently offered in prison (such as Custody to Work initiatives). The effectiveness of these programmes depends to a large extent on follow-up in the community (effective throughcare). Research and development of programmes on the role of criminal companions and how to avoid them is less advanced (Willmot 2000).

One of the major changes to have occurred in the Prison Service over the last decade has been the determination to introduce only the highest quality research-based offending behaviour programmes into establishments and to evaluate their effectiveness. They have to meet specified (research generated) criteria in order to be accredited.[7] Only accredited programmes count towards an establishment's Key Performance Indicators. Offending behaviour courses delivered in prison require a throughcare component in order to achieve accreditation. Some courses require a module to be delivered in the community in order for accreditation to be achieved. This development represents a major meeting of the findings from research with policy and a step change in the quality of the design and delivery of constructive work with prisoners aimed at reducing reoffending. The model of offending on which most of these offending behaviour programmes are based is cognitive-behavioural. This model assumes that behaviour is strongly linked to thinking, and that by addressing distorted thoughts, offenders will be less motivated to offend and develop more control over their behaviour. Most of the original programmes have been supplemented by booster and relapse prevention programmes aimed at reinforcing the learning accomplished on core programmes, and at rekindling the effects of such programmes after long periods in custody.

Seven programmes were in place at the time of writing: Reasoning and Rehabilitation; Enhanced Thinking Skills; a Problem-Solving Offending Behaviour course; RAPt (Rehabilitation of Addicted Prisoners trust); the Sex Offender Treatment Programme; Anger Management (CALM); and Cognitive Self-Change. Several other courses were at various stages of the acccreditation process: a version of Reasoning and Rehabilitation for young acquisitive offenders and a version for women; two programmes developed specifically for women – one on problem-solving, assertiveness and dealing with abusive relationships, the other on 'straight-thinking'. There is also a course for Violent Offenders, and some therapeutic community group work programmes aimed at tackling substance abuse.

Other programmes delivered in establishments have received 'interim' accreditation (which means the Panel will accredit them provided that identified amendments are made within 12 months, but meanwhile use is recommended; PSMB 2000). Interestingly, attending the Enhanced Thinking Skills course (which requires no admission of the offence) may increase willingness to volunteer for SOTP (which does require admission of the offence), so that individual prisoners may (where possible) work their way through those courses on offer in their establishments in different ways.

Establishments compete in a spending round for the resources required to host programmes – in this sense their distribution across the prison estate depends on a needs analysis carried out by area psychologists and, to a degree, on the enthusiasm and bargaining power of governors and staff with area managers, their populations and the business case made in the strategic planning process. There are more programmes offered at present in the south than in the north of the country, for example. Fifty-one per cent of SOTP programme tutors and 46 per cent of non-SOTP tutors are prison officers. Concern has been expressed that high numbers of prison officers are trained and then are not used, or gain rapid promotion (PSMB 2000). About two-thirds of establishments were delivering one or more programmes at the time of writing. Local prisons and open prisons with low staffing levels have the fewest programmes. There have been difficulties in the delivery in dispersal prisons – due to interruptions to the working day by searches, lock downs, etc. – so that accreditation is difficult to achieve against the constraints of the prison day. A new assessment system and a new determination to make programmes work in the dispersals estate has resulted in considerable progress in this area.

Reasoning and Rehabilitation (Cognitive Skills)

Studies of the longitudinal development of criminal careers have demonstrated that impulsivity is one of the main characteristics of chronic or persistent offenders (Farrington 1996, 1997). Impulsivity is linked to poor reasoning and decision-making (short-termism, lack of attention to consequences, low perceived locus of control, failure to avoid high-risk situations, etc.). Offending is seen as a consequence of 'faulty or immature reasoning'. Cognitive-behavioural techniques, such as the course developed by Ross and Fabiano in Canada, have been shown to be moderately successful in reducing impulsivity or increasing self-control (see Ross and Ross 1995; Ross *et al.* 1988). The Cognitive Skills (or Thinking Skills) programme includes interpersonal and social skills training. The aim of the 'Reasoning and Rehabilitation' programme originally developed in Canada but adopted in the UK, is to modify:

> the impulsive, egocentric, illogical and rigid thinking of the offenders and [to teach] them to stop and think before acting, to consider the consequences of their behaviour, to conceptualise alternative ways of responding to interpersonal problems and to consider the impact of their behaviour on other people, particularly their victims. (Ross *et al.* 1988: 31)[8].

Early research by the Prison Service's Programme Development Unit (OBPU) and the Research and Statistics Directorate found substantially reduced reconviction rates over 12 months after participation in prison accredited programmes (only). It found that of those who underwent the normal prison regime (no treatment), 40 per cent were reconvicted within two years; of those who took part in unaccredited programmes, 38 per cent were reconvicted within two years; of those who took part in accredited programmes, 18 per cent were reconvicted within two years (Clark, personal comment 1999). A more recent evaluation found that overall, the two-year reconviction rates for prisoners participating in Cognitive Skills Programmes compared to untreated prisoners was around 50 per cent lower for medium–high risk groups (see appendix 6.1 to this chapter).

The Sex Offender Treatment Programme (SOTP)

SOTP was launched in 1991 following adverse reports of the neglect of sex offenders and the impoverished regimes they experienced (Sampson 1994; Home Office 1991). Some sex offenders were receiving treatment prior to this but these courses were erratic and poorly supported in terms of training, resources and evaluation (Clark 1997). Before the introduction of Vulnerable Prisoner Units, sex offenders had been segregated 'for their own protection' and were subject to largely hostile and indifferent treatment by other prisoners and sometimes by staff (see, for example, Sparks, Bottoms and Hay 1996). This reinforced their beliefs that they were being victimised, and in some cases sex offenders were the victims of serious attacks. After the Strangeways disturbance in 1990, during which sex offenders became the target of hostile attacks, the Prison Service acknowledged that its policies towards sex offenders were inadequate and failed to protect either the public or the offenders (Terry 1999: 70). The Criminal Justice Act 1991 required the Prison and Probation Services to do more to protect the public from sex offenders.

As with many UK courses, the Prison Service developed its SOTP on the evidence of apparently successful treatment programmes developed in North America. Prisoners are rigorously assessed for their suitability for the programme, high-risk offenders being referred most frequently. The risk scale used is Risk Matrix 2000 and the factors used are: number of distinct court appearances where sentenced for a criminal offence including index offence; age at commencement of risk; any male victim of a sexual offence? any stranger victim of a sexual offence? ever had a live-in relationship lasting at least two years? And any non-contact sex offence? Those considered unsuitable are those suffering from acute mental illness, those at risk of self-injury, those suffering from severe paranoia or personality disorder, those with chronic brain damage or others considered unsuitable for medical reasons (Clark 1999). There is a separate programme for those with learning difficulties: the Adapted Programme. Twenty-seven establishments currently offer the SOTP, some offering the Core Programme only and others offering variations (the Extended Programme, the Booster Programme, the Rolling Programme and the Adapted Programme).

The Core Programme employs the 'Socratic' method of teaching – a motivational approach aimed at encouraging offenders to think for themselves by asking 'probing questions with a genuine tone of inquiry' (Mann and Thornton 1997: 11). It takes 180 hours to complete and is divided into 20 Blocks covering: Introduction (building group cohesion) (Blocks 1–4); Active Accounts of Offences (Block 5); Victim Empathy (including role-playing) (Blocks 6–9); and Relapse Prevention (Blocks 10–20). The Programme encourages offenders to understand why they committed their offences; to take responsibility for them; to modify their cognitive distortions (the false beliefs on which their behaviour is predicated); to develop an understanding of pro-social sexual fantasies, beliefs and behaviour; to learn social skills which may help them achieve normal adult relationships; to gain an understanding of the harm they have caused to their victims; and to control the negative emotional states which often underlie their offending (Terry 1999: 76; see also Beech et al. 1999).

Studies carried out to date show that treatment seems to be effective for some (particularly high-risk) individuals. Change has been demonstrated in relation to several aspects of offenders' thinking, for example: rape myths, child myths, submissiveness, benign control, social confidence, offence minimisation, self-esteem, victim-blaming, impulsiveness and hostility towards women (Terry 1999: 75–6). Two-year sexual and/or violent reconviction rates for treated released prisoners in medium-high risk groups (those who have completed the SOTP core programme) are significantly lower than for a comparison group (see Beech *et al.* 1999; and appendix 6.1 to this chapter).

What this review shows so far is that to be effective, programmes need to be carefully designed and implemented. They are resource intensive, and they need to unravel impulsive behaviour and risky thinking, normally over quite a long period of time. This approach became something of a 'holy grail', at one stage displacing other less formal approaches. Current developments include a more open and supportive approach to 'third way' or less easily accredited programmes. I want to turn to a slightly different type of programme – the recently accredited therapeutic approach.

Therapeutic and other effective regimes

The regime at HMP Grendon Underwood

Early evaluations of the effects of the therapeutic Grendon regime found no significant differences in the frequency or severity of post-discharge convictions from Grendon, using a matched control group (Gunn and Robertson 1987). In both samples, eight out of ten discharged prisoners were reconvicted within ten years. Genders and Player (1995), on the other hand, found that those prisoners who successfully complete the therapeutic process can be compared with those who do not and with control groups. The results from these comparisons showed a much more positive effect for those who completed the therapeutic programme. Their results suggested that reconviction studies should focus on prisoners who have successfully completed their therapeutic career rather than a random sample. Eric Cullen – using Genders and Player's therapeutic career model – followed up a random sample of 214 releases. He found that reconviction rates were lower (33.2 per cent reconvicted within two years compared with 44.7 per cent adult males released during the same period). He compared those who had stayed at Grendon for 18 months and found that 20 per cent were reconvicted compared to 40 per cent of those who had stayed less than 18 months. The probability of reconviction was even less when prisoners were released directly from Grendon (16 per cent) and when they were rated as a 'success' in therapy (7 per cent). It is of course possible that these results reflect selection and motivation (Cullen 1993). Taylor found lower reconviction rates among prisoners who had stayed for at least 18 months (Taylor 1999; also Marshall 1997). Partly as a result of these more positive evaluations, accreditation status has been sought (and achieved by one Grendon wing, to date) by prison-based therapeutic communities, previously considered to be out of step with the more favoured programme approach.[9] Grendon deals with high-risk sexual and violent offenders.

Genders and Player found evidence for the existence of distinct phases of therapeutic development.

1. *Settling in*: in this phase the prison culture was dismantled, prisoners acclimatised to the therapeutic community, and they began to experience a sense of acceptance, belonging, and social integration.

2. *Resocialisation*: in this phase, prisoners revised their modes of social interaction; they reported a greater degree of satisfaction in their relations with others, especially with authority.

3. *Consolidation*: this phase involved the furtherance of the intellectual component of therapy, and an increase in confidence and trust. Prisoners reported greater acceptance and exercised more social responsibility. They developed insight into the interrelated nature of their offending, and the underlying causes of their own problems.

As a result of their study, Genders and Player constructed a five stage career model, based on detailed observation of the assessment process: Recognition (definition of the problem); Motivation (expression of a desire to change); Understanding (recognition of interconnected and related aspects of life, and acknowledgment of underlying rather than surface causes); Insight (identification of solutions to problems); and Testing (putting into practice new ways of coping). Inmates moved through these stages at different speeds, but the process took about 18 months. Of those who left, 19 per cent of those spending less than 12 months at Grendon reached the final stage; 33 per cent of those spending between 12 and 18 months at Grendon reached the final stage; and 88 per cent of those who spent more than 18 months at Grendon reached the final stage.

This framework is helpful and has assisted in the evaluation process. Grendon may be a 'good prison' for all sorts of other reasons – its levels of safety, the high tolerance of Rule 43 prisoners, the atypical penal culture and the sense of direction felt by staff. Genders and Player describe its approach as distinct from a 'punitive control' model. It is not directed at stigmatisation but at 'reintegrative shaming'. Control is largely self-imposed. Staff at Grendon feel they are achieving the Prison Service Statement of Purpose. The Grendon model has 'survived', and is being expanded, where other quasi-therapeutic approaches (such as Barlinnie Special Unit and the open regime at Blantyre House) have not.

This account reinforces two important points:

- that in order for change to occur, penal cultures have to be appropriate; and

- this complex process takes place in stages.

Other structured therapeutic community approaches, for example towards substance abuse, have shown positive results, although like the study of Grendon above, results tend to support the finding that the longer the time spent in treatment, the better the outcome (this is particularly true for drug offenders). Studies also suggest that combined techniques work best. The fastest growing level of provision is in the therapeutic drug treatment area.[10]

Promising research results suggest that some prison programmes can help reduce offending. Interventions are more successful if the risk level is matched with the degree of intervention, if the focus is on criminogenic needs, if active, participatory methods are used, if offenders are accommodated in close proximity to their home and community, and if programmes are of sufficient breadth, are skills-oriented and cognitive methods are used. Programme integrity is crucial, and programmes are more successful if they are delivered in a context that is supportive of pro-social attitudes and behaviour.

Problems and limitations

There are practical and theoretical difficulties associated with the delivery and effectiveness of offending behaviour programmes in prison. First, the practical difficulties include fitting treatment programmes into the highly constrained prison day. There may be interruptions to the regime, difficulties in securing suitable rooms, problems getting prisoners unlocked at specific times and constant interruptions (Terry 1999: 68). Prisoners are not exposed to the normal environmental difficulties and triggers present in the community. When offenders who have successfully completed programmes in prison are released, there is rarely adequate follow-up via either close supervision or continuing courses (throughcare). It is likely that reinforcement of deviant lifestyles and thoughts occurs in prison, the effects of which may militate against treatment effectiveness. Prison staff do not always have the training, clear motivation or role definition to support programmes (Willmot 2000; Liebling and Price 2001), although considerable OBPU support is provided to establishments in order to address these issues. Short terms of imprisonment are the least likely to allow for formal offending behaviour programme interventions, under current arrangements.[11] Studies have found that positive treatment effects of prison (and other residential) programmes are rarely sustained for long in the community (e.g. Raynor and Vanstone 1996). As we know, the social environment into which offenders return has a highly significant impact on future behaviour (Haines 1990). This does support the case for high levels of supervision in the community following release.

What else works? The key ingredients of effectiveness

The 'What Works' literature is of interest, but tends to be narrow and technical in nature (Bottoms *et al.* 1998). The theories of crime on which they are based over-concentrate on individual/psychological deficits and not on social causes, despite the availability of convincing sociological explanations for crime (ibid.; also Vanstone 2000). Bottoms *et al.* suggest that four aspects of developing practice have emerged from investigations and professional practice as potentially valuable in attempts to reduce offending (Bottoms *et al.* 1998). They are:

1. efforts to reduce impulsivity;
2. efforts to strengthen offenders' pro-social community ties and to assist them in resolving personal and social problems contributing to their offending;
3. the development of pro-social modelling;[12] and
4. the fostering of legitimate practices by criminal justice agencies (see Tyler 1990; Sparks *et al.* 1996).

The first two concern substantive areas of *practice*, largely addressed above (see Bottoms *et al.* 1998) and the second two concern process. Bottoms *et al.* argue that the traditional 'What Works' literature has tended to emphasise (1) more than (2) or (3) and it has neglected (4). The recent review paper by Willmot on 'What Else Works?' suggests that a broader perspective is being developed, and that literacy, numeracy, drug treatment and employability (parts of 2), as well as the wider regime framework (4), are becoming major strands in the overall strategy to reduce reoffending. External evaluation of offending behaviour programmes is now underway and a new Strategy Board on What Works in Prison is, *inter alia*, addressing gaps in provision (such as programmes for women and young offenders, ethnic minority prisoners, short-termers and lifers: Newcomen 2000).

The remainder of this section looks at some of the broader developments aimed at making custody more effective, some of which may have more direct relevance to the shorter sentence.

What works with young people?

HMCIP's *Thematic Review of Juvenile Facilities* (HMCIP 1997) included a review of 'What Works and Fails in Custody'. The review drew on Little's work on 'belief rules' amongst young offenders – an identifiable code of street behaviour (Little 1990).[13] In custody, other 'belief rules' may be adopted:

- Do not rely on anybody other than yourself.
- Take your time working out who you can trust.
- Be especially wary of prison officers.
- Be careful that inmates do not steal from you.
- Work out the institutional regime.
- Copy experienced prisoners in the way they work the system.
- Keep your head down and do your time.
- Emphasise your independence
- Distinguish between, and attach status to, other groups of prisoners.
- Do not say where you have come from or what you have done.

There are dangers of custody for young people: that street cultures may predominate over rules and norms set by staff; institutions neglect the needs of individuals; bullying as a means of survival becomes a way of life; criminal habits and skills are learned; 'macho' behaviour masks low self-esteem and vulnerability; 'thick skins' develop so that change is resisted; family ties can deteriorate (custody becomes the point at which the family say 'we have had enough'; and reintegration into the community becomes more difficult. The positive advantages of custody for young people (adapted from a recent day conference for YOTs) are:

- the opportunity to interrupt a cycle of crime and associated lifestyle;
- time to think and plan;
- an opportunity to challenge attitudes and values, acquire skills and repair the lack of education and social skills;
- the opportunity to make a fresh start;
- the opportunity to develop self-esteem, and receive support in resisting peer pressure;
- less opportunity for drugs, alcohol and so on.

HMCIP argue that institutions for young offenders need to be fair (with clear and relevant rules and expectations observed by staff and prisoners). They should challenge offending-related attitudes. They should encourage personal responsibility, a work ethic and the development of individual potential. To be effective, young offender institutions need to meet the needs young people have for contain-ment, discipline and control. They need to ensure that they can tackle their offending behaviour, maintain positive contacts with families, experience positive human relationships with adults and other young people, and participate in education, employment and recreation. Individual assessment and custody planning is crucial (HMCIP 1997).

Restorative justice approaches

Many commentators believe there is an urgent need for a new model – some alternative to the 'techno-corrections' model of imprisonment. Arguably some programmes and therapeutic approaches incorporate aspects of these alternative models.

There have been some recent attempts to introduce restorative justice ideas into prison in England[14] and on a large scale in Belgium.[15] Pilot projects are being carried out at Holme House, Kirklevington and Deerbolt YOI (all in the north of England). These exploratory develop-ments may involve victim–offender mediation work, reparation, victim awareness programmes, teaching conflict resolution skills, family work and cultural change (see Edgar 1999; Willmot 2000; Liebling et al. 2001). The restorative justice approach also attempts to develop a meaningful relationship between the prison and the community. The aim of restorative approaches applied to prison is to 'change the relationship of the prison, the prisoner and the community' (ICPS 2001) and to organise the prison around different – if possible reintegrative – principles. Efforts are made, for example, to encourage prison staff to work (and base their lives) outside the prison. Early findings suggest that prisoners find these kinds of programmes and activities meaningful and that volunteering, for example, has a positive effect on their self-concept (Mace, in preparation; see also Bottoms 2000).

Other 'strength-based' approaches include pro-social modelling (which formed a central part of the regime in the public sector run Buckley Hall, constituting a major component of their successful bid against the private sector), Head Start projects, citizenship projects, volunteering (e.g. work done by the Inside-Out Trust), Dialogue and Appreciative Inquiry. All of these approaches actively involve participants in their own problem-solving, and seek a constructive solution to the problem of crime. There are clearly innovations around.[16]

Legitimacy and the prison regime

Attention is slowly turning to the context in which intervention programmes are carried out. The effectiveness of different types of prison regimes and cultures in supporting both the implementation of programmes and their treatment effects is currently being explored. Sparks et al. and others have shown that compliance with authority is likely to increase if the authority is regarded as legitimate (Sparks et al. 1996; see also Woolf 1991; Bottoms et al. 1998; Paternoster et al. 1997). Legitimacy includes consistency, impartiality, competency, correctability of low level decisions, representation (involvement in decision-making) and 'ethicality' – that is, the person in authority treats individuals with dignity and respect (Paternoster et al. 1997). A recent study of the quality of prison life supported by the Home Office Innovative Research Fund has devised a series of quantitative measures of 'legitimacy' and 'relationships' dimensions in prisons. These dimensions arose as a result of Appreciative Inquiry work, asking staff and prisoners to identify 'what matters' in prison.[17] The results show that prisons differ to a significant extent on these dimensions. The dimensions which discriminate most between establishments are: respect, humanity, relationships, trust, fairness, order, well-being and decency. There are also significant differences in the extent to which prisoners are able to maintain meaningful relationships with their families. Very large differences were found between prisons on well-being, with, for example, prisoners at one establishment rating the prison experience as much more painful than at other establishments (see Liebling and Arnold 2001: 110). Likewise, prisoners feared for their psychological safety much more at one prison than another. Differences in penal culture and 'moral performance' (or, as one prison put it, differences in the degree to which the prison can 'put in place a civic community') are of growing interest within establishments and amongst senior managers.[18] There is increasing recognition that modern management approaches require values as well as performance targets.

Future work is needed on whether prisoners' evaluations of their overall treatment in prison is linked to (a) their take up of and response to offending behaviour programmes; and (b) their prospects on release. Our hypotheses, based on our own developing work, are that prisons scoring highly on relationships and legitimacy dimensions will:

- be better at implementing OBPs and other constructive programmes;
- have staff who are more supportive of a culture of crime prevention/ pro-social behaviour;
- result in improved reconviction rates (or other measures of survival in the community).

The new 'decency' agenda is aimed at making regimes more legitimate – in part, possibly, to justify increasing use of it, but also (we can assume) to contribute to its effectiveness in both the implementation of constructive programmes and their success. It is important that we separate the questions of quality and quantity of imprisonment.[19]

Conclusions

In order to be sound and reasonable, the design and operation of prisons should be based not on any particular theory or ideology, but on some fundamental understanding of how imprisonment affects individuals. (Zamble and Porporino 1988: 2).

It is difficult to draw conclusions with so many apparently constructive new developments underway within individual establishments and areas, yet with what feels (to me) like a contradictory framework or set of conditions within which the prison is operating. What is the rationale for the new sentence of custody-plus? Do we know who imprisonment works for and who it doesn't work for? Do we have the evidence, for example, that prison 'works' for persistent offenders, or that short periods of custody can be made effective if followed by intensive supervision? The early days of custody are the most traumatic for the prisoner, and the most administratively complex for the establishment.

Halliday recommends short prison sentences with no follow-up for some offenders. There are risks with this approach: organisational (prisons become overwhelmed by the processing of short-stay offenders) and individual (suicide rates are high early in custody; short-term sentences may damage employment and family prospects). Studies suggest that punishment by itself is ineffective and can be counterproductive (MacKenzie 1994; Willmot 2000) and that change based on positive reinforcement works better.[20] For punishments to 'work' they need to be inevitable, immediate, severe and comprehensible, and alternative behaviours must be available (and should be reinforced). A long history of experiments with 'short sharp shock regimes' (Thornton *et al*. 1984); and with long-term versions (see Clare and Bottomley 2001) suggests that punitive approaches generally do not work but that 'rigorous' regimes which have an element of treatment-related work do better (Farrington *et al*. 2002).[21] Likewise, incentives-based regimes only improve institutional behaviour under certain circumstances, and little is known about the effects of compliance with regimes on future reoffending.

On the other hand, short stays in custody followed by effective supervision in the community may be preferable to medium-term stays in prison for large numbers of offenders. Some (now defunct) Detention Centres and the High Intensity Centre at Thorn Cross have or have had effective 'modular' regimes which cater for short stay prisoners (for example, offering phases in five-week cycles, in a 25-week programme). These regimes have detailed induction programmes, personal officer schemes, casework units, good probation links and highly motivated staff. They may offer basic literacy and numeracy programmes, drug treatment programmes, 'job clubs' and 'life skills' courses (use of leisure time, budgeting, health education and so on). They can be full and 'progressive', and generally, staff working in such centres feel a sense of purpose and direction often lacking in other establishments (HMCIP 1999). Community prisons, as envisaged by Woolf and others, could function in this way (Woolf Report 1991; Home Office 1991; HMCIP 1993). Consideration would need to be given to the administrative difficulties of high turnover and the role of the prison officer in this scheme. Other successful initiatives include the Portland On-Side Project, where high-risk young offenders are identified on reception, additional help is given throughout custody, and then project workers based in the prison (who operate as 'old fashioned social workers') follow released YOIs into the community, providing supervision, support and practical and family assistance. Early indications are that the scheme has some practical difficulties (a wide catchment area, key staffing changes, high emotional investment by the project workers in successful outcomes leading to burnout, etc.), but that 'treatment' YOIs do slightly better on release.

One of the difficulties in achieving positive treatment effects has typically been the lack of throughcare for offenders once they leave prison. Recent organisational changes (a joint head of psychological services for both prison and probation, a joint ombudsman, and a national reorganisation of probation services), the introduction of a joint assessment tool (OASys), a joint KPI on 'resettlement', and changes in the structure of sentences which will bring the prison and probation services much closer together suggest that 'joined up sentences', encompassing a 'shared vision', may be possible (however, see 'final thoughts' below).

The Halliday proposals make programmes for short-term prisoners more viable, as post-custodial supervision would allow for work started in custody to be continued on release. Developments are underway for a short-term offender programme. It is likely that Prison Service staff in policy areas and in establishments have some mixed feelings about short, unpredictable, repeat sentences ('we are not sure we want to be in this business', personal comment). The custody-plus sentence offers at best an opportunity to break out of or disrupt a peak in the cycle of offending. What is needed is the delivery of a sentence which retains pro-social or protective factors (employment, accommodation, family and community ties) while breaking criminogenic factors (drug addiction, impulsivity, criminal networks, etc.). Opportunities for (for example) short detoxification programmes, followed by links to future employment, may provide a focus for these short stays in prison. There are risks that the short sentence will be too appealing and will be overused (as the DTO has been).[22] Monitoring the use and effectiveness of this new sentence (and some of its problems) would provide considerable learning for the proposed 'custody-plus' sentence.[23] Custody-plus may be 'the perfect sentence for sentencers', but may pose a major organisational problem for the Prison Service.

Final thoughts

- There is a need for an explicit movement of resources from the prison to the community.

- Attention should be paid to the legitimacy (the moral climate) and effectiveness of prison regimes, including the 'failing prisons' initiative.

- The Prison Service should make an effective use of private and public sector competition to generate innovative and evidence-led interventions.

- We need a 'whole prison' approach to tackling offending behaviour (e.g. fully involving staff from employment, education services, etc.).

- Short prison sentences need a clear and achievable purpose (for example, assessment, drug treatment, first phase interventions).

- Since custody-plus is similar to the 'DTO', a review of its use, operation and effectiveness is urgently needed.

- There should be a review of the role of the local prison (with a new clarity of purpose around the concept of community prisons). There are some interesting examples.

- Consideration should be given to the use of reoffending and resettlement KPIs.

- To achieve joint working between the prison and probation services a unified vision of policy and practice is required.

- Thorough, ongoing evaluation of pilots, and of context, implementation and outcome, is needed.

- There are major headwinds: increasing prison population size, increasing prison size, cultural and organisational differences between prison and probation services, and scarce resources.

Appendix 6.1

Tables 6.3 and 6.4 are taken from an early version of Friendship *et al.* (forthcoming) and Friendship, Mann and Beech (forthcoming). See also Home Office Research Findings (2002).

Table 6.3   Two-year reconviction rates for prisoners participating in Cognitive Skills Programmes compared to untreated prisoners

Risk category	Comparison group*	Treated group	Significance	Reduction (percentage improvement on reconviction rates)
Low	14% of 88	4% of 115	$p < 0.05$	71%
Medium low	41% of 91	18% of 160	$p < 0.005$	56%
Medium high	79% of 61	44% of 167	$p < 0.0001$	44%
High	94% of 64	75% of 252	$p < 0.005$	20%

*A random sample of prisoners (excluding very short-termers) gathered by the Planning Group as part of their Criminogenic Needs study. See Friendship *et al.* (in press).

Table 6.4   Two-year sexual and/or violent reconviction rates for prisoners participating in the SOTP Core Programme compared to untreated sex offenders

Risk category	Comparison group*	Treated group	Significance	Reduction (percentage improvement on reconviction rates)
Low	2.6% of 969	1.9% of 263	NS	27%
Medium low	12.7% of 655	2.7% of 225	$p < 0.0001$	79%
Medium high	13.5% of 229	5.5% of 109	$p < 0.05$	59%
High	28.1% of 57	26.0% of 50	NS	7%

*Comprised of untreated sex offenders released from about the same period as the treated offenders were taking part in programmes (1992–96) following a sentence of at least four years.

Appendix 6.2

The following extract is taken from 'Sensible sentencing: curb short-term custody; end justice by geography', in *Youth Justice Board News* (October 2001).

> The Youth Justice Board is calling on youth courts to reduce the number of short custodial sentences and to make better use of new community penalties such as Intensive Supervision and Surveillance Programmes.

New information published in September shows that in the first year of availability 60 per cent of Detention and Training Orders (DTOs) were for six months or less, only three months of which are served in custody. Thirty-seven per cent of those were for only four months – where only two months are served.

There is little connection between the gravity of offences and the rate of custodial sentencing. Between April 2000 and March 2001 the number of DTOs imposed rose from 1,572 in the first quarter to 1,731 in the last quarter. Yet the number of recorded offences committed by juveniles in the eight categories most likely to attract a custodial sentence fell from 25,035 to 21,916.

The figures also reveal a significant 'justice by geography' effect. The ratio of custodial to community sentences varied between areas from 1:1 to 1:42. The impact of these wide variations is highlighted by the different sentencing decisions on the basis of similar facts between two neighbouring courts.

In May this year at Wimbledon youth court in South London a 16-year-old first-time offender was given a 12-month DTO for the theft of a mobile phone. In August at Brentford youth court in West London a few miles away, a 17-year-old first-time offender was given a 120-hour community penalty for the theft of a mobile phone in which the victim had been punched. The family of the former defendant appealed to the crown court who overturned the sentence, but not before the offender had served nearly four months and been forced to take his GCSEs in a Young Offenders Institution.

Norman Warner, chairman of the Board, said: 'This kind of justice by geography discredits our system; it makes justice a lottery dependent upon postcode.' He called on youth courts and YOTs to examine their local practices and to consider whether the widespread use of short custodial sentences is sensible, given the new option of ISSP.

He said: 'The courts and the YOTs need to consider whether the widespread use of short custodial sentences is appropriate or effective given the new community orders now available and the new range of supporting programmes that YOTs have been putting into place. Short custodial sentences disrupt the lives of young people and make it more difficult to implement effective educational and behaviour-changing programmes. And they waste resources.'

He said that overuse of short custodial sentences would not only have a negative impact on the work of the secure estate but would also be unlikely to be helpful in reforming offenders.

'If we are to achieve the quality of regimes for young people in custody which we all want and which are necessary to change offending behaviour, demand for places has to be managed. I hope the courts and their partner agencies in the community will reflect on these figures and consider carefully whether short custodial sentences are the most effective way to tackle offending.'

The Board will continue to monitor this issue and will be publishing tables showing levels of custody use and ratio to community sentences by YOT area every six months.

Notes

1 Helpful comments on a first draft of this paper were offered by Nigel Newcomen, Caroline Friendship and Sue Rex. I would also like to thank participants at the Cropwood conference in December 2001; and participants at two one-day symposia on Restorative Prisons organised by ICPS for useful discussions. I would like to thank Andrew Coyle for inviting me to join a delegation to Belgium to look at their restorative prisons work, and others (Louise Falshaw at OBPU and Fiona Byrne, Cropwood Fellow) who have supplied helpful data. Helen Griffiths and Sara Harrop assisted very ably with editing and tables.

2 Operational capacity is the 'maximum safe, overcrowded capacity of the prison estate'. The Certified Normal Accommodation figure (the uncrowded capacity) is 63,869.

3 The Prison Service operates with 138 establishments, with an average size of 500 places. Seven of these establishments are privately managed. Of these, six are privately owned.

4 This figure assumes that custody rates increase at 4 per cent per year for males and 9 per cent per year for females. The evidence suggests that while legislative and policy changes can account for some of the changes we have witnessed over the decade, very little is explained by changes in crime levels, and more is explained by changes in public and political *mood*.

5 This is a rapidly developing field. On making enquiries, I found an enormous level of activity (including a newly established 'short-term team' within OBPU), to which I cannot do full justice in this chapter.

6 Apart from the technical difficulties with reconviction rates (see below), there is the broader problem that comparing 'treated' offenders with 'non-treated' offenders in prison does not take account of the possible positive benefits of other aspects of a prison regime besides offending behaviour courses (Willmot 2000).

7 Accreditation of Prison Service offending behaviour programmes began in 1995 when a set of criteria for successful interventions was drawn up from the 'What Works' research. Initially two panels were set up, one for the

accreditation of general programmes and the second for the accreditation of the SOTP. The accreditation panels were comprised of key international research specialists. In 1999 these two panels were replaced by one joint panel known as the Joint Prison/Probation Accreditation Panel (JAP). The accreditation process occurs in two stages: (a) accreditation of the programme (is it appropriate?) and (b) accreditation or audit of the programme on site (is it delivered properly in this establishment?). The criteria are divided into four sections – programme management, treatment management, quality of delivery and throughcare. Each establishment is graded 0–4 on all four standards. All standards in both phases have to be satisfied. No programme has yet been accredited at the first attempt, and the process normally requires adjustments and improvements at the first stage before it reaches what are quite rigorous standards. The panel can make specific recommendations as part of the process. The purpose of the accreditation process is to meet the requirement of treatment integrity, found to be crucial to effectiveness in evaluations. Treatment integrity requires that the programme is strongly structured, and a supervisor monitors the programme so that all the treatment tutors abide by a consistent treatment approach.

8 Variations on this programme, for example the 'STOP' – Straight Thinking on Probation programme – are carried out and have been evaluated in the community; see Raynor and Vanstone (1996).

9 There are other (less well known) therapeutic communities at Wormwood Scrubs – the Maxwell Glatt Therapeutic Community; also for example, at Gartree, Highpoint Women's Prison, Winchester (planned) and at a newly opening private sector establishment at Peterborough.

10 There are also developments in work with personality disordered and borderline personality disordered offenders.

11 The shorter the programme, the less effective it is likely to be (ETS, at 20 two-hour sessions, is thought to be the shortest practicable; PSMB 2000). There is a two-week programme – MORE (Motivating Offenders to Rethink Everything) – currently under development.

12 A form of encouragement towards pro-social conduct through reinforcement, empathy and rewards; see Trotter 1996; Bottoms *et al.* 1998.

13 Use crime to meet financial needs; be assertive when offending; be competitive; offend in small gangs; steal things which are easily sold; learn how to sell the proceeds of crime; do not be concerned about the experiences consequent upon a court disposal; adopt short-term goals.

14 A Restorative Prison Project has been funded by the Northern Rock Foundation; see ICPS reports.

15 All Belgium prisons now have a 'restorative consultant' on the management team. Restorative Justice became a main plank of the Ministry of Justice response to public outrage after the 'Dutroux' affair. The work is described as a 'cultural revolution' (around the concepts of respect, trust

and dialogue) and provides a theoretical framework under which prison work is carried out.

16 Once I started asking, I unearthed countless stories of individual establishments pioneering positive work with short-stay offenders. Some of these projects are being carried out in close cooperation with the probation service. The practice of resettlement work is developing rapidly from the field, perhaps especially within establishments (see HMCIP 2001).

17 The dimensions are: respect, humanity, trust, relationships; support, safety, fairness, order, development in prison, development with family, decency and well-being. Staff and prisoners identified the same dimensions, suggesting that there is a broad consensus about values in prison (which resemble the values of civil society).

18 These developments are linked to the 'new decency agenda', which is providing a new sense of direction for the Prison Service.

19 It may also be important to distinguish, as the Belgians do, between 'what matters' because 'it works', and what matters because it's right.

20 MacKenzie found that so-called boot camps which devoted the most time to rehabilitative activities, and which had the highest levels of supervision, had the lowest reconviction rates, and that most did not reduce reconviction rates (MacKenzie 1994; MacKenzie et al. 1995). Recent work by Maruna also suggests that offending behaviour programmes which are too punitive and which demand full acceptance of responsibility for past actions can also undermine a redemptive self-concept (Maruna 2001).

21 Thorn Cross YOI, a High Intensity Training Centre, appears to achieve significant reduction in reconviction rates which are attributable to employment programmes and cognitive-behavioural skills training. A sentence allowing more than six months to be served is needed in order for young offenders to 'qualify' for the regime in practice.

22 Norman Warner has recently appealed to magistrates not to use the sentence so much. A 'bit of punishment and a bit of something constructive' is what 'every sentencer wants' (personal comment). Overuse of the shorter DTO sentences (three months and six months) has been linked to lack of training on the 'tariff' and on alternatives. See appendix 6.2.

23 On a recent visit to HMYOI Brinsford, a large young offenders institution near Wolverhampton, staff in reception complained to us about what was happening to their prison. Magistrates, they said, had 'gone mad with this new, short Detention and Training Order sentence'. Prisoners were arriving 'by the bus load', who only had two months to serve. Staff at the prison were requesting longer terms of imprisonment – a minimum of eight months. That way, they said, 'at least we can do something with them, and maybe these short sentence ones, who probably shouldn't be here at all, can be diverted'.

References

Beech, A., Fisher, D. and Beckett, R. (1999) *STEP 3: An Evaluation of the Prison Sex Offender Treatment Programme: A Report for the Home Office.* London: Home Office.

Bottoms, A.E. (2000) *Restorative Justice in Sociological Perspective,* paper given at Restorative Justice Symposium, Cambridge, 7–8 October.

Bottoms, A.E., von Hirsch, A. and Rex, S. (1998) 'Pro-Social Modelling and Legitimacy: Their Potential Contribution to Effective Probation Practice', in Rex, S. and Matravers, A. (eds), *Pro-Social Modelling and Legitimacy: The Clarke Hall Day Conference.* Cambridge: Institute of Criminology.

Clare, E. and Bottomley, K. (assisted by Grounds, A., Hammond, C.J., Liebling, A. and Taylor, A.) (2001) *Evaluation of Close Supervision Centres,* Home Office Research Study 219 London: Home Office Research, Development and Statistics Directorate.

Cullen, E. (1993) 'The Grendon Reconviction Study, Part 1', *Prison Service Journal,* 90, 35–7.

Edgar, K. (1999) 'Restorative Justice in Prison Prison', *Service Journal* 123, 6–7.

Farrington, D. (1996) 'Individual, Family and Peer Factors in the Development of Delinquency', in Hollin, C. and Howells, K. (eds), *Clinical Approaches to Working with Young Offenders.* Chichester: Wiley.

Farrington, D. (1997) 'Human Development and Criminal Careers', in Maguire, M., Morgan, R. and Reiner, R. (eds), *Oxford Handbook of Criminology,* 2nd edn. Oxford: Clarendon Press.

Farrington, D., Ditchfield, J., Hancock, G., Howard, P., Jolliffe, D., Livingstone, M.S. and Painter, K.A. (2002) *Evaluation of Two Intensive Regimes for Young Offenders.* Home Office Research Study, 239. London: Home Office Research Development and Statistics Directorate.

Friendship, C., Mann, R. and Beech, A.R. (forthcoming) *An Evaluation of a National Prison Based Treatment Programme for Sexual Offenders in England and Wales.*

Friendship, C., Blud, L., Erikson, M. and Thornton, D. (forthcoming) *Cognitive Behavioural Treatment for Imprisoned Offenders: An Evaluation of HM Prison Service's Cognitive Skills Programme.*

Friendship, C., Blud, L., Erikson, M. and Travers, R. (2002) *An Evaluation of Cognitive Behavioural Treatment for Prisoners,* Home Office Research Findings, 161.

Gallo, E. and Ruggiero, V. (1991) 'The "Immaterial" Prison: Custody as a Factory for the Manufacture of Handicaps', *International Journal of the Sociology of Law,* 19, 273–91.

Genders, E. and Player, E. (1995) *Grendon: A Study of a Therapeutic Prison.* Oxford: Clarendon Press.

Gray, C. and Elkins, M. (2001) *Projections of Long-Term Trends in the Prison Population to 2008.* London: Home Office.

Gunn, J. and Robertson, G. (1987) 'A Ten Year Follow-Up on Men Discharged from Grendon Prison', *British Journal of Psychiatry,* 151, 674–8.

Haines, K. (1990) *After-Care Services for Released Prisoners: A Review of the Literature*. Cambridge: Institute of Criminology.

HMCIP (1993) *Doing Time or Using Time: Report of a Review by Her Majesty's Chief Inspector of Prisons for England and Wales of Regimes in Prison Service Establishments*. London: Home Office.

HMCIP (1997) *Thematic Review of Juvenile Facilities by HM Chief Inspector of Prisons for England and Wales*. London: Home Office.

HMCIP (1999) *Report on a Full Inspection of HM Young Offender Institution Thorn Cross, September 7–11 1998*. London: Home Office.

HMCIP (2001) *Through the Prison Gate: A Joint Review by HM Inspector of Prisons and Probation of Resettlement*. London: Home Office.

Hollin, C. and Howells, K. (eds) (1996) *Clinical Approaches to Working with Young Offenders*. Chichester: Wiley.

Home Office (1991) *White Paper: Custody Care and Justice*. London: HMSO.

Home Office (1999) *Reconvictions of Offenders Sentenced and Discharged from Prison in 1995, England and Wales*. London: Home Office.

Home Office (2000) *Prison Statistics England and Wales 2000*. London: HMSO.

Home Office (2001) *Making Punishment Work: Report of a Review of the Sentencing Framework for England and Wales* (the Halliday Report). London: Home Office.

ICPS (2001) Restorative Prison Project papers.

Kershaw, C., Goodman, J. and White, S. (1999) *Reconvictions of Offenders Sentenced or Discharged from Prison in 1995, England and Wales*, Statistical Bulletin 19/99. London: Home Office.

Liebling, A. and Arnold H. (2001) 'Measuring the Quality of Prison Life', report submitted to Home Office.

Liebling, A. and Price, D. (2001) *The Prison Officer*. Leyhill: Prison Service and Waterside Press.

Liebling, A., Arnold, H. and Elliott, C. (2001) 'Transforming the Prison: Romantic Optimism or Appreciative Realism?, *Criminal Justice* 1(2), 161–80.

Little, M. (1990) *Young Men in Prison: The Criminal Identity Explored Through Rules of Behaviour in Adolescence*. Dartmouth: Dartmouth.

Lloyd, C., Mair, G. and Hough, M. (1994) *Explaining Reconviction Rates: A Critical Analysis*. Home Office Research Study No. 136. London: HMSO.

Losel, F. (1995) 'The Efficacy of Correctional Treatment: A Review and Synthesis of Meta-evaluations', in McGuire, J. (ed.), *What Works: Reducing Reoffending*. Chichester: Wiley.

Mace, A. (forthcoming) The Restorative Prison Project.

McGuire, J. and Priestly, J. (1995) 'Reviewing What Works: Past, Present and Future', in McGuire, J. (ed.), *What Works: Reducing Reoffending*. Chichester: Wiley.

MacKenzie, D.L. (1994) 'Boot Camps: A National Assessment', *Overcrowded Times*, 5(4), 1, 14–8.

MacKenzie, D.L., Brame, R., McDowall, D. and Souryal, C. (1995) 'Boot Camp Prisons and Recidivism in Eight States', *Criminology*, 33, 327–57.

Mann, R. and Thornton, D. (1997) 'The Evolution of a Multi-site Offender Treatment Programme', in Marshall, W.L., Hudsen, S.M., Ward W. and

Fernandez, Y.M. (eds), *Sourcebook of Treatment Programme for Sexual Offenders*. New York: Pleunum Press.

Marshall, P. (1997) *A Reconviction Study of HMP Grendon Therapeutic Community*, Home Office Research Findings No. 53. London: Home Office.

Martinson, R. (1974) 'What Works? Questions and Answers about Prison Reform', *Public Interest*, 35, 22–54.

Maruna, S. (2001) *Making Good: How Ex-convicts Reform and Rebuild their Lives*. Washington, DC: American Psychological Association.

Newcomen, N. (2000) Unpublished paper.

Palmer J. (1975) 'Martinson Revisited', *Journal of Crime and Delinquency*, 12(2), 133–52.

Paternoster, R., Bachman, R., Brame, R. and Sherman, L.W. (1997) 'Do Fair Procedures Matter? The Effect of Procedural Justice on Spouse Assault', *Law and Society Review*, 31, 163–204.

Prison Reform Trust (2001) *Strangeways – Ten Years On*. London: PRT.

Prison Service (2001) *Corporate Plan 2001–2002 to 2003–2004*. London: Prison Service.

Prison Service Management Board (2000) 'Towards a Strategy for Accredited Offending Behaviour Programmes', unpublished paper.

Raynor, P. and Vanstone, M. (1996) 'Reasoning and Rehabilitation in Britain: The Results of the Straight Thinking on Probation (STOP) Programme', *International Journal of Offender Therapy and Comparative Criminology*, 40, 272–84.

Ross, R.R. and Ross, R.D. (1995) *Thinking Straight: The Reasoning and Rehabilitation Program for Delinquency Prevention and Offender Rehabilitation*. Ottowa: Air Training and Publication.

Ross, R.R., Fabiano, E.A. and Ewles, C.D. (1988) 'Reasoning and Rehabilitation', *International Journal of Offender Therapy and Comparative Criminology*, 32, 29–36.

Sampson, A. (1994) *Acts of Abuse: Sex Offenders and the Criminal Justice System*. London: Routledge.

Sampson, R.J. and Laub, J.H. (1993) *Crime in the Making: Pathways and Turning Points Through Life*. Cambridge, MA: Harvard University Press.

Sparks, R. Bottoms, A.E. and Hay, W. (1996) *Prisons and the Problem of Order*. Oxford: Clarendon Press.

Taylor, R. (1999) *A Seven-Year Reconviction Study of HMP Grendon Therapeutic Community*, Home Office Research Findings No. 115. London: Home Office.

Terry, K.J. (1999) *Analysing the effects of motivation on sex offenders in a Cognitive-Behavioural Treatment Programme*. PhD Thesis, University of Cambridge.

Thornton, D., Curran, L., Grayson, D. and Holloway, V. (1984) *Tougher Regimes in Detention Centres*. London: HMSO.

Trotter, C. (1996) 'The Impact of Different Supervision Practices in Community Corrections: Cause for Optimism', *Australian and New Zealand Journal of Criminology*, 29, 29–46.

Tyler, T. (1990) *Why People Obey the Law*. New Haven, CT and London: Yale University Press.

Vanstone, M. (2000) 'Cognitive-Behavioural Work with Offenders in the UK: A History of Influential Endeavour'. *Howard Journal*, 39(2), 171–83.

Willmot, P. (2000) 'What Else Works? Applying the Research on Reducing Recidivism to Prison Regimes', unpublished paper.

Woolf, Lord Justice (1991) *Prison Disturbances April 1990: Report of an Inquiry by the Rt Hon. Lord Justice Woolf (parts I and II) and His Honour Judge Stephen Tumim (part II): Presented to Parliament by the Secretary of State for the Home Department by Command of Her Majesty February 1991*. London: HMSO.

Zamble, E. and Porporino, F.J. (1988) *Coping, Behaviour and Adaptation in Prison Inmates*. New York: Springer.

Chapter 7

Reinventing community penalties: the role of communication

Sue Rex

Why 'reinvent'?

Many offenders are dealt with in the community, using penalties such as probation, community service and curfews backed by electronic monitoring. In 2000, nearly 100,000 people sentenced for indictable offences received a community sentence.[1] The range of community measures has been extended very recently.[2] Yet, in the absence of a clear conceptual framework for community orders, we have failed fully to exploit the opportunities offered by these penalties. In this chapter, I first establish the case for a rethink about community penalties by sketching the contemporary scene. I then examine the solution offered by the Halliday Report (Home Office 2001a) to the lack of clarity surrounding the use of community orders, namely a generic community punishment order. My argument is that this proposal will not enhance public – or offenders' – understanding of what happens when someone is supervised in the community.

The rest of the chapter – the bulk of it – considers the possible application to community orders of penal theory in which the emphasis is on communication with the offender. I use empirical findings from interviews with magistrates and victims, offenders and probation staff to illuminate what they saw punishment communicating and how they saw offenders responding to that communication. Drawing out from this material how people perceived the role that community penalties might play, I hope to show the potential that these kinds of penalties have to promote constructive responses to the messages conveyed in the act of sentencing. Rather than a change in legal form to produce a generic community punishment order whose meaning is obscure to the public and to offenders, I would suggest that efforts would be more profitably directed at the substance of community penalties to maximise the opportunities they offer to engage offenders positively in processes of change.

Conceptual confusion

In the 25 years since the collapse of the Rehabilitative Ideal in the 1970s (Allen 1981), the underlying rationale for non-custodial penalties has undergone major transformations (from 'penal-welfarism' to 'alternatives to custody' to 'punishment in the community' to 'public protectionism'). These rapid and significant shifts in thinking have left considerable instability and uncertainty about the purpose and status of community orders. It is not surprising that there has been little impact on the use of custody. Superficially, over the 1990s, community penalties have been on an upward trend: 98,000 offenders were sentenced to community orders for indictable offences in 2000 compared with 72,000 in 1990. Yet, a closer examination of the sentencing trends reveals a somewhat different picture, so that the proportions sentenced to probation and community service for indictable offences have dropped over the decade,[3] and a lower proportion of those sentenced to community orders now have prior records.[4]

Contrast the views of community penalties expressed in speeches made on the same day (31 January 2001) by the then Home Secretary, Jack Straw, and by the Lord Chief Justice, Lord Woolf. Whereas the Home Secretary saw little promise in community penalties for persistent offenders who have 'almost without exception been through the mill of community sentences and still reoffended', Lord Woolf described a short custodial sentence as 'a very poor alternative to a sentence to be served in the community'. These comments reflect one theme that has endured throughout the recent history of non-custodial penalties – what Worrall (1997) calls their 'subordinate' relationship with custody. Yet, the reintegrative and rehabilitative possibilities offered by community penalties – as outlined below – surely mean that they merit our serious attention in their own right.

These are propitious times for community penalties. In addition to the proliferation of new orders, we have seen the establishment of a National Probation Service for England and Wales.[5] And we are in the heyday of the 'What Works' movement. The Joint Prisons/Probation Accreditation Panel has been tasked with approving a core curriculum of demonstrably effective programmes for offenders.[6] In pursuit of the goal of reduced recidivism, a range of evaluated 'Pathfinder' projects have been funded under the Crime Reduction Programme – the resettlement of prisoners, the acquisition of basic skills and community service – as well as the cognitive-behavioural programmes more traditionally associated with reducing offending.[7] This initiative undoubtedly gives considerable impetus to probation work. However, its exclusive focus on rehabilitation may eclipse other aims of community-based options, one of which is to impose certain restrictions to mark the fact that an offence has been committed. The recent sentencing trends referred to above point to two dangers in this approach. One is that a focus on reoffending will erode the relationship between the gravity of the offence and the severity of the order, showing once again how difficult it is to reconcile the requirements of rehabilitation and desert.[8] A further danger is that the emphasis on recidivism may ironically draw in offenders the nature of whose crimes does not justify – or require – the use of probation resources.

Generic community punishment?

The Review of the Sentencing Framework in England and Wales – widely known as the Halliday Report – recognised the need for urgent clarification of the purposes of the various community orders and how they should be used. The solution offered is a single community punishment order, whose punitive weight would be proportionate to the gravity of the offence, taking account of previous convictions (Home Office 2001a: Recommendation 27). The new order would comprise the ingredients best suited to meeting the needs of crime reduction and exploiting opportunities for reparation. Courts would be able to select from the whole range of requirements available: currently, compulsory work, offending behaviour programmes, treatment for substance misuse and mental illness, curfews and exclusions, and reparation to victims and communities.

Proposals for a 'generic' community order have been considered twice before (Home Office 1988; Home Office 1995), latterly to give sentencers greater flexibility to impose more appropriate community orders and because a single 'community sentence' might command greater public confidence. In the event these proposals were not pursued, the government apparently persuaded by some respondents to the consultation process that the current range of community penalties already provided a sufficient range of options (Home Office

1996). Instead, 'demonstration' projects were to explore what could be achieved to promote judicial and public confidence in community options within the current legal framework. Reporting the results of those projects, the researchers found that sentencers were more satisfied with the information they received and felt more informed about probation programmes following the projects (Hedderman *et al.* 1999). The most significant impact on sentencing, in both higher and lower courts, was not on the use of custody, but an increase in the use of probation orders with additional requirements, largely at the expense of other community penalties, and especially relating to summary cases (in other words, net-widening).

So why revive the proposal for a generic order again now? The context has certainly changed since 1996, partly because of major extensions to the range and combinations of community penalties available to the courts. As the National Probation Directorate commented in its response to the Report, the relevant legislation has become highly complex and we have moved some way towards a single sentence through the Criminal Justice and Court Services Act 2000 (National Probation Directorate 2001). But what of the objection raised against the 1995 proposal by Ashworth *et al.* (1995): that a 'pick 'n' mix' generic order would represent a serious threat to a reasonable relationship between the gravity of the offence and the overall severity of the order? Here, the Halliday Report offers some fairly detailed proposals aimed at preserving proportionality, which go some way towards the agreed understanding of the comparable restrictiveness of different community orders advocated by Ashworth *et al.* It also envisages that greater 'rationality' in sentencing might reduce the risk of 'condition creep' (Home Office 2001a: para. 6.13). An 'outline tariff' is provided (Home Office 2001a: 41), the aim of which is to illustrate how such arrangements could work. In discussing restrictions, the Report emphasises the more measurable physical (or financial) deprivations imposed by the various requirements; there is no reference to the demands, for example, of attempting 'lifestyle' changes such as refraining from alcohol or drugs, or restraining aggressive reactions to particular situations. The sheer number of hours for which an offender attends an accredited programme may not reflect the efforts he or she has to make outside the sessions if programme objectives are to be met.

The proposed name for the new order – a community *punishment* order – does not acknowledge the aims of crime reduction and reparation, as well as punishment, identified by the Report for community-based sanctions. If the intention is to make the public believe that a community order is indeed a 'punishment' by calling it such, one suspects that this will prove futile. Worse, such a name may well obscure the constructive aspects of the sanction that might attract public support, for example the reparation to the community in performing compulsory work. It seems unlikely to enhance public understanding of what happens when an offender is sentenced to a community order. The public, and offenders, seem more likely to understand what an order means when its name describes the activity involved, such as a *curfew* order or a *community service* (or perhaps *compulsory work*) order. The deficiencies identified by the Review could be addressed by simplifying the range of orders, increasing their flexibility and specifying their purposes, and using National Standards to bring the arrangements for their administration and enforcement into line.

Rethinking community penalties – communicative theory

The tensions between rehabilitation and desert mirror those between the consequentialist and retributive penal theories in which they have their origins. That is, between an approach that looks backwards to the offence for which it exacts retribution and one that looks forward to the crime reductive consequences secured through deterrence, incapacitation and rehabilitation. Penal theory has developed considerably in recent decades, and most contemporary theorists favour a hybrid approach combining elements of both.[9] However, we have yet to achieve real synthesis between these ideas – and an adequate resolution of the extent to which proportionality should act as a constraint.

A third kind of penal theory claims to move beyond mere compromise between retribution and consequentialism. This is a communicative theory, developed most fully by Anthony Duff,[10] who accords punishment a forward-looking goal – the reform of the offender through 'moral persuasion'. Material forms of punishment should be intrinsically appropriate to the aim of bringing offenders to recognise the wrongfulness of their crimes and the need to reform. Punishment is also retributive in the sense that the communication condemns or censures the crime, requiring a reasonable relationship between the severity of the punishment and the relative gravity of the offence. This is not a purely expressive communication, but one that appeals to the offender as a rational moral agent capable of responding. Duff (2000) defines punishment as a 'secular penance', justified as part of a morally communicative process that aims to persuade offenders to repent of their crimes, to communicate their reparative apology to others, and to undertake to reform their future conduct.[11] Others struggle with this somewhat 'religious' terminology, as becomes obvious below.

What is particularly relevant to this chapter is the re-conceptualisation that Duff (2000) offers of community penalties. In his account, a *probation order* reminds the offender that the offence cast doubt on the offender's commitment to the community's public values and threatened to undermine the mutual trust on which the community depends. The conditions attached to a probation order aim to bring home to the offender the character and implication of the offences as public wrongs, and to persuade the offender that he or she must (and can) modify his or her future behaviour. *Community service*, as public reparation, enables the offender to express his or her understanding of what he or she has done and his or her renewed commitment to the community, as well as requiring him or her to perform apologetic reparation.

It is useful to contrast Duff's account of punishment with that offered by von Hirsch, which also incorporates backward- and forward-looking perspectives but has a very different understanding of the nature of the communication. Penal censure, as punishment is characterised in desert theory, 'gives an individual an opportunity to respond in ways that are typically those of an agent capable of moral deliberation: to recognise the wrongfulness of the action, feel remorse, make efforts to desist in the future – or else to try to give reasons why the conduct was not actually wrong' (von Hirsch 1999: 69). The implication here is that whether and how to respond to the punishment is left to the offender, and von Hirsch doubts whether the state is authorised to impose the secular penance envisaged by Duff.[12] He sees the deprivations of punishment as providing instead a supplementary prudential reason for refraining from crime, which must always be secondary to the censure element to avoid treating offenders like tigers in a circus (see von Hirsch 1993, 1999). While efforts might be made at 'reform', these are 'additional permissible activities' rather than an actual justification for punishment (von Hirsch, 1999: 78).

For Bottoms (1998), what distinguishes these two writers is that von Hirsch has an 'external' view of the offender, whereas Duff is concerned with the individualised internal states induced by punishment (and by the material forms that punishment therefore takes). Bottoms (drawing on Lucas 1980) offers another possibility: dialectically defensible censure, comprising a moral dialogue in which the offender's point of view is fully considered and where a decision adverse to the offender is reached for reasons that he or she ought to be able to acknowledge as cogent. A more future-oriented and more

143

individualised view of the offender is implied than in von Hirsch's account, without involving the direct attempt to induce penitence envisaged by Duff. While a response from the offender – in the form of a change in attitude or reformed behaviour – might be encouraged, it is not formally part of the point or process of punishment.

This has largely been a theoretical debate. Indeed, Duff (2000) is careful to offer his account as an ideal, and to argue (convincingly) that it does not represent criminal justice processes as they operate in practice. However, it is valid to explore its possible application to how state punishment is actually delivered, or could be delivered, in practice, on the basis that effective thinking about punishment requires a closer relationship between high-level normative thinking and ground-level practical decision-making (Raynor 1997). In other words, theory should be used to help us in making decisions about offenders.

In research funded by the Economic and Social Research Council, I am exploring how the ideas discussed above actually apply to people's perceptions and experiences of community-based options, relating this to a discussion of their broad understandings of punishment and how community sentences contribute to penal aims. I have started with 65 in-depth interviews with victims, offenders, magistrates and probation practitioners, in which they discussed: what punishment com-municated; how offenders responded to that communication; and how community orders do or could contribute to the process. Having completed the analysis of those interviews, I have used them to construct questionnaires with which I am now examining the views of larger numbers within each group. In the rest of this chapter, I shall draw on the interviews to discuss how people characterised the messages conveyed to offenders in the act of sentencing and how they saw offenders responding. A useful starting point is how people prioritised the aims of punishment.

Prioritising punishment

Generally, where interviewees expressed a 'priority aim' for punish-ment, they favoured the prevention of further offending over what we might understand as retribution. Punishment should serve a socially useful function, beyond marking the fact that the person had commit-ted an offence, though the distinction between these aims was often not clear cut. One magistrate conveyed an aspiration quite often expressed by others in wishing to secure a positive outcome through what was quite clearly 'punishment': 'although you're punishing them, you have to try to do the best to help them stop reoffending and [to] learn by their mistakes'.

A victim articulated particularly positive ambitions, and others shared the underlying sentiments:

> Once they've become an offender a lot of people would say that's too late. I don't. I say now is our opportunity. They've got to this point in their lives where they've offended, let's look at what we can do to stop them offending again. Rather than saying 'well, OK, we'll give them a punishment, once they've done their punishment they can go on their way, that's the end of the matter.' Let's follow it through.

People combined elements of retributive (or desert) thinking with consequentalist (or crime reductive) aims in their understandings of punishment. They saw securing a response from the offender as central to the court's aim in sentencing. The emphasis on this by probation officers and offenders might well be a product of the current policy emphasis on preventing reoffending, much promoted within the Probation Service and likely to have made an impression on offenders. However, magistrates and victims also placed a high priority on the sentence having a positive impact on offenders' attitudes and behaviour. There seems little support here for an argument that securing such a response is secondary to the aim of expressing censure for the offence; in von Hirsch's terms that it is an 'additional permissible activity' rather than a justification for punishment.

Communicating penal messages

Messages seen as actually communicated to the offender in the act of sentencing seemed to fall into two main categories: normative or 'moral' expressions of disapproval of wrongdoing; and 'instrumental', intended to secure a particular reaction from the offender. Interviewees' failure to distinguish clearly between these two ideas supports a formulation of punishment as both normative and forward-looking.

Looking first at the 'moral' messages, predominant was what von Hirsch (1993) would understand as censure: the expression of disapproval, and disavowal of the behaviour, in some cases with specific reference to the harm or suffering caused. What theorists characterise as 'hard treatment' (something painful or inconvenient) needed to be imposed to bring home the fact that the behaviour was wrong and to make that message impinge on offenders. There was cautious endorsement of the need for proportionality – for the punishment to correspond to the gravity of the offence. Views were complex on this point, reflecting the difficulties experienced in the academic literature in settling the question of how far sentencing should be constrained by desert.

'Instrumental' messages, implying the response expected from the offender, took varied forms. The idea of a 'threat' resonated particularly with magistrates, who wanted offenders to understand that nasty consequences would follow continued offending. Offenders, too, detected the message that continued offending would lead to a harsher response, implicitly or explicitly custody, which they seemed to accept as what von Hirsch (1993) has called a 'prudential disincentive' to further offending: 'What the magistrates are saying is "if you go out and burgle this bloke's house and you get caught, we're going to put you in prison. And if you do it again, we'll step up a little bit, or we'll put you in prison if you haven't been in before".'

Similarly popular was the idea that the court was indicating that the offender had crossed a boundary into unacceptable behaviour – a message that conveyed both censure and that the behaviour should stop. This had most resonance for probation officers: some specifically referred to boundaries; others that offenders were being shown that they could not behave as they had – society would not accept it, or this was how society would respond. Magistrates referred to society's inability to tolerate offending behaviour; offenders should refrain and perhaps be assisted in doing so. The following magistrate doubted offenders' capacity to comprehend the point: 'I'm trying hard to say "your behaviour is anti-social. If you want to live in our community, then we expect you to abide by some reasonable guidelines". I suspect that's probably a bit deep for most of our offenders.'

Such instrumental messages were often couched in more positive language. A prominent theme, particularly among magistrates, was of giving the offender a second chance, expressed in varied terms. On the one hand, the offender was warned: 'don't step out of line again', 'it's almost the end of the line', 'if you trip up again . . .'. More frequently, there was some expectation of apology, reparation or repentance: the sentence represented a chance 'for a new beginning', 'to put something right' or 'to prove that this isn't your normal behaviour'. The fact that they usually ascribed this function to a conditional discharge suggests that magistrates related the idea most strongly to first-time offenders. Probation officers expressed the same idea in comparatively positive terms, giving more prominence to probation orders.

Offenders saw a community order as being given a chance to change; a 'slap' on the hand not to do it again; a chance to get rehabilitated (by not going to prison); or a recognition of a clean record. Victims tended to apply the idea to the first-time offender, or to people who were the product of a bad environment, where the offence might be seen as out of character: 'There is almost a "we'll give you a second chance" approach to the first time offender: "you've got to choose now whether to commit yourself to a life of crime or to go back the other way, and we'll try and help you do that".'

Indeed, there was often anticipation of a positive reaction on the part of offenders to the experience of being sentenced. Thus, having to pay, or to put the harm right in some way, or to put something back into society through community service or a reparation order, enabled the offender to make amends for his or her behaviour. More broadly, the intention might be to encourage the offender to move forward in a positive way, in effect to reform themselves by making a 'go' of their life or seeking to become a better person – an aspiration associated particularly with a non-custodial penalty. For example, the experience of undertaking community service was seen by magistrates and probation staff as promoting a sense of self-belief or self-efficacy, through the realisation that they had a contribution to make to society.[13] Both community service and probation enabled offenders to gain a sense of achievement.

Some people saw punishment as seeking to 'educate' or 'persuade' offenders to change their behaviour. Probation and community service might be used to explain or to develop the offender's awareness of the impact of his or her behaviour. One person saw the 'law as teacher'; another commented that probation was almost like going back to school, and a third thought that CS supervisors might be in a position to show offenders that others were worse off than them.

Probation staff and magistrates were most likely to discuss the reinforcement of the sentence in supervisory processes. One probation officer saw contact with a penal agent (prison or probation) as reinforcing the message that this was a court sentence and a responsibility to be taken seriously; a curfew order – where such contact was absent (or restricted to staff monitoring the tag) – might fail to convey that more subtle message. A number of others pointed to the difficulties of getting offenders to see the order as continuing processes that began at court, partly because the court hearing might become a distant memory for people on longer orders. One probation officer thought that comments made by magistrates when passing sentence might be discussed with offenders at various points of their orders.

147

The contrasting lack of reference to these reinforcing processes by offenders suggested that court and supervisory stages were fairly discrete in their eyes. Probation staff and magistrates were also more likely than offenders to describe how supervisory processes continued specific elements of the communication that started in court, for example that behaviour was wrong and harmful. Magistrates sometimes saw probation as involving a demanding review of the offender's lifestyle and pattern of behaviour. A process of reasoning was depicted by some probation officers, though they were conscious of the sheer difficulty of getting some offenders to attend to the wrongfulness of their behaviour. Offenders recounted receiving helpful advice or 'straight talk', or having their thinking endorsed (for example, in group work programmes), but it would be stretching the point to argue that they saw themselves as the recipients of moral persuasion as understood by Duff (2000). The following offender seems to be recounting the provision of clear advice about decision-making rather than an attempt to persuade him about the nature of his offences as public wrongs and the need therefore to modify his future behaviour: 'I can come and talk to my probation officer. I've known her for a long time and she's straight with me. She'll tell me what I need to hear not just what I want to hear.'

Responding to the penal message

Ideally, the penal messages discussed above would prompt offenders to accept responsibility, both for their offending and for the behaviour in which it was implicated. A sense of responsibility was not expected to develop in immediate response to the sentence: this was a process that might start or continue after the court hearing, possibly during supervision or as a result of 'mature' reflection. It was recognised that offenders' experiences within the criminal justice system often militated against their taking responsibility. Prison, in particular, was seen as enabling offenders to avoid responsibility, both for their behaviour and for what was going on in their lives.

One aspect of accepting responsibility was the realisation that one had caused harm. Victims, quite naturally, wanted the impact on them to be brought home to offenders. Probation staff saw an acknowledgment that their behaviour had hurt others as part of offenders' progress towards rehabilitation. It was less of a theme for magistrates, but some thought that the cold light of day, or community reparation, might help offenders see the impact of the offence on other people. Offenders reported admitting in a variety of ways the harm caused to victims, themselves and their families – some before coming to court and others as a result of experiences on probation. One commented that probation 'does make you sit back and think: "would I like my things to be smashed or taken".'

There was also a hope that the realisation that one had caused harm would stimulate feelings of remorse, which might propel decisions to change one's behaviour (another instance of the blend between the normative and the instrumental elements of the communication with offenders). Magistrates discussed signs of remorse in court, such as body language or some act of reparation, which were more plausible from a first-time offender. Remorseful offenders might prompt a different sentence – a conditional discharge, or a community service order rather than a combination or probation order, because they did not need to be deterred or persuaded to stop offending. Victims saw remorse as indicating that offenders had punished themselves, had learnt their lesson or might be 'easier to reach', sometimes as a prerequisite to change. Offenders described remorse as a natural process, which promoted acceptance of the sentence. For probation staff, remorse was indicative of a lower risk of reoffending or provided a basis for rehabilitation; therefore it might justify a probation order. One probation officer discussed using remorse in post-sentence processes:

I think there is room for using remorse in sentencing after the event . . . Yes I do think that [the process of remorse is a necessary part of people not offending in the future]. I think that probation's responsibility is to motivate them to get to that point where they can start to look at what they did and why they did it.

Differing views were expressed on whether a display of remorse justified a reduced sentence (for example, in response to an early guilty plea). One viewpoint was that society's expectation of punishment minimised the amount by which the sentence could be reduced; another that magistrates would show leniency towards the remorseful, deferential offender who displayed the right reactions in court. This is known to be a vexed question, on which Duff (2000) opposes a reduced sentence, partly because it encourages dishonesty and sends the wrong messages about crime, but more significantly because repentance and reparative apology need to 'complete' the process begun by remorse. The reservations expressed both by probation officers and magistrates on this point seemed symptomatic of their wider resistance to making decisions on the basis of what were seen as profoundly intimate and internal processes, where it was difficult to tell that the 'remorseful' offender was sincere rather than self-pitying. One victim expressed the tension well in portraying real remorse as inducing a deep sense of shame that was difficult to articulate – the person getting drunk at a party who was unable to face anyone the following day.

It was seen as desirable for offenders to come over time to accept the punishment because they recognised they had done wrong and deserved to be punished. Offenders described coming to recognise that they did the crime so had to do the punishment, and that the experience might be beneficial. It seemed important to magistrates that offenders accept the punishment as fair, proportionate and deserved; this was seen as promoting compliance and perhaps law-abiding behaviour. Probation staff discussed the barriers to that acceptance by offenders, who might find it difficult to acknowledge the court's authority or experience resentment, alienation or denial.

The aspirations discussed so far – for offenders to accept responsibility and the justification for punishment – seem close to 'dialectically defensible censure', as theorised by Bottoms (1998). Hopes clearly went further: that their acceptance of these normative messages would prompt offenders to take positive steps, or to refrain from activities, and to stop offending. Such efforts might be motivated by a wish to make amends or to pay one's dues, which found expression in various ways: expiating guilt through 'hard treatment'; going through processes of rehabilitation; offering some recompense (possibly symbolic); putting something back into the community. However, a number of people made a similar point to this probation officer about how prison might impede such a process:

> You certainly hear offenders say 'well I've been to prison. I've paid the price. I don't see why that should be brought up again'. So they feel you do something wrong and you pay for it and then it's finished with. So that kind of message is given to them.

The experience of being punished was seen as having the potential to make offenders think twice, possibly by being deterred, but also through a more reflective process. The latter was closely related to the idea that offenders might chose to reform themselves, where views varied over the extent to which offenders were 'in the driving seat' or were driven by external factors. For probation staff, offenders had to be prepared to change; it was patronising, punitive and ineffective to do things to people. One probation officer was relieved not to be in a position to probe people's internal states:

I suppose there is an expectation that the person will examine themselves and what has contributed to their being in that place and how they can take steps to change their attitudes. [Have you encountered people who have gone through that process?] I've had experience of people who said they had. You can't see inside a chap's soul, thank god.

Magistrates portrayed a rational, thinking offender with responsibility to change him or herself in response to varying stimuli – avoiding custody, family responsibility, wishing to avoid causing harm to others. There was an element of deterrence in this thinking, coupled with the awareness that 'you can take someone to court but only they can change themselves'. Offenders expressed a strong sense of their own independence: the decision to change, and the effort, was for them to make, albeit prompted by a variety of factors including the wish to make something of their lives:

So it wasn't what the courts did to me, it was within me that I wanted to stop all the stuff I've done, petty things, criminal damage and drink driving . . . [And what makes you think it's got to stop?] Because I want to get somewhere in life. I didn't want to be in and out of prison.

Closely related to the idea of reform, but associated with feelings of regret rather than a 'rational reappraisal', was repentance. One victim was clearly discomforted by the religious connotation, but could not think of a more appropriate way to express the underlying determination not to reoffend:

It's more than remorse because remorse can just mean feeling sorry for yourself, so it's the feeling sorry for what you've done and its effects on others. The word repentance means changing, a giving up of one side and moving to another. I can't think of a word that doesn't have any religious connotation.

Linked to this was the notion of making 'apology', the sincerity of which might be demonstrated by reparative or reformative activity in recognition of accountability for one's actions. Tavuchis (1991) discusses the sociological significance of an apology as an acknowledgment of responsibility and expression of genuine regret and remorse, and the impact of bringing third parties into what is more naturally a private realm. His observation that '[third party] intervention . . .

typically militates against a mutually acceptable and morally satisfying resolution insofar as it interferes with the normal unfolding of the process' (1991: 51) could explain the dissatisfaction I encountered with processes of remorse and apology within the criminal justice setting.

Conclusions

A number of points emerge from the above discussion of interviewees' views about the role of communication in punishment. First, securing a response from the offender – sometimes through deterrence – seemed central to their understandings of the aims of sentencing. However, although the need for the punishment to achieve a 'social purpose' seemed paramount to most people, this cannot be equated with a simple 'consequentialist' position. Strong elements of retributive thinking – a sense of fairness and cautious endorsement of proportionality – were evident, in addition to an almost universal perception of punishment as an expression of disapproval and disavowal of the offence(s). Offenders were widely portrayed as active, thinking, decision-making agents, and revealed a strong sense of their own volition; these perceptions would be inconsistent with an assertion that they were being treated like 'tigers in a circus' (von Hirsch 1993) or their behaviour otherwise manipulated. It is difficult to disentangle retributive from consequentialist thinking in people's understandings, and they seem at least to support a justification for punishment that combines elements of each, in other words, a conceptualisation that is both normative and forward-looking.

The penal messages described in interview often anticipated a positive reaction from offenders, and community orders figured quite prominently in explanations of how particular disposals could be used to reinforce those messages. For example, community service (and the reparation order) enabled offenders to make amends by putting something back into the community, though understandings did not extend to Duff's (2000) model of apologetic reparation (which he accepts might be formal rather than sincere). More broadly, the aspiration that sentencing could be used to encourage the offender to achieve positive change was quite strongly associated with a community sentence. Community service enabled offenders to see that they had something to contribute to society, and therefore to gain 'grounded increments in self-esteem' (Toch 2000), and offenders described themselves as gaining a sense of achievement through probation as well as community service.

Their experiences in undertaking community service or being supervised on a probation order were both seen to have the potential to develop offenders' awareness of the impact of their behaviour on other people. In relation to probation, this idea seems close to Duff's (2000) conceptualisation of the aims of the conditions attached a probation order as communicating to offenders the character and implication of their offences as public wrongs, and therefore to persuade them to modify their future conduct. However, although probation officers saw themselves as getting offenders to attend to the wrongfulness of their behaviour, offenders themselves portrayed a more morally neutral process in which they received advice or were assisted in their decision-making. Community service supervisors were seen as having the opportunity to show offenders that others were worse off, echoing McIvor's (1998) reflection on her study of community service in Scotland. This might actually be a richer and more subtle understanding than offered by Duff, who portrays community service as 'constituting an attempt to persuade [the offender] to face up to the wrong she has done' (2000: 105).

In keeping with the current vogue for probation programmes to 'confront offending behaviour', probation officers clearly saw their task as to promote offenders' acceptance of responsibility. They also perceived a link between offenders' experiencing remorse and resolving not to offend in the future; their function was to help stimulate the necessary processes of self-examination. However, probation officers were also aware of the inherent contradiction between trying to get people to take responsibility for themselves while simultaneously supervising certain aspects of their behaviour. For offenders, although supervision might help them realise the harm caused by their offending, they placed considerable emphasis on developing their own sense of responsibility, and saw remorse as a natural – rather than an induced – process. The understandings expressed by the offenders I interviewed might have fallen short of a conception of probation as aiming to secure their penitent understanding of their wrongs, and therefore their repentance (Duff 2000). But they could still see the experience as helping them to develop an understanding of their offending and its consequences, and as helping them to engage in processes of change and reform.

I hope to develop and elucidate the above discussion through further empirical work. However, provisionally, the experiences and understandings disclosed in interview suggest that community orders have rich communicative potential. There seems scope here for work undertaken with offenders supervised in the community to promote constructive responses to the messages communicated in sentencing: that they should take responsibility for what they have done, gain an understanding of the harm caused, make amends and move forward in a positive way.

This findings suggests, perhaps, that what is needed is not the change in legal form proposed by the Halliday Report (Home Office 2001a) to produce a generic community punishment order whose meaning is obscure to the public and to offenders. What might be more profitable is to focus on the substance of community penalties to maximise the opportunities they offer to engage offenders positively in processes of change. However, the interviews highlight one major obstacle to engaging offenders in those processes: the disconnection between what happens at court and what happens on a community order. They argue for closer integration between offenders' experiences in court and their experiences on supervision, the benefits of which emerged in the pilots of Drug Treatment and Testing Orders (Turnbull *et al.* 2000).[14]

Notes

1 See *Criminal Statistics England and Wales 2000* (Home Office 2001b) – just under 80,000 were sentenced to immediate custody.

2 The Crime and Disorder Act 1998 introduced the Drug Treatment and Testing Order and, for young offenders, the Reparation Order and the Action Plan Order. The Criminal Justice and Court Services Act 2000 has introduced the Exclusion Order and Drug Abstinence Order.

3 See *Criminal Statistics England and Wales 2000* (Home Office 2001b). The proportion of probation orders imposed for indictable offences was 72 per cent in 1990 and 66 per cent in 2000; for CSOs the respective proportions were 69 per cent and 60 per cent.

4 According to *Probation Statistics England and Wales 2000* (Home Office 2002), 25 per cent of those sentenced to probation in 2000 had no previous convictions compared with 12 per cent in 1990; the equivalent proportions for CS were 47 per cent and 14 per cent respectively.

5 Again, under the Criminal Justice and Court Services Act 2000.

6 The target being to get 60,000 offenders through accredited programmes in 2003/4 – see Probation Circular 60/2000 for 'What Works' Strategy.

7 Probation Circular 35/1999 announced the selection of Community Service, Resettlement and Basic Skills Pathfinder projects under the Crime Reduction Programme.

8 The tensions between rehabilitation and desert were exposed following the Criminal Justice Act 1991; in practice, there seem real difficulties in

achieving a balance between these ideas, with the consequence that one consideration tends to overrule the other (see Rex 1998).

9 See von Hirsch (1993) for a discussion of hybrid models that allow exceptional departures from the requirements of desert for the purposes of crime prevention, or which contemplate a range of sanctions that are not excessive or manifestly too lenient. Von Hirsch's own model interlocks both 'censure' and 'crime prevention' in its General Justifying Aim, so that 'the preventive function of the sanction should be seen, I think, as supplying a prudential reason that is tied to, and supplements, the normative reason conveyed by penal censure' (1993: 13).

10 See, for example, Duff (2000, 1999 and 1996).

11 Duff (2000) distinguishes moral persuasion from 'moral education', which might be justified because it benefits the offender. He rejects an interpretation of punishment as education on the grounds that it is objectionable and paternalistic to impose punishment for the offender's own good – following Mills' famous dictum that the only purpose for which coercive power can be rightfully exercised over a citizen is to prevent harm to others. Moreover, it is unclear why punishment should be the preferred method of moral education – even if this form of intervention is what most offenders need. 'Education' implies that offenders are rather like children who have yet to receive the education they need rather than responsible moral agents who need to be persuaded to attend to the wrongfulness of their behaviour.

12 Yet von Hirsch has gone further to suggest that 'some kind of moral response *is expected* on [the offender's] part ... A reaction of indifference would, if the censure is justified, itself be grounds for criticising [the offender]' (von Hirsch, 1993: 10 – my emphasis).

13 A perceived impact in line with Toch (2000), who argues that prisoners can gain 'grounded increments' in self-esteem by assisting the underprivileged, possibly with rehabilitative implications, and that altruistic activity can produce teaching points similar to cognitive skills training that emerge from experience rather than academic exercises.

14 In Liverpool, two stipendiary magistrates took on the review of drug treatment and testing orders, holding a dedicated fortnightly afternoon court session. According to the researchers, the clear oversight of an individual case and a growing relationship between the drug-using offender and sentencers seemed effective both in reinforcing positive progress and in swiftly addressing problems.

References

Allen, F.A. (1981). *The Decline of the Rehabilitative Ideal: Penal Policy and Social Purposes*. New Haven, CT: Yale University Press.

Ashworth, A., von Hirsch, A., Bottoms, A.E. and Wasik, M. (1995) 'Bespoke Tailoring Won't Suit Community Penalties', *New Law Journal*, 145, 970–2.

Bottoms, A.E. (1998) 'Five Puzzles in von Hirsch's Theory of Punishment', in Ashworth, A. and Wasik, M. (eds), *Fundamentals of Sentencing Theory: Essays in Honour of Andrew von Hirsch*. Oxford: Clarendon Press.

Duff, R.A. (1996) 'Penal Communications: Recent Works in the Philosophy of Punishment', *Crime and Justice: A Review of the Research*, 20, 1.

Duff, R.A. (1999) 'Punishment, Communication and Community', in Matravers, M. (ed.), *Punishment and Political Theory*. Oxford: Hart Publishing.

Duff, R.A. (2000) *Punishment, Communication and Community*. Oxford: Oxford University Press.

Hedderman, C., Ellis, T. and Sugg, D. (1999) *Increasing Confidence in Community Sentences: the Results of Two Demonstration Projects*, Home Office Research Study No. 194. London: Home Office.

Home Office (1988) *Punishment, Custody and the Community*, Cm. 424. London: HMSO.

Home Office (1995) *Strengthening Punishment in the Community*, Cm. 2780. London: HMSO.

Home Office (1996) *Protecting the Public*, Cm. 3190. London: HMSO.

Home Office (1999) *Crime Reduction Programme – Pathfinder Selection*, Probation Circular 35/1999. London: Home Office.

Home Office (2000) *What Works Strategy for the Probation Service*, Probation Circular 60/2000. London: Home Office.

Home Office (2001a) *Making Punishments Work*. London: HMSO.

Home Office (2001b) *Criminal Statistics England and Wales 2000*. London: HMSO.

Home Office (2002) *Probation Statistics England and Wales 2000*. London: HMSO.

Lucas, J.R. (1980) *On Justice*. Oxford: Clarendon Press.

McIvor, G. (1998) 'Pro-Social Modelling and Legitimacy: Lessons from a Study of Community Service', in Rex, S.A. and Matravers, A. (eds), *Pro-Social Modelling and Legitimacy: The Clarke Hall Day Conference*. Cambridge: Institute of Criminology.

National Probation Directorate (2001) *Consultation on Sentencing Reform: National Probation Service Response*, Probation Circular 145/2001. London: Home Office.

Raynor, P. (1997) 'Some Observations on Rehabilitation and Justice', *Howard Journal*, 36, 253.

Rex, S.A. [1998] 'Applying Desert Principles to Community Sentences: Lessons from Two Criminal Justice Acts', *Criminal Law Review*, 381.

Straw, J. (2001) 'Next Steps in Criminal Justice Reform', Speech to the Social Market Foundation, 31 January 2001 (unpublished).

Tavuchis, N. (1991) *Mea Culpa: A Sociology of Apology and Reconciliation*. Stanford, CA: Stanford University Press.

Toch, H. (2000) 'Altruistic Activity as Correctional Treatment', *International Journal of Offender Therapy and Comparative Criminology*, 44, 270–8.

Turnbull, P.J., McSweeney, T., Webster, R., Edmunds, M. and Hough, M. (2000) *Drug Treatment and Testing Orders: Final Evaluation Report*, Home Office Research Study No. 212. London: Home Office.

von Hirsch, A. (1993) *Censure and Sanctions*. Oxford: Clarendon Press.

von Hirsch, A. (1999) 'Punishment, Penance and the State', in Matravers, M. (ed.), *Punishment and Political Theory*. Oxford: Hart Publishing.

Worrall, A. (1997) *Punishment in the Community: The Future of Criminal Justice*. London: Longman.

Woolf, Lord Justice (2001) 'The Woolf Report: A Decade of Change?', Address to the Prison Reform Trust, 31 January (unpublished).

Chapter 8

Revisiting ex-prisoner re-entry: a buzzword in search of a narrative

Shadd Maruna and Thomas P. LeBel[1]

Ex-prisoner 're-entry' has become 'the new buzzword in correctional reform' (Austin 2001: 314) both in the United States (Office of Justice Programs 1999; Travis 2000) and increasingly in the United Kingdom (Halliday 2001; Morgan and Owers 2001). The US Department of Justice, which lists 're-entry' as one of two 'hot topics' on its website, has launched a large-scale 'Re-entry Initiative' that will provide over 100 million dollars in funding for localised programmes for released prisoners. While she was Attorney General of the United States, Janet Reno (2000: 1) referred to ex-prisoner re-entry as 'one of the most pressing problems we face as a nation'. She further argued that 'we are not going to end the culture of violence until we address this problem'.

While the problems of adjusting to life after prison are not at all new (see Soothill 1974), the size and scope has certainly expanded in recent decades. In the United States, over 600,000 individuals will be released from prison this year (over 1,600 per day) compared to 170,000 releasees in 1980. In addition, re-entering society seems to be more difficult and precarious a transition than ever before. In 1980, 27,177 released ex-prisoners were returned to state prisons in the US. In 1999, this number was 197,606. As a percentage of all admissions to state prison, parole violators more than doubled from 17 per cent in 1980 to 35 per cent in 1999 (In California, a staggering 67 per cent of prison admissions were parole failures.) Between 1990 and 1999 the number of parole violators rose by 50 per cent while the number of new court commitments rose by only 7 per cent (Hughes, Wilson and Beck 2001). This indicates that the re-entry problem is not only a product of the

1990s incarceration boom in the United States, but was actually a leading cause of the boom as well.

Arguably, the situation for ex-prisoners in the United Kingdom is less dire. Certainly, Britain has a longer and more substantive history of addressing the housing, employment and counselling needs of released prisoners (Haines 1990). Still, this support will be badly stretched as the prison population increases. The UK prison population has jumped from around 40,000 in 1992 to over 68,000 today, and may reach as high as 90,000 in the near future (Grove, Godfrey and McLeod 1999). Moreover, substantial difficulties remain for returning ex-convicts (see Hagell, Newburn and Rowlingson 1995; Metcalf, Anderson and Rolfe 2001; Paylor 1995). In fact, 57 per cent of all prisoners in England and Wales discharged in 1996 were re-convicted for a standard list offence within two years of their release (Home Office 2001a). In a joint thematic review on resettlement issues, HM Inspectorates of Prisons and Probation conclude: 'The resettlement needs of many prisoners are being severely neglected' because of the lack of an overall strategy for reintegration (Morgan and Owers 2001: 1).

As such, the renewed focus on re-entry in the United States and United Kingdom is extremely welcome and much needed. Still, questions remain as to just what the new 're-entry' buzzword actually implies and whether or not the proposals being put forth are indeed as new and exciting as the buzz suggests. The use of the term 're-entry' is generally confined to the United States, although the word has also crept into contemporary British discussions (see Halliday 2001). As such, this chapter will focus primarily on the developments around re-entry in the United States, with attention given to the implications for recent British proposals for reform.

The need for new narratives

> Bullets kill and bars constrain, but the practice of supervision inevitably involves the construction of a set of narratives which allows the kept, the keepers, and the public to believe in a capacity to control [crime] that cannot afford to be tested too frequently.
> (Simon 1993)

As a buzzword, 're-entry' appears to connote something similar to previous terms such as 'prisoner aftercare' (Haines 1990), 'throughcare' (McAllister, Bottomley and Liebling 1992), 'discharged prisoners' aid' (Soothill 1974), 'reintegration', 'integration', 'parole' and the currently preferred term in Britain, 'resettlement' (see Morgan and Owers 2001). At the same time, 're-entry' lacks the element of support or nurturance implicit in root words like 'care', 'aid' and even 'settle'. Indeed, 're-entry' is an intentionally vague, largely descriptive term that can imply different things to different listeners. For evidence of just how slippery this variously named concept is, consider the UK Association of Chief Officers of Probation's definition of what they call 'resettlement':

> A systematic and evidenced-based process by which actions are taken to work with the offender in custody and on release, so that communities are better protected from harm and re-offending is significantly reduced. It encompasses the totality of work with prisoners, their families and significant others in partnership with statutory and voluntary organisations. (Cited in Morgan and Owers 2001: 12)

In other words, nearly anything can be called re-entry (or resettlement or whatnot) as long as it works.

In his tremendous history of parole in the United States, Simon (1993: 9) writes, 'One of the primary tasks of an institution that exercises the power to punish is to provide a plausible account of what it does and how it does what it does'. This might be particularly important for community corrections, which, as Fogel (1984: 85) notes, 'lacks the forceful imagery that other occupations in criminal justice can claim: police catch criminals, prosecutors try to get them locked up, judges put them in prisons, guards and wardens keep them there, but what do probation officers do?' Simon argues that a good correctional narrative needs some rather obvious components. Basically, it requires a plausible theory of criminogenesis (what causes people to commit crime?), and then a set of practices that appear capable of reversing this process and therefore controlling the crime problem. Simon and others argue that re-entry policy in the United States currently lacks any such coherent narrative.

Indeed, a 'growing conviction that the system no longer represents a credible response to the problem of crime' (Rhine 1997: 71) has led to several new proposals to severely curtail or even abandon parole supervision[2] entirely in the United States (e.g. Austin 2001). One of the invited participants at a US conference on 'Rethinking Probation' stated this matter quite bluntly: 'Public regard for probation is dangerously low ... We have to realise that we don't have broad public legitimacy' (Dickey and Smith 1998: 3). Another participant described the public mood toward community corrections as a 'malaise'. 'Even more importantly, there is a malaise in our own house [among probation professionals]' (Dickey and Smith 1998: 5).

In recent years, the British probation service has undergone its own period of feeling 'uncomfortable, threatened, unsure of its role, and not at all confident of its social or political credibility' (Garland 1997: 3). This period of uncertainty, of course, was one of the factors leading to the 'repositioning' of probation and the formation of the unified 'National Probation Service' with the explicit goal of restoring public acceptance. In her keynote address to members of the National Probation Service, Probation Minister Beverley Hughes said, 'Public credibility is crucial to our success. Only if, together, we can convince communities of your role and your reliability will you be able to do your important job effectively' (Teague 2001: 218). One of the first priorities for reform may be in resettlement cases where the National Probation Service is still weak (see Morgan and Owers 2001). According to the Halliday Report (2001: 28), 'Resettlement cases are viewed as the 'poor relations' compared with community sentences and very little pre-release planning is being undertaken'.

The re-entry buzz

It is in this climate that the new re-entry reform proposals have emerged. Perhaps the most significant of these is the new concept of a 're-entry court', based on the drug court model, which would cast judges as 're-entry managers' (Travis 2000: 8).

> A re-entry court is a court that manages the return to the community of individuals being released from prison, using the authority of the court to apply graduated sanctions and positive reinforcement and to marshal resources to support the prisoner's reintegration, much as drug courts do, to promote positive behaviour by the returning prisoner. (Office of Justice Programs 1999: 1)

In the United Kingdom, a similar proposal has been made for expanding the role of judicial oversight in the re-entry process, placing the courts in an unprecedented case-management and supervisory role. In this 'sentence review capacity', the judiciary would be charged with planning and reviewing the progress of a prisoner's re-entry into the community 'under conditions geared to "seamlessly" completing work begun in prison to reduce re-offending and managing risks to the public' (Halliday 2001: iv).

These are significant reforms that would require substantial changes in the traditional functions of the judiciary in both the United States and the United Kingdom. Essentially, the court system would be 'engaged in the ongoing monitoring of defendants instead of leaving this job to probation or community-based organisations or – in too many cases – to no one at all' (Berman and Feinblatt 2001: 136–7). Moreover, this importation of the drug court model into the re-entry arena is, frankly, about as enterprising as one can hope for in criminal justice reform. The public approves of so little of what is done in the name of corrections that if some new programme attracts positive, popular attention, as the drug court model has, then it gets used in as many areas as possible. In the same way that the popularity of 'community policing' led to 'community prosecutors', 'community courts' and that ilk, the media hype surrounding Dade County's drug court in the early 1990s has been a catalyst for numerous 'problem-solving' courts, of which the 're-entry court' is only the latest version.

Yet, as with any transplantation of a model from one context to the next, there is a problem with applying this drug court model to the re-entry process. Richard Gebelein (2000), a pioneering drug court judge, tried to explain the popularity of drug courts in an era in which there is allegedly little support for the rehabilitative ideal. He argues that the main reason is that, unlike the earlier failed movement of rehabilitation programmes, the drug court movement has been able to provide a clear explanation of what has caused the criminal behaviour of the drug court clients and what they need to get better. Essentially the slogan that addiction is a disease and, as such, needs to be treated by professionals is one that makes sense to the public at this point in history.

Is there a similar narrative for re-entry? There are certainly a lot of new words being used: 're-entry courts', 'seamlessness', 'sentence management'. Yet, new jargon does not necessarily imply the development of a new narrative. In fact, the discourse around these new re-entry initiatives reveals surprisingly little that is new. Halliday (2001: 28), for instance, argues that, 'A great deal can be done to make release planning, and management of prisoners' return to the community, more effective'. This includes 'buttressing curfews, and electronic monitoring where necessary, with programmes to meet identifiable needs'. Similarly, according to Reno (2000: 3):

> The re-entry court is modelled on the ... theory of a carrot and stick approach, in using the strength of the court and the wisdom of the court to really push the issue ... The message works with

us: stay clean, stay out of trouble, and we'll help you get a job, we'll help you prepare in terms of a skill. But if you come back testing positive for drugs, if you commit a further crime, if you violate the conditions of your release, you're going to pay.

These 'new' visions for re-entry (involving tighter control and more assistance) will have a familiar ring to those involved in prison reform. Indeed, they have probably been around since the first carrot met the first stick. (Stow (2002) points out that the metaphor of controlling humans 'like donkeys, by carrots and sticks' suggests a rather 'undignified status'.) Moreover, except for the part about the strength and wisdom of the judiciary,[3] this combination sounds suspiciously like 'simply another word for traditional parole supervision, which many have tried to discredit and dismantle' over the last 35 years (Austin 2001: 314). According to Bazemore (forthcoming: 4):

An important indicator of the current state of the field is the fact that long established, empirically grounded admonitions to focus at least as much on services as on surveillance, and to avoid overloading offenders with sanctions, are often viewed in these models as profound new insights.

Traditional narratives of re-entry

Reno's stick and carrot represent the key symbols of the two reigning paradigms in parole practice over the last 100 years, which can be broken down into the familiar dichotomy of punishment and welfare, monitor and mentor, or cop and social worker (Barry 2000). We refer to these as 'risk-based' and 'need-based' justifications, respectively. Both are deficit models – that is, they emphasise ex-prisoners' problems – but they require very different technologies and connote different meanings. Below, we briefly assess both narratives, focusing explicitly on the messages they communicate to the public and to ex-prisoners themselves (see Duff 2001).

Control narratives (risk-based)

The February 2000 press release from US Senator Joseph Biden's office announcing the 'first-ever' re-entry court in Delaware began with the macho headline 'Biden Introduces Tough New Court Program for Released Inmates'. Getting 'tough' on those who have already 'paid their debt' to society has become a standard, if not always coherent, re-entry narrative. The basic story, here, seems to be that ex-prisoners are dangerous, and they need to be watched carefully and controlled. Indeed, this implication is clear in the new name given to the Re-entry Initiative in the United States. Originally titled, 'Young Offender Re-entry Initiative', under the Clinton Administration, the Bush Administration transformed the project into the 'Serious and Violent Offender Re-entry Initiative' and have 'toughened' up the language accordingly throughout their version of the proposal.

Underlying the control narrative is the assumption that criminal behaviour is freely chosen and that ex-prisoners will likely respond to the threat of sanctions (or, at any rate, if they do not, then they are too dangerous to be out of prison). This explanation suggests the need for an 'electronic panopticon' (Gordon 1991) or 'pee 'em and see 'em' (Cullen 2002) approach to re-entry involving electronic monitoring, intensive supervision (i.e. additional home and office visits), random drug testing, home confinement, behaviour restrictions, curfews and expanded lengths of supervision. Empirically, this sort of intensive community supervision has failed to live up to its promises. Petersilia and Turner's (1993) nine-state, random-assignment evaluation found no evidence that the increased surveillance in the community deterred offenders from committing crimes. At the same time, this research quite conclusively showed that heightened supervision could increase the probability that technical violations would be detected, leading to greater costs and use of incarceration.

Further, the control narrative has little support from the psychological literature on planned change. Kelman (1958), for instance, discusses three means of changing behaviour: change via compliance, change via identification and change via internalisation. The first strategy, utilising power-coercive means, may achieve instrumental compliance, Kelman says, but is the least likely of the three to promote 'normative re-education' and long-term transformation once the 'change agent' has been removed (see also Bottoms 2000). Indeed, this hypothesis was recently confirmed in MacKenzie and De Li's (2001) study of intensive supervision probation. They found some deterrent effect during the period of probation, but found that this seems to 'wear off when they are no longer under supervision' (37–8).

Additionally, overly strict control tactics can undermine the perceived legitimacy in paroling authorities among clients. For instance, parole conditions that include prohibitions against associating with fellow ex-prisoners or entering drinking establishments are often viewed as evidence that the entire parole process is a joke. Persons returning from the trauma of prison with few resources and little hope are likely to become 'defiant' (Sherman 1993) at such heavy-handed treatment. Ex-prisoners often feel they have 'paid their debt to society' already and should therefore 'be left alone' (Halliday 2001: 28). Far from endorsing a 'seamless' transition from prison control to community control, 'No one wants the separation of prison and parole more urgently than do prisoners', according to Mobley and Terry (forthcoming: 22). 'When people "get out", they want to *be out*. Any compromise or half-measure, any "hoops" or hassles placed in their path, breeds resentment'. The extent of this resentment is apparent in the fascinating, and apparently somewhat widespread, phenomenon of prisoners choosing to 'max out' of their sentence inside a prison rather than be released early and face high levels of supervision (Petersilia and Deschenes 1994).

Most importantly, however, the control narrative suffers from the 'deeply entrenched view' that 'equates punishment and control with incarceration, and that accepts alternatives as suitable only in cases where neither punishment nor control is thought necessary' (Smith 1984: 171). Essentially, if parolees are such 'dangerous men' and need so much supervision, then why aren't they still in prison? The average US parole officer – who has a caseload of 69 parolees each averaging 1.6 face-to-face contacts per month (Camp and Camp 1997) – simply cannot compete with the iron bars, high walls and razor wire of the prison when it comes to securing constraint-based compliance (see Bottoms 2000: 92–3).

Support narratives (need-based)
The traditional counter to a risk-based re-entry system is a need-based system of aftercare. Here the story is that ex-prisoners are people with multiple deficits (many of which are the result of the prison experience itself!). The most important of these are 'criminogenic' needs (or those deficits related to offending). In order to promote conformity, according to the narrative, these needs must be met by requiring released prisoners to attend programmes in addiction counselling, cognitive therapy, life skills training, anger management and the like.

There is a well-known body of empirical support for the claim that such rehabilitative interventions can marginally reduce recidivism rates when treatment is correctly matched to a client's criminogenic needs (see McGuire 1995). Yet, there is a difference between measures of recidivism reduction and the concept of reintegration. Bazemore (forthcoming: 8) argues that the support paradigm can actually be a 'barrier to meaningful offender reintegration' because of the way this assistance is viewed by the wider community. 'The notion of someone who has hurt another citizen . . . getting help or service without making amends for what has been damaged flies in the face of virtually universal norms of fairness'.

Combination-deficit narratives

The traditional, middle-ground position, which appeals to Reno and many of the contemporary re-entry reformers is to resolve the pendulous mentor or monitor debate by trying to do both.[4] Basically, the idea is that if one combines a control approach (which does not really work but is assumed to have public support) with a treatment approach (that works a little but is thought to lack widespread support), the end result will be a programme that is both popular and effective. Instead, more often than not, the result of mixing such disparate goals is a 'muddle' (Dickey and Smith 1998). As Fogel (1978: 10–11) famously quipped, 'A parole officer can be seen going off to his/her appointed rounds with Freud in one hand and a .38 Smith and Wesson in the other . . . Is Freud a backup to the .38? Or is the .38 carried to "support" Freud?'

Theoretically, control strategies are intended to encourage instrumental compliance during the supervisory period, while the treatment strategies are designed to help participants internalise new, moral values. That is, the therapy or the job training is what is really going to work, but without the heavy coercion, the ex-prisoners will not show up for the treatment (for support of this hypothesis see MacKenzie and Brame 2001; Petersilia and Turner 1993). Unfortunately, combining coercive supervision with treatment can send 'mixed messages' to returning ex-prisoners (Mobley and Terry forthcoming) and can compromise the welfare provision of the treatment agency (Garland 1990: 180). Coerced treatment is often resented by correctional consumers, who prefer self-help groups to state-sponsored, top-down reform programmes (Irwin 1974). Mobley and Terry (forthcoming: 5) write, 'Certainly ex-cons need access to social services and community resources, but they should not have to engage with law officers to get them. Agencies designed for purposes of social control should be kept apart from those developed for social support'. Although parents and parental guardians are comfortable combining a disciplinary role with a social support role, this cop-and-counsellor combination may not be possible in the much more limited relationship between parole officer and parolee. Indeed, more often than not, interventions premised on a combination-deficit model end up becoming 'almost all stick and no carrot' and ignoring the 'individuality of human beings' (Prison Reform Trust 1999).

Importantly, 'carrot and stick' models of re-entry assign a largely passive role to the ex-prisoner (Bazemore 1999). The individual is expected 'simply to be (to exist) and to obey. There is nothing expected of him other than co-operation and good behaviour' (Scharf 1983: 117). Critics argue that the operant conditioning implied in the 'carrot and stick' metaphor confounds blind conformity with responsible behaviour. This argument has been best developed in Stephen Pryor's thought-provoking report *The Responsible Prisoner* (2001), in which he examines the extent to which prisons reward and demand passive compliance instead of moral choice. For instance, Pryor (2001: 98) quotes one prisoner as saying, 'Keeping your head down is what is rewarded, not challenging or stretching yourself.' When asked to describe the type of behaviour that was most rewarded in the prison system, prisoners in Stow's (2002: 70) study similarly responded almost uniformly with descriptions of 'toeing the line', 'not questioning', 'just being quiet', 'like a robot', 'be subservient' and 'kow-tow'. Pryor (2001) argues that 'an assumption of reciprocal responsibility and trust' would be more likely to instil a sense of personal responsibility in the returning prisoner.

Finally, the carrot and stick model of re-entry fails to assign a meaningful role to the community. Although the process of reintegration has always had as much to do with the community as it has with the individual, carrot and stick reintegration models focus almost exclusively on the individual case (see Smith 2000). If re-entry is to be a meaningful concept, presumably it implies more than physically re-entering society, but also includes some sort of 'relational reintegration' back into the moral community. That is, the reintegrated person should be re-accepted as a full-fledged member in and of the wider community. Social dependency and intensive supervision (or so-called carrots and sticks) seem to be the opposite of this sort of moral inclusion (Taylor 1997).

Strengths-based re-entry: an emerging narrative?

An alternative paradigm is emerging (actually re-emerging) in social service areas related to re-entry but has not been a large part of the new discussion around re-entry (Bazemore 1999 is one exception). For the sake of consistency (and not just to invent another new term), we will refer to this as a 'strengths-based' paradigm.[5] Strengths approaches ask not what a person's deficits are, but rather what positive contribution the person can make (see Grant 1968). How can their lives become useful and purposeful? In Jeremy Travis's (2000: 7) formulation: 'Offenders are seen as assets to be managed rather than merely

Table 8.1   Practice implications of the needs and strengths models

Needs models	Strengths models
Individual and group therapy	Community service, peer counselling, leadership development
Job readiness and job counselling	Work experience, service crews
Outdoor challenge	Conservation projects, community beautification
Remedial education	Cross-age tutoring (juvenile offender tutoring younger children)
Message to offender: 'You have problems and need our help'	*Message to offender:* 'You are needed in your community'

liabilities to be supervised'. This shift represents a move 'away from the principle of entitlement to the principle of social exchange' (Levrant *et al.* 1999: 22) or to what Bazemore (1999) calls 'earned redemption'. Table 8.1, adapted from Bazemore (1999), provides a contrast between this approach[6] and a need-based model.

The 'strengths narrative' begins with the assumption that ex-prisoners are stigmatised persons, and implicitly that this stigma (and not some internal dangerousness or deficit) is at the core of what makes ex-prisoners likely to reoffend. The 'narrative of criminogenesis' that Simon (1993) calls for, then, is clearly based on a labelling/social exclusion story – on which, of course, the very idea of 'reintegration' is also premised. Johnson (2002: 319) writes, 'released prisoners find themselves "in" but not "of" the larger society' and 'suffer from a presumption of moral contamination'.

To combat this social exclusion, the strengths paradigm calls for opportunities for ex-prisoners to make amends, demonstrate their value and potential, and experience success in support and leadership roles. In the language of the 1960s New Careers movement, the goal is to *'devise ways of creating more helpers!* Or to be more exact: how to transform receivers of help (such as welfare recipients) into dispensers of help; how to structure the situation so that receivers of help will be placed in roles requiring the giving of assistance' (Pearl and Riessman 1965: 88–9, emphasis in original). Finally, these contributions need to be recognised and publicly 'certified' in order to symbolically 'de-label' the stigmatised person (see Maruna 2001: chapter 8).

Focusing on reparation and earned redemption, strengths-based re-entry would communicate a quite different message to the community than deficit models. According to Bazemore (forthcoming: 24): 'Such demonstrations send a message to the community that the offender is worthy of further support and investment in their reinteg- ration, and to the offender that s/he has something to offer that is of value to others'. Basically, the premise is that a good neighbour is not someone with a straitjacket on, nor is she or he a socially supported dependant. A good neighbour is a contributing member of society.

To focus on the 'strengths' of a population that is clearly swimming in needs and risks seems naive or Pollyannish, yet the reciprocal implications of the strengths narrative – that one needs 'to do something to get something' (Toch 1994: 71) – make it intuitively appealing. A participant in the 'Rethinking Probation' conference summarised this appeal concisely:

> Let me put it this way, if the public knew that when you commit some wrongdoing, you're held accountable in constructive ways and you've got to earn your way back through these kinds of good works, ... [probation] wouldn't be in the rut we're in right now with the public. (Dickey and Smith 1998: 36)

This symbolic appeal of transforming the probationer into a 'giver rather than a consumer of help' is also evidenced by the enthusiasm around community service as a sanction in the 1970s in Britain.[7]

Rationale for a 'strengths' approach

The central, theoretical premise behind 'strengths-based' practice can be found in the 'helper principle' of the New Careers Movement: essentially, that it is better (or more reintegrative) to give help than to receive it (see also Cullen 1994: 543–4). The alleged benefits of assuming the role of helper include 'the self-respect he gains from doing a meaningful job and the sense of competence obtained for the learning of skills' (Pearl and Riessman 1965: 82–3). Similarly, Toch (2000: 270) argues that among the benefits of altruistic behaviour include a sense of accomplishment, grounded increments in self- esteem, meaningful purposiveness and a cognitive restructuring to- ward prosocial goals.

Recent research on desistance from crime provides the most direct and intriguing evidence in support of these principles. For instance, as is well known, Sampson and Laub (1993) found that one-time offenders who were responsible for providing for their spouses and children were significantly more likely to desist from crime than those who made no such bonds. A less well known finding of their research, as pointed out by Cullen (1994), was that desistance was strongly correlated with assuming financial responsibility for one's ageing parents or siblings in need as well (Sampson and Laub 1993: 219–20). The implication seems to be that nurturing behaviours are inconsistent with a criminal lifestyle. Indeed, Lynne Goodstein speculates that women's traditional responsibility for other family and community members may be one reason that females are so dramatically under-represented in criminal statistics (cited in Cullen 1994).

Sampson and Laub's (1993) other key finding – the role of steady, legitimate employment as a transition out of criminal offending cycles – also suggests that assuming roles of responsibility may have reformative value. Uggen and Janikula (1999) investigated the question of whether involvement in unpaid volunteer work can also induce a change in a person's likelihood of antisocial conduct. They found a robust negative relationship between volunteer work and arrest even after statistically controlling for the effects of antisocial propensities, prosocial attitudes, and commitments to conventional behaviour. Citing Tocqueville (1956: 197), Uggen and Janikula (1999: 334) conclude that, 'By dint of working for one's fellow-citizens, the habit and the taste for serving them is at length acquired'. Indeed, participants in community service work almost always rate the experience as a positive and beneficial experience (McIvor 1992: 177).

Finally, Maruna's (2001) research on the psychology of desistance from crime offers perhaps the most direct evidence of a link between a 'generative' identity and criminal reform. In a clinical comparison of successfully and unsuccessfully reformed ex-prisoners, Maruna found that those who were able to 'go straight' were significantly more care-oriented, other-centred and focused on promoting the next generation. Frequently, these sample members based their self-conceptions on identities as 'wounded healers'. That is, they have tried to find some meaning in their shameful life histories by turning their experiences into cautionary or hopeful stories of redemption, which they share with younger offenders in similar situations.

What would strengths-based re-entry look like?

Like any good re-entry model, this one would begin almost immediately after a determination of guilt. The default sentencing outcome in any strengths-based paradigm would be community service – although of a different nature than that which is currently employed. Virtually all US and UK probation departments have had some experience with community service as a sanction, and it has been widely viewed as a rare penal success story (see Whitfield and Scott 1993). Yet despite its origins as a rehabilitative panacea, dating back to the Wootton Committee (Advisory Council on the Penal System 1970: 13), community service is no longer exclusively justified using a strengths narrative. According to Bazemore and Maloney (1994), 'Punishment now appears to have become the dominant objective of service sanctions in many jurisdictions'. This shift is made explicit in the UK context (see Halliday 2001: 40) by the much criticised relabelling of community service as a community *punishment* order. Some critics have gone so far as to suggest that community service orders in the United Kingdom tend to be 'almost exclusively manual, menial and arduous' (Caddick 1994: 450; see also Blagg and Smith 1989), although this trend seems to be changing (see Home Office 2001b). Indeed, Johnson and Rex (forthcoming) argue convincingly that regardless of its new name, community service work in the United Kingdom is 'rediscovering reintegration' and undergoing a return to its origins as a rehabilitative and educational intervention (Advisory Council on the Penal System 1970).

In a strengths-based framework, community service work would be voluntarily agreed upon, and would involve challenging tasks that could utilise the talents of the offender in useful, visible roles.

> Probation and parole projects in which offenders visibly and directly produce things the larger community wants, such as gardens, graffiti-free neighbourhoods, less dangerous alleys, habitable housing for the homeless . . . have also helped build stronger communities, and have carved channels into the labour market for the offenders engaged in them. (Dickey and Smith 1998: 35)

Such volunteer activities could be encouraged even in cases in which incarceration is deemed necessary. In a partnership programme with Habitat for Humanity, prisoners from 75 prisons (working alongside volunteers from the community) built over 250 homes for low-income Americans in 1999 (Ta 2000). Groups of prisoners frequently volunteer their skills for projects like Toys for Tots, training dogs for the seeing impaired, repairing aging public buildings and churches, and so forth. Perhaps most impressive among the contributions made by prisoners is the little publicised but essential work that teams of prisoners have voluntarily undertaken in fighting the forest fires ravaging America's national parks.

With the support of the Inside-Out Trust, British prisoners volunteer to repair wheelchairs, furniture and bicycles, audiotape information for blind listeners and perform other good deeds. Since 1997, the

Samaritans have trained convicts to become 'prison listeners' and befriend other prisoners who want to talk about their feelings or may be suicidal. Prisoners in New York State have been involved in the crucial work of providing respite care to fellow prisoners dying of AIDS and other illnesses in the prison system. As one of Stephen Pryor's interviewees stated in the Responsible Prisoner report, 'It is amazing how much talent prisoners have when they are allowed to show it. Officers' jobs would be much less stressful if they learned how to make use of us scumbags; there are so many things we could do for ourselves, and them' (Pryor 2001: 101).

One of the most important ways prisoners and ex-prisoners can make positive contributions is through increased involvement in the raising of their children. Surveys of prisoners in the United States show that 55 per cent of state and 63 per cent of federal prisoners have children under the age of 18, and almost half of those parents were living with their children at the time they were incarcerated (US DOJ BJS 2000). The United States Department of Justice, Bureau of Justice Statistics (2000: 2) estimates that these 667,900 incarcerated fathers left behind approximately 1,372,700 children under age 18. A key strengths-based aspect of reintegration would involve the facilitation of active relationships and traditional parental responsibility among prisoners (see especially Lanier (forthcoming) for specific policy proposals). Active engagement in parenting while incarcerated provides a 'stability zone' for offenders that 'softens the psychological impact of confinement' (Toch 1975), and studies find a strong and consistent positive relationship between parole success and maintaining strong family ties in prison (e.g. Holt and Miller 1972).

A strengths-based re-entry court

The work of re-entry, then, becomes the facilitation of opportunities to make useful contributions and reparation to one's family and community. Just as important as developing these opportunities, for symbolic reasons, is the public recognition of this work. Re-entry as it is currently practised focuses almost entirely on detecting and punishing failure – even though the 'what works' principles suggest that positive reinforcement should outweigh punishment by a 4:1 ratio (Gendreau, Cullen and Bonta 1994). As conformity is all that is required of deficit-based parole, it makes little sense to commend or acknowledge persons simply for doing what they are supposed to and following the rules. Indeed, the primary 'reward' available in parole today is to 'get off' parole, a particularly strange and unceremonious process.[8]

The role of the re-entry court in a strengths-based paradigm would not involve the application of additional sanctions as in the traditional court, but instead would be to dispense 'reintegration'. This would not just mean a release from prison or supervision (as is the traditional role of the parole board), but rather a release from the stigma of the original conviction through ceremonies of reintegration (see Maruna 2001). The court then might be modelled on Braithwaite's (2001: 11) notion of 'active responsibility': 'Passive responsibility means holding someone responsible for something they have done in the past. Active responsibility means the virtue of taking responsibility for putting things right for the future'. The re-entry court would act as a 'public recognition ceremony' acknowledging 'a milestone in repaying [one's] debt to society' (Travis 2000: 9). The court's role would be to officially acknowledge and reward the types of positive actions described previously (volunteer work, counselling, parenting) and to determine at what stage the ex-prisoner should be officially 'forgiven'.

The notion of rewarding success is already implicit in the re-entry court idea. Travis (1999: 133) asserts that 'the court should use positive judicial reinforcement by serving as a public forum for encouraging pro-social behaviour and for affirming the value of individual effort in earning the privilege of successful reintegration'. And in fact, jurisdictions are required to outline milestones in the re-entry process that would trigger recognition and an appropriate reward (Office of Justice Programs 1999).

In drug treatment courts, 'applause is common' and in some courtrooms 'even judicial hugs are by no means a rare occurrence' (Wexler 2001: 21). According to Makkai and Braithwaite (1993), such praise can have 'cognitive effects on individuals through nurturing law-abiding identities, building cognitive commitments to try harder, encouraging individuals who face adversity not to give up ... and nurturing belief in oneself'. They find substantial evidence in favour of a 'radical redesign of regulatory institutions so that they are more praise-driven than punishment-driven' (74). Braithwaite and Braithwaite (2001: 15) write: 'Obsessed with the evil side of life, criminologists neglect the more important domains where regulatory objectives are about nurturing excellence'.

A strengths approach would probably take this further and, following Johnson (2002: 328), would recast the re-entry court process as 'a mutual effort at reconciliation, where offender and society work together to make amends – for hurtful crimes and hurtful punishments – and move forward'. Braithwaite and Braithwaite (2001) have argued that praise may work in the exact opposite way that shaming does.

173

That is, while it is better to shame an individual act and not the whole person, it may be better to praise the whole person rather than the specific act.

[P]raise that is tied to specific acts risks counter productivity if it is seen as an extrinsic reward, if it nurtures a calculative approach to performances that cannot be constantly monitored . . . Praising virtues of the person rather than just their acts . . . nourishes a positive identity. (Braithwaite and Braithwaite 2001: 16)

As such, the primary work of the re-entry court would not be to reward specific acts, but rather to act as a sort of 'elevation ceremony' (Lofland 1969) or 'certification process' (Meisenhelder 1977). Lofland (1969: 227) suggests that elevation ceremonies 'serve publicly and formally to announce, sell and spread the fact of the Actor's new kind of being'. These include the ex-offender's 'public appearance before a formally assembled group, [and] the public profession of one's personal transformation' (228). Ideally, like the 1974 Rehabilitation of Offenders Act, this delabelling would also involve the 'expiration' of the individual's criminal history allowing the person freedom from having to declare previous convictions to potential employers and other authorities. The ultimate reward, then, for reactive 'good behaviour' should be permission to legally move on from the past.

Last words and hesitations

As opposed to more sober analyses of the current state of re-entry (e.g. Simon 1993), we have offered what is clearly a rather optimistic picture of an emerging trend in contemporary practices. Yet, if nothing else, the co-optation and demise of the original New Careers Movement in the United States and the United Kingdom[9] suggests there is much reason to temper our enthusiasm for the likelihood of success for a strengths-based re-entry initiative.

Above all, while strengths rhetoric has a nice ring to it, in actual practice strengths-based activities can often be perceived as a threat to the correctional establishment. Irwin (1974: 142–3) writes:

If a program is successful or partially so in orienting a group of prisoners toward the active conception of rehabilitation, toward being self-sufficient, self-actualised, socially aware, and socially involved, the clients are perceived as threats to the unstated concerns of the [prison] organisation. Some of the clients will try to change established routines; criticise and generate outside criticism toward the correctional organisation; make claims to moral equality or superiority; and attempt to bring themselves . . . into the organisation's policy and decision-making routines. These activities . . . are intolerable. What follows when this occurs is that the active definition of rehabilitation is rooted out, and the program is forced to adopt the passive definition, that of promoting conformity to existing social contexts.

The ideal role of the criminal justice system in a strengths-based future, then, may be to simply stay out of the way and not cause too much trouble.

Notes

1 The authors would like to thank Gordon Bazemore, Ros Burnett, Sue Rex and Hans Toch for their insights and comments on earlier drafts.
2 These should be seen as distinct from previous efforts to abolish parole release structures, which largely left post-incarceration supervision intact.
3 Premising a re-entry narrative on the 'strength and wisdom' of the judiciary sounds odd in the context of the United Kingdom where surveys consistently reveal a widespread lack of confidence in the court system. Indeed judges receive 'more negative evaluations than any other criminal justice professional' (Hough and Roberts 1999: 12).
4 In the United Kingdom, the Criminal Justice and Court Services Act 2000 has now made these narratives explicit by re-naming existing community penalties: the 'Community Punishment Order', the 'Community Rehabilitation Order' and the combination 'Community Punishment and Rehabilitation Order'.
5 However, this should be seen as an umbrella term that encompasses approaches that go by many other names – most notably Restorative Justice, but also the New Careers movement, relational rehabilitation/relational justice, and the New Recovery Movement. The strengths-based message is also central to the London-based 'Payback' organisation that aims to help victims and communities benefit from the constructive work of non-violent offenders.
6 We make no pretension to 'discovering' (and most certainly not inventing) this paradigm. Strengths-based themes have been a staple of progressive criminal justice reforms at least since the time of Maconochie's Mark System (see Morris 2001). After a recent rejuvenation in the 1960s and 1970s, however, programmes inspired by this theme decreased significantly and in many cases disappeared from correctional practice and (importantly)

correctional rhetoric, which focuses almost exclusively on principles of risk, need and occasionally 'responsivity'. The case being made in this chapter is only that there are signs that a 'strengths' narrative is coming back in multiple guises in the social services (see Saleebey 1997; White 2000), and that this theme may be an appropriate one to introduce into the re-entry debate.

7 Rutherford (1993) describes community service as the 'Big Idea' of the 1970s in the United Kingdom. He argues that a new vision of similar magnitude is needed for today.

8 When one of this chapter's authors earned his freedom after 56 months of parole supervision, he was offered not so much as a 'congratulations' or a 'good luck' from the officer who had such power over his life. In fact, he only found out that he had been released from parole supervision when he had to call his PO to get a travel pass to visit family out of state. The memorable dialogue proceeded something as follows: 'So, does that mean I'm free?' 'Yes, you don't need to report anymore.' 'Do I have all of my rights back?' 'I don't know anything about that.' 'Thanks.'

9 The last remaining UK New Careers Project, in Bristol, was phased out in 1992 just as the Criminal Justice Act was coming into force (see Caddick 1994).

References

Advisory Council on the Penal System (1970) *Non-Custodial and Semi-Custodial Penalties*. London: HMSO.

Austin, J. (2001) 'Prisoner Re-entry: Current Trends, Practices, and Issues', *Crime and Delinquency*, 47(3), 314–34.

Barry, M. (2000) 'The Mentor/Monitor Debate in Criminal Justice: What Works for Offenders', *British Journal of Social Work*, 30, 575–95.

Bazemore, G. (1999) 'After Shaming, Whither Reintegration: Restorative Justice and Relational Rehabilitation', in Bazemore, G. and Walgrave, L. (eds), *Restorative Juvenile Justice: Repairing the Harm of Youth Crime*. Monsey, NY: Criminal Justice Press, 155–94.

Bazemore, G. (forthcoming) 'Reintegration and Restorative Justice: Toward a Theory and Practice of Informal Social Control and Support', in Maruna, S. and Immarigeon, R. (eds), *After Crime and Punishment: Ex-Convict Re-Entry and Desistance from Crime*. Albany, NY: SUNY Press.

Bazemore, G. and Maloney, D. (1994) 'Rehabilitating Community Service: Toward Restorative Service Sanctions in a Balanced Justice System', *Federal Probation*, 58(1), 24–35.

Berman, G. and Feinblatt, J. (2001) 'Problem-Solving Courts: A Brief Primer', *Law and Policy*, 23(2), 125–40.

Blagg, H. and Smith, D. (1989) *Crime, Penal Policy and Social Work*. Harlow: Longman.

Bottoms, A. (2000) 'Compliance and Community Penalties', in Bottoms, A., Gelsthorpe, L. and Rex, S. (eds), *Community Penalties: Change and Challenges*. Cullompton: Willan.

Braithwaite, J. (2001) 'Intention Versus Reactive Fault'. Unpublished paper.

Braithwaite, J. and Braithwaite, V. (2001) 'Part One', in Ahmed, E., Harris, N., Braithwaite, J. and Braithwaite, V. (eds), *Shame Management Through Reintegration*. Cambridge: University of Cambridge Press.

Caddick, B. (1994) 'The "New Careers" Experiment in Rehabilitating Offenders: Last Messages from a Fading Star', *British Journal of Social Work*, 24, 449–60.

Camp, C. and Camp, G. (1997) *The Corrections Yearbook*. South Salem, NY: Criminal Justice Institute.

Cullen, F.T. (1994) 'Social Support as an Organizing Concept in Criminology: Presidential Address to the Academy of Criminal Justice Sciences', *Justice Quarterly*, 11, 527–59.

Cullen, F.T. (2002) 'Rehabilitation and Treatment Programs', in Wilson, J.Q. and Petersilia, J. (eds), *Crime: Public Policies for Crime Control*. Oakland, CA: Institute for Contemporary Studies.

Dickey, W.J. and Smith, M.E. (1998) Dangerous Opportunity: Five Futures for Community Corrections: The Report from the Focus Group. Washington, DC: US Department of Justice, Office of Justice Programs.

Duff, R.A. (2001) *Punishment, Communication and Community*. Oxford: Oxford University Press.

Fogel, D. (1978) 'Foreword', in McCleary, R. *Dangerous Men: The Sociology of Parole*. Beverly Hills, CA: Sage, 7–15.

Fogel, D. (1984) 'The Emergence of Probation as a Profession in the Service of Public Safety: The Next Ten Years', in McAnany, P.D., Thompson, D. and Fogel, D. (eds), *Probation and Justice: Reconsideration of Mission*. Cambridge, MA: Oelgeschlager, Gunn, and Hain, 65–99.

Garland, D. (1990) *Punishment and Modern Society: A Study in Social Theory*. Chicago: University of Chicago Press.

Garland, D. (1997) 'Probation and the Reconfiguration of Crime Control', in Burnett, R. (ed.), *The Probation Service: Responding to Change*. Oxford: University of Oxford, Centre for Criminological Research, 3–10.

Gebelein, R.S. (2000) *The Rebirth of Rehabilitation: Promise and Perils of Drug Courts*. Washington, DC: National Institute of Justice, Papers from the Executive Sessions on Sentencing and Corrections.

Gendreau, P., Cullen, F.T. and Bonta, J. (1994) 'Intensive Rehabilitation Supervision: The Next Generation in Community Corrections?', *Federal Probation*, 58, 173–84.

Gordon, D. (1991) *The Justice Juggernaut: Fighting Street Crime, Controlling Citizens*. New Brunswick, NJ: Rutgers University Press.

Grant, J.D. (1968) 'The Offender as a Correctional Manpower Resource', in Riessman, F. and Popper, H.L. (eds), *Up From Poverty: New Career Ladders for Nonprofessionals*. New York: Harper and Row, 226–34.

Grove, P.G., Godfrey, D.A. and McLeod, J.F. (1999) *Long Term Prison Population Projection: Operational Research Unit Model 1999*. London: Home Office RDSD.

Hagell, A., Newburn, T. and Rowlingson, K. (1995) *Financial Difficulties on Release from Prison*. London: Policy Studies Institute.

Haines, K. (1990) *After-care Services for Released Prisoners: A Review of the Literature*. London: Home Office.

Halliday, J. (2001) *Making Punishments Work: Report of a Review of the Sentencing Framework for England and Wales*. London: Home Office.

Holt, N. and Miller, D. (1972) *Explorations in Inmate-family Relationships*. Sacramento, CA: California Department of Corrections.

Home Office (2001a) *Prison Statistics England and Wales, 2000*. London: Home Office.

Home Office (2001b) *Community Punishment Pathfinders – Interim Evaluation Report: Executive Summary*. London: Home Office.

Hough, M. and Roberts, J.V. (1999) 'Sentencing Trends in Britain: Public Knowledge and Public Opinion', *Punishment and Society*, 1, 11–26.

Hughes, T.A., Wilson, D.J. and Beck, A.J. (2001) *Trends in State Parole, 1990–2000*. Washington DC: US Department of Justice, Bureau of Justice Statistics: Special Report.

Irwin, J. (1974) 'The Trouble With Rehabilitation', *Criminal Justice and Behaviour*, 1(2), 139–49.

Johnson, C. and Rex, S. (forthcoming) 'Community Service: Rediscovering Reintegration', in Ward, D. and Lacey, M. (eds), *Probation: Working for Justice*, 2nd edn. London: Whiting & Birch.

Johnson, R. (2002) *Hard Time*, 3rd edn. Belmont, CA: Wadsworth.

Kelman, H.C. (1958) 'Compliance, Identification and Internalization: Three Processes of Opinion Change', *Journal of Conflict Resolution*, 2, 51–60.

Lanier, C.S. (forthcoming) 'Who's Doing the Time Here, Me or My Children?: Addressing the Issues Implicated by Mounting Numbers of Fathers in Prison', in Ross, J.I. and Richards, S.C. (eds), *Convict Criminology*. Belmont, CA: Wadsworth.

Levrant, S., Cullen, F.T., Fulton, B. and Wozniak, J.F. (1999) 'Reconsidering Restorative Justice: The Corruption of Benevolence Revisited?', *Crime and Delinquency*, 45, 3–27.

Lofland, J. (1969) *Deviance and Identity*. Englewood Cliffs, NJ: Prentice-Hall.

McAllister, D., Bottomley, K. and Liebling, A. (1992) *From Custody to Community: Throughcare for Young*. Aldershot: Ashgate.

McGuire, J. (1995) *What Works: Reducing Re-offending*. London: John Wiley & Sons.

McIvor, G. (1992) *Sentenced to Serve: The Operation and Impact of Community Service by Offenders*. Aldershot: Avebury.

MacKenzie, D.L. and Brame, R. (2001) 'Community Supervision, Prosocial Activities, and Recidivism', *Justice Quarterly*, 18(2), 429–48.

MacKenzie, D.L. and De Li, S. (2001) 'The Impact of Formal and Informal Social Controls on the Criminal Activities of Probationers'. Retrieved on 15 October 2001, from http://www.bsos.umd.edu/ccjs/corrections/Doc/BondandCrime.pdf.

Makkai, T. and Braithwaite, J. (1993) 'Praise, Pride and Corporate Compliance', *International Journal of the Sociology of Law*, 21, 73–91.

Maruna, S. (2001) *Making Good: How Ex-convicts Reform and Rebuild their Lives.* Washington, DC: American Psychological Association.

Meisenhelder, T. (1977) 'An Exploratory Study of Exiting from Criminal Careers', *Criminology*, 15, 319–34.

Metcalf, H., Anderson, T. and Rolfe, H. (2001) *Barriers to Employment for Offenders and Ex-offenders.* London: Department for Work and Pensions Research.

Mobley, A. and Terry, C. (forthcoming) 'Dignity, Resistance and Re-entry: A Convict Perspective', in Maruna, S. and Immarigeon, R. (eds), *After Crime and Punishment: Ex-Convict Re-entry and Desistance from Crime.* Albany, NY: SUNY Press.

Morgan, R. and Owers, A. (2001) *Through the Prison Gate: A Joint Thematic Review by HM Inspectorates of Prisons and Probation.* London: HM Inspectorate of Prisons.

Morris, N. (2001) *Maconochie's Gentlemen: The Story of Norfolk Island and the Roots of Prison Reform.* New York: Oxford University Press.

Office of Justice Programs (1999) *Re-entry Courts: Managing the Transition from Prison to Community. A Call for Concept Papers.* Washington DC US Department of Justice, Office of Justice Programs.

Paylor, I. (1995) *Housing Needs of Ex-offenders.* Aldershot: Avebury.

Pearl, A. and Riessman, F. (1965) *New Careers for the Poor: The Nonprofessional in Human Service.* New York: Free Press.

Petersilia, J. and Deschenes, E.P. (1994) 'What Punishes? Inmates Rank the Severity of Prison vs. Intermediate Sanctions', *Federal Probation*, 58, 3–8.

Petersilia, J. and Turner, S. (1993) 'Intensive Probation and Parole', in Tonry, M. (ed.), *Crime and Justice: An Annual Review of Research*, Vol 19. Chicago: University of Chicago Press, 281–335.

Prison Reform Trust (1999) *Prison Incentives Scheme.* London: Prison Reform Trust.

Pryor, S. (2001) *The Responsible Prisoner: An Exploration of the Extent to which Imprisonment Removes Responsibility Unnecessarily and an Invitation to Change.* London: Home Office.

Reno, J. (2000) 'Remarks of the Honorable Janet Reno, Attorney General of the United States on Reentry Court Initiative', John Jay College of Criminal Justice, New York, 10 February 2000. Retrieved on 23 June 2000, from http://www.usdoj.gov/ag/speeches/2000/doc2.htm.

Rhine, E.E. (1997) 'Probation and Parole Supervision: In Need of a New Narrative', *Corrections Management Quarterly*, 1(2), 71–5.

Rutherford, A. (1993) 'Time for Another Big Idea', in Whitfield, D. and Scott, D. (eds), *Paying Back: Twenty Years of Community Service.* Winchester: Waterside, 150–4.

Saleebey, D. (ed.) (1997) *The Strengths Perspective in Social Work Practice*, 2nd edn. New York: Longman.

Sampson, R.J. and Laub, J. (1993) *Crime in the Making: Pathways and Turning Points through Life*. Cambridge, MA: Harvard University Press.

Scharf, P. (1983) 'Empty Bars: Violence and the Crisis of Meaning in the Prison', *Prison Journal*, 63, 114–24.

Sherman, L.W. (1993) 'Defiance, Deterrence, and Irrelevance: A Theory of the Criminal Sanction', *Journal of Research in Crime and Delinquency*, 30, 445–73.

Simon, J. (1993) *Poor Discipline: Parole and the Social Control of the Underclass, 1890–1990*. Chicago: University of Chicago Press.

Smith, M.E. (1984) 'Will the Real Alternatives Please Stand Up?', *New York University Review of Law and Social Change*, 12(1), 171–97.

Smith, M.E. (2000) 'What Future for "Public Safety" and "Restorative Justice" in a System of Community Penalties', in Bottoms, A., Gelsthorpe, L. and Rex, S. (eds), *Community Penalties: Change and Challenges*. Cullompton: Willan.

Soothill, K. (1974) *The Prisoner's Release: A Study of the Employment of Ex-Prisoners*. London: Allen & Unwin.

Stow, B. (2002) *Outcomes and Process in Incentives and Earned Privileges: Does Justice Matter?* MST thesis in Applied Criminology and Management, Institute of Criminology, University of Cambridge.

Ta, C. (2000) 'Prison Partnership: It's About People', *Corrections Today*, October, 114–23.

Taylor, J.B. (1997) 'Niches and Practice: Extending the Ecological Perspective', in Saleebey, D. (ed.), *The Strengths Perspective in Social Work Practice*, 2nd edn. New York: Longman, 217–27.

Teague, M. (2001) 'Launching the National Probation Service', *Probation Journal*, 48, 218–19.

Toch, H. (1975) *Men in Crisis: Human Breakdowns in Prisons*. Chicago: Aldine.

Toch, H. (1994) 'Democratising Prisons', *Prison Journal*, 73, 62–72.

Toch, H. (2000) 'Altruistic Activity as Correctional Treatment', *International Journal of Offender Therapy and Comparative Criminology*, 44(3), 270–8.

Tocqueville, A. (1956) *Democracy in America* [1835]. New York: Knopf.

Travis, J. (1999) 'Prisons, Work and Re-Entry', *Corrections Today*, 61(6), 102–33.

Travis, J. (2000) *But They All Come Back: Rethinking Prisoner Re-entry*. Washington, DC: US Department of Justice, National Institute of Justice, Research in Brief – Sentencing and Corrections: Issues for the 21st Century.

US Department of Justice, Bureau of Justice Statistics. (2000) *Incarcerated Parents and their Children* (NCJ 182335). Washington, DC: US Government Printing Office.

Uggen, C. and Janikula, J. (1999) 'Volunteerism and Arrest in the Transition to Adulthood', *Social Forces*, 78, 331–62.

Wexler, D.B. (2001) 'Robes and Rehabilitation: How Judges Can Help Offenders "Make Good"', *Court Review*, 38(1), 18–23.

White, W.L. (2000) *Toward a New Recovery Movement: Historical Reflections on Recovery, Treatment and Advocacy*. Retrieved 2 December 2001, from http://www.recoveryadvocacy.org.

Whitfield, D. and Scott, D. (eds) (1993) *Paying Back: Twenty Years of Community Service*. Winchester: Waterside.

Chapter 9

The Halliday Report and persistent offenders

Peter Jones

The Halliday Report (Home Office 2001) offers ambitious proposals for refashioning sentencing law and practice in England and Wales. Some of these address the special challenge presented by persistent offenders. Others propose an expansion of judicial involvement and oversight of the administration of sentence. These proposals are the subject of this chapter based on my experience as a Stipendiary Magistrate (now District Judge (Magistrates Court)) for South Yorkshire until June 2001. The views expressed are my own and should not to be taken to be those of the District Bench as a whole or any other group. They are based on working in my local courts, which I have no reason to believe are unrepresentative of the country as a whole. My aim is to produce a paper for discussion which is a practical rather than an academic document. I have therefore kept footnotes and references to a minimum. Those who are very familiar with the courts will, I hope, forgive my use of detailed case histories. I have, of course, changed the names of actual defendants.

Unless the context indicates otherwise, the masculine form of pronouns is used to cover both masculine and feminine throughout.

Introduction

My intention is to look, in particular, at two of the recommendations made in *Making Punishments Work: Report of a Review of the Sentencing Framework for England and Wales* (hereafter the 'Halliday Report') (Home Office 2001).

- The Halliday Report recommends that the existing 'just deserts' philosophy be modified by incorporating a new presumption that severity of sentence should increase when an offender has sufficiently recent and relevant previous convictions. I wish to examine the effect of this recommendation from the point of view of the treatment of the typical low-level persistent offender who appears on a regular basis for sentence in the magistrates' court.

- The Halliday Report suggests that courts should develop a new 'sentence review' capacity which would deal with breaches of community sentences, hear appeals against recall to prison, authorise pre-release plans for offenders on release from custody and review progress during community sentences and the community part of custodial sentences.

I also make reference to the recommendations for a new generic community punishment order and interim review order and consider the proposals for the production of a code of sentencing guidelines for all the main criminal offences.

Previous convictions

Chapter 2 of the Halliday Report considers sentencing principles and, while arguing that the principle of proportionate punishment ('just deserts') needs to be sustained (2.6), recommends the adoption of a clear presumption that sentence severity should increase as a consequence of sufficiently recent and relevant previous convictions. One of the justifications for this approach is that a continuing course of criminal conduct, in the face of repeated attempts by the state to try and correct it, calls for increasing denunciation and retribution, notwithstanding that earlier crimes have already been punished (2.7). Thus, it is argued, not only should the severity of the sentence be governed by the seriousness of the offence and its degree of harmfulness, but it should also be increased to reflect previous convictions, taking account of how recent and relevant they are (2.8). Chapter 8 provides for these principles to be enshrined in statute with the creation of a codified guide for all the main criminal offences, providing 'entry points' of sentence severity and for 'how escalating sentence severity for increasing numbers and types of previous conviction should operate and subject to what limits' (8.9).

Before considering how the proposal might operate in practice, we need to bear in mind the present position. It was only just over ten years ago that the Criminal Justice Act 1991 (CJA 1991) at s.29(1) provided that an offence *shall not* be regarded as more serious by reason of any previous convictions of the offender, although s.1(2)(a) did allow the court to take account of the offence and one other associated with it in deciding whether the offence was so serious that only a custodial sentence could be justified. Not unnaturally such an artificial situation, which, in effect, compelled the court to assume that no defendant was a recidivist or a habitual criminal, did not survive for very long. Section 29(1), CJA 1991, as amended by the Criminal Justice Act 1993 (now reproduced at s.151(1), Powers of the Criminal Courts (Sentencing) Act 2000 (PCC(S)A)) provided that, in considering the seriousness of any offence, the court *may* take into account any previous convictions of the offender. In addition, the effect of s.2(2), CJA 1991 (now s.80(2), PCC(S)A) is to provide that the term of any custodial sentence for a non-violent, non-sexual offence shall be for such term as is commensurate with the seriousness of the offence and any offence associated with it.

In practice, all courts obtain information about the defendant's criminal record (or lack of one) before sentence and, in appropriate cases, take it into account. However, for many years it has been a basic tenet of sentencing practice that the court does not sentence on the defendant's record but rather for the offence itself. This principle was recognised by the House of Lords in *R. v. Ottowell* (1968) [1] Thus, the offence may be regarded more seriously because the defendant has offended before and has not changed his offending ways but this should not result in him receiving a sentence which bears no relationship to the seriousness of the offence he has committed. Otherwise, it could be said that he was being sentenced for his record of previous offending, for which, of course, he has already been punished.

However, with the aim of incapacitation and/or deterrence, that principle may be departed from, for instance where the court detects an habitual offender at work. In *R. v. Gwillim-Jones* (2002),[2] a 47-year-old man with 100 previous convictions, who had recently been placed on probation, had a three-year sentence of imprisonment upheld on appeal following his conviction for the attempted theft of a handbag in a pub. The sentence was said to be within the established tariff.

If the Halliday proposals are intended to replicate this sort of approach across a wide range of offences, there may well be a substantial change in sentencing practice, driven by codified guidelines, with considerable implications for judicial discretion and, presumably, the numbers and make-up of the prison population. Before work begins on any such guidelines, it will be important to understand how previous convictions are presently taken into account by the courts and whether any consistent and principled approach underpins the effect which the offender's record has on sentence.

The following is an example of the sort of persistent offender that in recent years has become all too common in the lower criminal courts.

John is 22. From age 10 he was received into the public care system on a number of occasions. He missed a great deal of schooling and is just about numerate and literate. He became involved with drugs from age 15 and has had a chronic heroin habit for five years. To support this he has stolen from his parents and other family members and now has no family support. He has no settled accommodation and no job. He has no supportive relationship or friendship group other than those involved in the supply and use of drugs. He is a regular dishonest offender, these days usually shoplifting large quantities of toiletries and the like, which can be sold on within a matter of hours to raise money for his next drug purchase. He is before the court for sentence for six shoplifting matters. They are spread over a period of three weeks. He has been arrested three times and twice re-bailed. On the third occasion he pleaded guilty to all matters and was remanded in custody for three weeks for pre-sentence reports. When he appears for sentence he is said to be free of drugs. Whether or not that is true, he is certainly still psychologically dependent and, if he does not receive further custody, will return to the only home he knows which is with those who are heavily involved in the drug culture. At present he says he wants to stay free of drugs. He is a vulnerable young person with extremely limited personal and intellectual resources. The court would no doubt wish (as he has already served the equivalent of a six week custodial sentence) to assist him to address his habit and to prevent him reoffending by considering a Drug Treatment and Testing Order (DTTO) backed up, perhaps, by a condition of residence in a probation hostel so as to give him structure, routine and support and remove him as far as possible from unhelpful influences.

However, his criminal record shows recent and relevant previous convictions. He has 55 previous convictions, mostly for dishonesty. They cover the last six years. This year alone he has been before the court on three separate occasions for sentence (always for dishonesty) and for a total of 13 offences has received (in order) a conditional discharge, custody (to reflect time spent on remand) and a Community Rehabilitation Order (CRO) to which he is still subject and with which he is struggling to comply.

At present, John's criminal record discloses a clear cycle of interventions starting with a discharge or fine, moving onto probation or an appropriate community sentence and then, when all non-custodial alternatives have been tried and his offending is obviously out of control, a period in custody commensurate with the seriousness of the offences. When, on release, John, in due course, returns to similar offending, the court is reluctant to simply return him to custody (often the argument is that he has not returned to drug use but is offending to pay off drug debts incurred prior to his last prison sentence) and so the sentencing cycle begins again.

In the future, how is John, who now falls to be sentenced for what will include his 60th conviction for dishonesty, to be dealt with? In a codified sentencing framework which provides for escalating entry points based on recent and relevant previous convictions, he may well face as a starting point a sentence well above the new short-term prison sentence proposed in the Halliday Report, Chapter 3 and also above the current maximum sentencing powers of the magistrates' court. I acknowledge that there is an argument that, had such a sentencing regime already been in effect, John would never have built up such a record since he would have spent most of the last few years in custody and the public would have been spared his offending. Nevertheless, in considering the implications of the recommendation, it must be remembered that, while John is certainly culpable because he quite deliberately shoplifts, his offending typically consists of stealing bottles of shampoo or cans of deodorant, while the Halliday Report itself reminds the Court to bear in mind the seriousness and harmfulness of the offence when making recommendations for intermediate sanctions (Chapter 5) and more effective non-custodial disposals (Chapter 6).

At 6.6 the Halliday Report recommends a new generic community punishment order whose punitive weight would be proportionate to the current offence and *any additional severity for previous convictions*. Such an order would be flexible and draw on a menu of available requirements and interventions. It is of course to be hoped that any guidelines will permit the court to consider seriously the appropriateness of a non-custodial disposal, even in a case such as John's, if such a 'package' seems to be the most appropriate approach at that time to reducing the risk of reoffending.

However there would appear to be the potential for conflict between the proposals for a widening range of non-custodial alternatives to custody and the possible rigidity of a sentencing framework which gives considerable weight to previous convictions. The guidelines can of course be widely drawn but that might rather undermine the aim of bringing a more principled approach and greater transparency to the way in which previous convictions impact on sentence. In addition, it is difficult to see how someone like John would escape a severe sentence without the retention of a considerable element of judicial discretion, which itself has suffered some erosion in recent years, e.g. by the introduction of prescribed minimum sentences in the PCC(S)A. It will be necessary too for the guidelines to possess an overall coherence and establish a principled interrelationship between offences. The greater the weight accorded to previous convictions the greater the risk of the level of sentence for the persistent petty non-violent, non-sexual offender approaching or overlapping the sentencing level for the one-off offence of serious personal violence or sexually abusive behaviour.

As far as the proposals for non-custodial powers and the community elements of the intermediate sanctions (Chapters 5 and 6) are concerned, much will depend on the package of measures available and whether it includes, in addition to supervision, courses and other interventions, the provision of appropriate accommodation in the community. In relation to young offenders (not specifically dealt with in the Halliday Report) I would argue that the criminal justice system needs to concentrate its attention on that group of persistent and prolific offenders who commit the majority of juvenile crime. The profile of most of these young people is that they are estranged from their family, homeless or living in unsuitable surroundings, abusing illegal drugs and/or alcohol, have a background of abuse and neglect, have experience of the public care system and are itinerant, vulnerable and at risk with a chaotic lifestyle. What is needed for them is a network of centrally funded, locally administered, supported lodgings/remand foster-carers/specialist secure and semi-secure accommodation available throughout the country which has immediate access to health, psychiatric, psychological, education and drug and alcohol treatment services together with work opportunities for those who are older. These resources should be available to prevent reoffending during the court process as a remand option for the court and to prevent a return to offending after sentence by the court as a supportive base from which either a community order can be properly worked and completed or, on release from custody, from which the supervision part of that order can be operated.

I would suggest that all that is equally true of someone like John who is still only 22 and without family or other support or adequate accommodation within the community. Halliday acknowledges this need in Chapter 5. However, its importance cannot be underestimated, not only to enable interventions commenced with offenders in prison to be maintained in a 'seamless' way on their return to the community (which will require proper cooperation and liaison between the probation and prison services), but also as a vital part of any non-custodial package, since so many of such orders fail. This is not necessarily because of poor motivation on the part of offenders but because their lack of personal resources and suitable accommodation and support in the community prevents them from responding positively to the demands of many non-custodial disposals. If the requirements of community orders are to be made even more rigorous and intrusive with the expectation of speedy enforcement and custodial sentences already 'pencilled in' (Halliday 5.18) in default of full compliance, it is important that any package of interventions with the offender is tailored appropriately. A balance needs to be maintained between making proper demands of him to demonstrate effort and commitment, while at the same time recognising that it is in the interests of the defendant and the community in general that the order is given every chance of being successfully completed.

Here, too, there is a tension between the desire to demonstrate to the public that the order is sufficiently punitive and a legitimate alternative to custody while allowing the offender a reasonable chance to succeed. Some defendants, however, will, as now, prefer a period in custody rather than undergo the rigours and demands of a community sentence. Whether or not formal consent to a non-custodial package is to be required from the defendant, there seems little point in imposing a sentence with which the defendant makes it clear he will not comply. At present, there are a number of offenders who choose to spend a period of time in custody rather than commence the long haul of a DTTO which in their case will be the only alternative to custody. For these defendants a DTTO is not recommended as a disposal to the court and cannot be made. Equally it is not unknown for youths to risk a sentence of the youth court by entering a not guilty plea thus avoiding a Referral Order which is perceived as more rigorous and lengthy than any likely court sentence for the offence. That attitude, of course, may change if the alternative (taking into account previous convictions) is a lengthy period of custody.

On the other hand, a genuine desire to reform and to comply with a non-custodial disposal may not coincide with the commission of an offence for which, even now, a non-custodial sentence can be made available. What if, for instance, in John's case he moves from shoplifting to burglary, albeit a low-level daytime sneak-in to a dwelling-house where there is no confrontation with the householder and a purse or bag is taken. After, say, four months on remand awaiting disposal in the Crown Court, all spent on a drug-free wing and having already taken counselling and relevant courses, John may well be ready with support in the community to finally address his addiction. At present the court may be persuaded to take the chance but in future will it effectively be precluded from imposing a community sentence because this is a serious offence and John has 'recent and relevant convictions' for dishonesty, or perhaps in another case, the offender has two previous burglary convictions so that the sentence entry point is now a substantial custodial sentence?

This latter situation will soon be a live issue for the courts as the provisions of s.111 of the PCC(S)A start to bite. The court is not obliged to impose the statutory minimum sentence of three years on third-time domestic burglars if there are particular circumstances which relate to any of the offences which would make it unjust to do so in all the circumstances. Will a finding that it is 'unjust' allow a non-custodial sentence to be passed and how will the prescribed custodial sentence regime in the PCC(S)A fit within the code of guidelines proposed by Halliday? Paragraph 8.6 envisages that the guidelines would have such force and be so informed by the offender's previous record that once they are available 'it would be sensible to look again at the need for mandatory minimum sentences based on previous convictions'. The proposals for the production of codified sentencing guidelines raise the possibility of a much more extensive set of, in effect, mandatory minimum sentences for all the main offences, geared to the number of recent and relevant previous convictions, while, on the other hand, imaginative proposals are made in Chapters 5 and 6 for new intermediate sanctions and non-custodial powers. Where and how these latter proposals fit into the sentencing code will be of crucial importance. Will the presumption of increasing sentence severity based on recent and relevant convictions proposed in Chapter 2 lead to guidelines which effectively preclude the court from imposing community sentences even where, in the exercise of its discretion, it feels that such a disposal holds out the best hope of preventing reoffending despite recent and relevant criminal convictions? In cases such as John's of persistent non-violent, non-sexual offending, will lengthy custodial sentences be inevitable despite the availability of a broad regime of non-custodial options supported by appropriate non-secure accommodation and ongoing support in the community?

Judicial involvement in sentence design and management

Under further Halliday proposals, whether or not John receives a custodial or non-custodial sentence, he will not be free of continuing judicial oversight. At 7.26 it is recommended that courts develop a sentence review capacity involving dealing with breaches of community sentences, together with appeals against prison recall, authorising pre-release plans for longer-term prisoners and reviewing progress during community sentences or the community part of custodial sentences, including the power to vary the intensity of such a sentence.

Courts presently have a continuing involvement with non-custodial orders in dealing with breach proceedings and from time to time sentencers call for regular reports from the probation service on the progress of certain non-custodial sentences, although not, as far as I am aware, in any systematic way. In addition, the Crown Court can order that any breach proceedings in relation to a community sentence which it imposes should be directed back to the Crown Court. The treatment and testing provisions of DTTOs can be amended after advice from the providers and with the consent of the defendant. Action Plan Orders in the youth court may provide for a hearing within 21 days of sentence to allow for the order to be 'tweaked' by the court so as to allow experience gained during its early days to inform the final shape of the order.

The Halliday proposals would involve much greater judicial involvement in the content of the sentence imposed by the court and an extensive and enhanced role thereafter throughout the life of the sentence, whether custodial or non-custodial or a combination of both. Much of this will be wholly new and represents a radical departure from the traditional role of the judge as an independent figure who hands down a sentence to be implemented by others after considering the facts of the offence as outlined by the prosecution or as ascertained at trial, the submissions of the defence and any reports, usually in writing, prepared by relevant professionals. These proposals call for a more 'hands-on', interventionist and proactive approach which is one for which some parts of the judiciary may be neither prepared nor equipped.

My experience of such a role in relation to persistent offenders to date has mainly been with DTTOs. These Orders are made for between six months and three years and, typically, direct the defendant to attend five days per week to provide specimens for analysis and to participate in a treatment programme which aims at reducing/ eliminating the use of drugs and putting an end to the consequent offending behaviour. Provision is made for review hearings at 28-day intervals after sentence with the defendant directed to attend, although the court has power in the case of good progress to widen the intervals between reviews and to conduct them on paper. Also, with the agreement of the defendant, the original treatment and testing requirements may be amended. In my experience reviews are conducted by the court which imposed the sentence. The probation officer responsible for the order provides the court with a report on progress which is seen by the defendant. The probation officer attends the hearing, often with the nurse attached to the testing centre and any other relevant worker involved with the case. The defendant appears and is rarely represented. The hearing is in open court but often at a time convenient to all concerned when the court is not busy. The essential ingredients of any review hearing are, in my view, judicial continuity, dialogue, frankness, a willingness to compromise and full participation by the defendant.

Jeff is 32. His heroin habit dates back twelve years. His offending covers a period which mirrors almost exactly his addiction. Courts have over the years dealt with him by every means at their disposal. Jeff lives with his brother who is also an addict. Jeff shoplifts to fund his addiction. Almost as soon as DTTOs were available Jeff was considered suitable. Against a backdrop of c.70 previous convictions he fell to be sentenced for four counts of shoplifting. Jeff is intelligent, mature and sick of the addiction. He welcomes the order. At the first review he is said to be motivated but struggling. He receives a methadone prescription (a heroin substitute) but the test results show he is still using illegal drugs. He has not been charged in relation to his use of drugs but, of course, the court must be prepared to live with the fact that he is admitting continuing breaches of the Misuse of Drugs legislation. He keeps each and every appointment (about 22/23 in any monthly period) but, crucially, he needs help to move to his own accommodation, away, not only from his brother who is not minded to give up drugs, but also from the only supportive environment he has known for years, i.e. the drug culture. Neither the court nor the officer responsible for the order can provide direct help with this. The case goes out for review in another 28 days. At the next hearing Jeff has stopped taking cocaine (he is a polydrug user), has kept all appointments but has shoplifted on two separate occasions. This, he says, was to pay off old drug debts. On balance he is cooperating, is still motivated and, after a mixture of 'carrot and stick' approach, the court adjourns to the next review in 28 days time and sentencing on the new matters is put off to that date. Next time the report is rather pessimistic. Jeff has still not been rehoused, has missed some appointments and is losing heart, but he has not offended. The report recommends perseverance, particularly as in the context of a twelve-year addiction and his long criminal record he is making progress (albeit slowly). The court deals with the new offences by way of discharges and adjourns for another 28 days. Next time Jeff looks much better, is more positive, has a date to move into his own accommodation in a new area and the report is much more optimistic – *but* he has shoplifted twice!

This is the sort of case that courts are learning how to deal with in the context of DTTOs. The Halliday proposals will mean many more such hearings requiring judicial discretion, direct interaction with the offender and representatives of those agencies working with him, both in the community and where relevant in prison, and a certain amount of nerve! Halliday suggests that the review process would be mainly paper-based. I acknowledge that there will be cases and times where this is appropriate and that the use of TV links etc. must be developed. However, it seems to me important, particularly in the early days of a demanding community order, that the court establishes a dialogue with the offender and the provider so that concerns can be directly addressed and good progress acknowledged face to face. My view is that there is a proper role for the judiciary in keeping certain sentences under review and in being willing to embrace the sort of judicial involvement envisaged in Chapter 7. This task is easier for the professional judiciary to perform than the lay magistracy. On a practical level, it is difficult to reconvene the same bench of three magistrates at the best of times, let alone for regular review hearings, and it is likely that lay magistrates who are often unable to sit regularly will have less experience than their professional colleagues in the imposition and management of a range of orders. It may also be more difficult for a bench of three to agree their approach on each occasion when the decision is by no means clear-cut and what the defendant requires above all is a clear and consistent judicial message.

The DTTO course providers also, I believe, welcome regular and consistent judicial input. It is something around which they can structure their work under the order and assists them by providing an overview from a source independent of their day-to-day work and involvement with the defendant. The defendant also needs to see that the sentencer has a commitment to the order being successfully completed. If a sentencer imposes a community sentence such as a DTTO it is because that order is seen as providing the best chance at that time of preventing further offending and bringing about the long-term rehabilitation of the defendant. The sentencer has therefore judged it to be in the public interest, as well as the defendant's, that the order is imposed and that it succeeds. The difficult decision, of course, is when to pull the plug. Some defendants make the decision easy for the court by not attending for treatment or by absconding or (as in one case I dealt with) by appearing at the review hearing complete with the three bags of belongings he deemed necessary for the lengthy prison stay he asked me to impose! In other cases the decision is less straightforward.

The present power to defer sentence often throws up the sort of difficulties which will be encountered under the new proposals. The court can defer passing sentence for any offence with the defendant's consent for up to six months and can set requirements or objectives to be complied with in the meantime. These targets are not part of the sentence but at the end of the period of deferment the court must judge how far the defendant has or has not measured up to expectations in deciding how he should be sentenced for the offence. The difficulty arises when there has been partial compliance with the requirements (the majority of cases) and the court must decide whether the failures are so fundamental as to require the abandonment of further consideration of a community sentence or whether the defendant has made a sufficiently substantial effort to comply with the sentencer's conditions so as to avoid a custodial sentence.

> Jamie, who is 19, has been the subject of a six-month deferred sentence by the magistrates' court. He had pleaded guilty to an unpleasant assault on another lad outside a night-club. The offence merited custody. However, since the date of the offence, he had been placed on a CRO by the Crown Court and had got his first job. He had moved back to live with his mum who provided much-needed stability. The conditions of the deferment were to stay out of trouble, to stay in employment, to comply with the CRO, to pay compensation to the victim at £10 per week and to write letter of apology to the victim who was prepared to receive it. Six months later Jamie has written the letter but three months ago he was laid off from his job through no fault of his own. However, even before then he was not paying the compensation regularly and has only paid £50 in all. His mum has thrown him

out, he has missed five appointments under the CRO but no breach proceedings have been issued because he is appearing on the deferment. He has, however, kept out of trouble and has another job (confirmed in writing) to start on Monday. He has had two previous convictions for violence in the last two years.

I acknowledge the sense in a continuing role for the court in monitoring the progress or otherwise of a sentence. The picture which the court gets of the offender on the day of sentence is, of course, a snapshot in time when good intentions are to the fore, promises are made, assurances are given and there is always a job to start on Monday! However, one of the weaknesses of a deferred sentence has been that because sentence is 'put off', unless, as in Jamie's case, he is already subject to an order imposed for a separate offence, the defendant is left to his own devices without formal input or support. The suggested 'interim review order' recommended at Halliday 6.21 envisages a more active role for the probation service and proper safeguards. However, the decision which the court has to make at the end of the interim review period may very well be no easier or clear-cut than under the present regime.

These, then, are the sort of issues which the court faces when exercising its present, limited powers of review. Though not easy to resolve, the court addresses them as boot it can. Such sentencing problems are likely to be repeated over a much wider area given the proposals at Halliday 7.26. and, in the case of disputed allegations of breach of community sentences or recalls to custody, will require the court to undertake a fact-finding exercise and, presumably, conduct hearings at which evidence is adduced.

An important element in any system of review and sentence management is judicial continuity. That may be much less easy to achieve in the Crown Court than the magistrates' court where most district judges (magistrates' court) have a base court at which they can conduct regular sentencing reviews.

There are many advantages in having the sentencer who imposed the sentence conduct the review. He will know how close or otherwise the defendant came to custody, how much leeway, given the defendant's personal circumstances, can properly be allowed during the life of the order, and he will have a sense of ownership of the sentence. By way of example, professional benches in the youth court are sometimes able, by a series of constructive adjournments, to establish a dialogue with the youth, his carers, the Youth Offending Team and other agencies involved with the child. So long as proper boundaries are maintained, it is possible to make use of the youth court (in a way which is at present not really possible in the magistrates' court) as a forum in which all appropriate agencies are brought together. Disposals can be made in relation to offending behaviour which recognise that, for many young people, their criminal activities are a manifestation of a wider problem and so deal with them in ways which acknowledge the need for a broader, more long-term and welfare-orientated approach. It is also sometimes possible in this setting for the court to apply some leverage as far as the resources which a particular agency is prepared to make available to a young offender in need (and/or his carers) are concerned. However, in the area of the public law relating to children, the courts have been wary of finding themselves in the position of having to adjudicate on the way in which agencies should allocate their funds and have intervened only rarely and then on a case-by-case basis.

In my view, there is no reason why the approach outlined above should not be replicated in review and sentence management hearings in relation to persistent adult offenders, given the obvious public interest in putting an end to their offending and bringing about a permanent change in behaviour. However, there needs to be a considered debate about the proper role which the court should play in partnership with other agencies, in particular on the question of how far, if at all, the judiciary, whether as individual decision-makers or as a body, should be involved in the allocation and use of those funds for which, at present, others in the criminal justice system are responsible.

The Halliday proposals for judicial involvement in sentence review and management are likely to have substantial resource and cost implications. Consideration should be given to which types of case require it and, where it is justifiable, judges, court rooms and court staff will need to be made available to carry out the functions envisaged. Judges will have to be given time to consider reports and other documentation. Perhaps they will need to be available to speak with or meet the agencies involved with the offender or be provided with staff who can do so. They will need access to appropriate support services.

Judges will also have to be provided with information about available sentencing options. The court cannot give proper consideration to the appropriate sentence unless it has clear information as to the options available by statute, the availability locally of courses, interventions, accommodation, support in the community, etc. and about what disposals have been considered by the report-provider and, if rejected, the reasons why. In this regard, the prosecution's role at the sentencing stage may need to be reconsidered, together with the question of appropriate legal representation (if any) at each stage of the review process. The sentence of the court must be an informed decision based on the provision of full information about the menu of options available and with assistance from all the agencies who will be involved in sentence delivery. There needs to be flexibility too in how reviews are conducted. Where appropriate, court appearances could be kept to a minimum and use made of paper, telephone or electronic reviews as well as a video link for serving prisoners. Courts will need to adopt consistent procedures for sentence management whether on paper or with the defendant present and thought will need to be given to the assistance which the court is to receive, however the process is conducted.

The proposals will also require judicial commitment at all levels and an acceptance that these functions are a proper exercise of the judicial role. Not all judges will agree that it is or welcome such involvement. Those who do will benefit from discussion and the sharing of information and experiences. It is essential that they are provided with training, e.g. in how to conduct the hearings and to exercise their new powers, together with information about the way in which such hearings are conducted in other jurisdictions.

Proper judicial discretion must be allowed. The review courts should be able to exercise wide and flexible powers. They should be able not simply to replace a community order with a custodial sentence of some length, but also to amend the requirements of the community order and choose from among a broad menu of possible interventions, targeted to the particular offender, as part of a continuous process. This would recognise that there may be no single programme or method which will necessarily bring about change and that the approaches which seemed appropriate when the sentence was imposed may need to be modified as the defendant's circumstances alter (as they so often do) during the life of the order. One of the strengths of review is the provision of appropriate, up to date information for the court. In this way it may be possible for the original sentencer's long-term aim of successful community intervention to be maintained. Continuous review would also allow for good progress to be acknowledged by a relaxation of restrictions or requirements and, ultimately, by early discharge of the order or formal acknowledgment of its successful completion, with the important symbolic involvement at that point of the judge who imposed the sentence in the first place.

In conclusion, I would suggest that, in implementing the Halliday proposals, it will be important:

1. To ensure that the establishment of codified sentencing guidelines, which seek to provide for differential sentencing entry points based on the offender's previous convictions, does not circumscribe judicial discretion to such an extent that they become a straitjacket preventing the imposition of non-custodial sentences, where appropriate, in the cases of persistent, low-level, non-violent, non-sexual offenders who are presently dealt with within the sentencing powers of the magistrates' court.

2. In the context of judicial involvement in sentence management, to build on the experiences of the courts to date and adequately equip and prepare members of the judiciary for their new roles by the selection, training and proper resourcing of those who are committed to the extension of their judicial role and to working in partnership with other agencies in carrying out their new functions.

3. To acknowledge the demands which the new proposals will make on all the criminal justice agencies, including the court service, and the need for these initiatives to be adequately supported.

Notes

1 See *DPP* v. *Ottewell* (1968) 52 Cr App R. 679.
2 See *R.* v. *Gwillim-Jones* (2002) 1 Cr App R. 6.

Reference

Home Office (2001) *Making Punishments Work: Report of a Review of the Sentencing Framework for England and Wales*. London: Home Office Communications Directorate.

Chapter 10

Record-enhanced sentencing in England and Wales: reflections on the Halliday Report's proposed treatment of prior convictions

Andrew von Hirsch[1]

Introduction

A new framework for criminal sentencing is under consideration for England and Wales. In a policy paper published in February 2001, the Home Office (2001a) announced it was considering basic changes in sentencing policy which would place substantially more emphasis on the offender's previous criminal record than has been permissible under the desert-oriented approach embodied in the Criminal Justice Act 1991.[2] There followed, in the summer of the same year, a 'Sentencing Framework Review' by a senior civil servant, John Halliday (Home Office 2001b, hereafter referred to as the 'Halliday Report'), which offers various options for change, but ones in which this increased emphasis on the criminal record is an assumed central element.

This chapter examines the desirability of giving augmented weight to the criminal record. Rather than addressing the numerous specifics of the Halliday Report, I shall concentrate on this general question: *how could a substantially larger recidivist premium be rationalised?* The Report offers two main kinds of reasons for this step: that it would better reflect what repeat offenders deserve; and that it would provide wider scope for efforts to reform criminals. Each of these claims, to be given adequate scrutiny, will require us to consider questions of sentencing rationale, and it is such questions that I shall try to address here.[3]

This chapter consists of three main parts, dealing with the three principal claims made by the Halliday Report. The first of these concerns whether offenders can be said to deserve substantially more punishment in virtue of having an extensive record of previous convictions. The second deals with whether the principle of proportionality of sentence may properly be redefined to embrace the criminal record as well as the seriousness of the current offence, as the Report claims it should. The third part considers the Report's assertion that record-enhanced sentencing will provide a better opportunity for the reform of offenders.

Do the Report's prior-record proposals reflect a new penological paradigm?

On two occasions since the Second World War, extensive alterations have been made in the framework of criminal sentencing. The first, beginning mainly in the 1940s, involved the introduction of the 'welfare' model, according to which the offender's rehabilitative needs were to be given significant weight in determining certain sanctions.[4] The second, embodied in the Criminal Justice Act 1991, involved the introduction of a 'just deserts' rationale for deciding severities of punishment.[5] Neither of these changes was revolutionary – traditional sentencing approaches continued to influence law and practice in many important respects. But substantial they undoubtedly were.

These changes in the sentencing framework were influenced by significant shifts in criminological thinking: the first, in criminologists' increasing interest in rehabilitative strategies and individualised treatment; the second, in a greater concern with fairness and proportionate penal responses. This meant that the changes could be supported by extensively articulated reasons. Whatever one ultimately might think of the welfare or desert models, these were at least conceptions colourably backed by an articulated theory and (in the case of rehabilitation) by some empirical research.

A notable feature of the present proposals, however, is that they reflect no such shift in criminological thinking. There is no new penological literature that explains why record-driven sentencing would better reflect what convicted offenders might deserve or why it would succeed in better preventing crime. The Home Office's proposals appear to derive mainly from ideas put forward by Mr Jack Straw in the mid-1990s when he was Shadow Home Secretary.[6] Neither these sources nor the Home Office's recent discussions, including the Halliday Report, provide any real articulation of the rationale for the proposed shift of emphasis toward previous offending. These proposals are vigorously urged, but their conceptual and empirical underpinnings remain scarcely explored.

In examining the Halliday Report's proposals on the role of the criminal record, it should be recalled that England and Wales, only a few decades ago, did have schemes in place that called for extended imprisonment of repeat offenders. These efforts began with a 'preventive detention' statute enacted in the early twentieth century, and continued in various statutory forms through the mid-1960s.[7] They yielded little more than terms of imprisonment for recidivists involved in minor property crimes (often marginalised figures who posed little significant threat to public safety), and eventually were abandoned as unworkable. If record-based sentencing is to be reintroduced, it would need to be explained why it can be expected to work better, or operate more justly, than those failed efforts.

Does repetition make the offence substantially more serious?

One of the Halliday Report's central claims is that putting greater emphasis on an offender's criminal record would better reflect what they deserve: a repeater, this argument runs, acts much more reprehensibly than a first offender and hence deserves substantially more punishment.

The Criminal Justice Act 1991 gave statutory authority to the doctrine of 'progressive loss of mitigation' (see Wasik and von Hirsch 1994). This doctrine holds that a modest degree of mitigation should normally be extended to first offenders (or those having limited criminal records), but after the offender has been before the court on several occasions, the 'ceiling' for the offence is reached and all such mitigation is used up. Further repetitions should be dealt with by imposition of the full measure of penalty, but there ordinarily should be no substantial further increases on account of the criminal record. In this view, the criminal record would have limited weight, and the main determinant of severity would be the gravity of the current crime.

What justifies 'progressive loss of mitigation'? Desert theorists have sketched the following account (see von Hirsch 1998b; von Hirsch 1986, ch. 7). Our everyday moral judgments include the notion of a lapse. A transgression is judged somewhat less strictly when it occurs against a background of prior compliance. The idea is that even an ordinarily well-behaved person can have his or her inhibitions fail in a moment of weakness or wilfulness. Such a temporary breakdown of self-discipline is a kind of human frailty for which some understanding should be shown. In sentencing, the relevant lapse is an infringement of the criminal law rather than a more commonplace moral failure, but the logic of the first offender discount remains the same – that of dealing with a lapse more tolerantly. A further reason for so treating a lapse is respect for the process by which people can attend to, and respond to, censure for their conduct. A first offender, after being confronted with censure or blame, is capable, as a human being presumed capable of ethical judgments, of reflecting on the morality of what he or she has done and making a greater effort to show self-restraint. In thus granting the discount, we show respect for this capacity, and thereby give the offender a 'second chance'. With repetitions, however, the discount should begin to diminish, and eventually disappear. The repeated offence can less and less plausibly be described as a mere lapse, and repetition after confrontation with penal censure suggests a failure to make that extra effort at self-restraint which was the basis for granting the discount.

In the Halliday Report, this theory of progressive loss of mitigation is rejected, and it is proposed, instead, to give substantially increased stints of punishment to repeat offenders (albeit not quite so large increases as a purely cumulative approach would call for).[8] The Report claims that a greater emphasis on the criminal record would better reflect what repeat offenders deserve. In the Report's words, 'A continuing course of criminal conduct in the face of repeated attempts by the State to correct it, calls for increasing denunciation and retribution, notwithstanding that earlier crimes have already been punished' (Halliday Report, 2.7). No reasons are advanced, however, in support of this claim. So what might those reasons be?

Increased culpability?

One possible rationale is that repetition could be said to increase the personal culpability of the offender, and hence his deserts. But why? The report does not provide an explanation, but one might possibly be constructed – based on notions of awareness of wrongdoing.[9] Before an offender has been convicted, the argument runs, he is simply part of the general audience to whom the legal prohibition is addressed. He may not have paid the prohibition much attention, understood its scope or have fully grasped that it really applied to himself. The censure embodied in the punishment for the first offence, however, serves as a dramatic way of confronting the actor with the wrongfulness of the conduct. Thereafter, claims to possible ignorance or inattention become progressively less plausible. Prior convictions thus support the imputation of greater awareness of wrongdoing.

Desert theorists have become sceptical of this argument, because prior convictions would at most provide evidence of such greater awareness, that could be contravened by other evidence (see von Hirsch 1986: 79). But even if the argument were valid in its own terms, it still would give scant support to the degree of emphasis on the prior criminal record that the Report proposes. Personal awareness of wrongdoing, like other culpability factors, bear on the extent to which the harm done in offending may fairly be imputed to the actor's choices. Greater awareness, therefore, can do no more than permit the actor to be held more fully answerable for his criminal act and its consequences. But holding the actor more fully accountable for the harm of the act still should not warrant greatly increased penal censure. Consider the offender convicted of a routine theft, such as stealing a CD player from a shop. If he has an extensive record of convictions for prior thefts, this might, according to the 'greater awareness' thesis, show that he was or should have been entirely cognisant that such behaviour is reprehensible when he committed the present act and hence may be held fully answerable for the theft. However, if the conduct involves no more than modest harmfulness, it remains a relatively minor infraction. Raising that conduct's penalty significantly on account of the offender's supposed added culpability would tend to make its punishment comparable to that for 'normal' cases of significantly more injurious crimes (see Roberts 2002 for how the Halliday proposals would take penalties out of rank-ordering in severity with respect to the degree of harmfulness of the offences involved). Stealing a CD player from a shop, even with supposed malice, is still just stealing a CD player and escalating the applicable sanction on account of this imputed malice would make this seem like a much bigger theft.

Defiance of law?

Another possible reason relates to the notion of defiance: the offender who reoffends after having repeatedly been subjected to penal censure shows a contempt for law that should substantially increase his deserts for his current crime. (This, indeed, seems reflected in the Report's locution about 'a continuing course of criminal conduct *in the face of repeated attempts of the State to correct it*': 2.7, italics supplied). Whether the mere fact of repetition actually shows defiant attitudes is itself debatable. People reoffend for all kinds of reasons (economic and social circumstances, perceived immediate need, weakness of character, hopelessness) that have little to do with defiant attitudes. However, suppose it were the case that repetition was evidence of defiance. Would this warrant giving this imputed attitude a central role in the determination of an offender's deserts? We need to consider why defiance might arguably matter.

One argument might be that defiance affects the offender's culpability: if the offender is deliberately flouting the prohibition, this shows still more strongly than mere knowledge of the prohibition that the act's harmfulness can fully be imputed to the offender's choice. But this takes us little further, as it merely might show that the actor may be held yet more clearly answerable for the harm done or risked by his act. That, however would hardly warrant much further augmentation in the penalty. Theft of a CD player from a shop, with the animus shown by a deliberate flouting of the rule against theft, is still just stealing an article of modest value.

An alternative explanation is that the contemptuous stance supposedly evidenced through repetition is itself an evil against which the penal system should convey substantially increased penal censure. In this view, the repeat offender who steals the appliance actually does two things. First, he deliberately misappropriates the article – for which not much censure is due, as the harm is not great. Second, he shows his lack of respect for the legal system and for the community whose norms that system embodies – which is a flagrant kind of bad citizenship, for which much more blame should be expressed in the punishment. In other words, he should be punished substantially more for daring to reoffend after having been officially censured before through his prior punishment.

The difficulty with such a 'how dare you' theory is that it is doubtful that, in a free society, defiance of authority should itself be deemed to constitute a wrong that substantially should enhance what an offender deserves. Treating defiance as an evil in itself that warrants substantial extra punishment presupposes authoritarian assumptions about the state, the community and the criminal law. Granted, subsystems exist in which such assumptions might properly operate, such as discipline within the military services. If a sergeant gives an order to a soldier in his charge and the latter refuses, that refusal itself is grounds for disciplinary action irrespective of any risks or injurious consequences of the conduct itself. However, this is precisely what makes military life and military discipline so different from normal existence in a free society. The law should not be seen as imposing some kind of quasi-military regime on citizens.[10]

Redefining proportionality to include the criminal record?

The Halliday Report adopts yet another strategy for giving substantially added weight to the criminal record, one that is not so much an argument as an exercise in definition. It attempts to redefine the Principle of Proportionality as embracing the offender's record as well as his current offence of conviction. The severity of the punishment, it is stated, is to be proportionate to the seriousness of the current crime *and* 'recent and relevant' prior convictions (2.40). As a result, prior convictions could receive much more weight than the principle of progressive loss of mitigation would allow. In his critique of the Halliday Report, Julian Roberts (2002) shows how such a formulation could lead to criminal records becoming the primary determinant of the severity of the penalty.

The Report does not give the seriousness of the *current* offence (as opposed to the record) any distinct constraining role, because its formulation of the principle of proportionality contains no explicit limitation based on the current offence alone.[11] In providing illustrations of the principle's implementation (2.20), it does say that the 'effects of previous convictions should always be subject to outer limits resulting from the seriousness of offences'. Yet this fails entirely to specify how permissive these 'outer limits' would be or what their supposed rationale is.

Is this a 'modification' of the principle of proportionality?

The Report treats this redefinition as a 'modification' of the principle of proportionality. The modification, however, consists in jettisoning the essence of the principle. In sentencing, the offender is facing punishment for the offence for which he now stands convicted; he is not being resentenced for crimes for which he has been convicted previously. The principle of proportionality concerns the relationship between the degree of blameworthiness (i.e. seriousness) of the offence for which he is facing punishment – that is, the current offence – and the degree of penal censure to be expressed by the severity of that punishment. Prior offences might bear to some degree on the penal censure due for the current offence, for some of the reasons discussed in the previous section. However, increased penal censure, and thereby increased punishment, cannot directly and straightforwardly be attributed to the character of past offences – for the offender has been convicted and punished for those offences already. To make such direct attribution to past offences possible, the basic structure of the criminal law would have to be changed, so that offenders are no longer punished for particular offences for which they stand convicted.

Would such a change be desirable? There are contexts in everyday life where we address the merit or demerit of a person's career as a whole. A prime example of career-desert are honorary degrees awarded by universities for distinguished scholarship. Such desert-judgments, however, have a different logic from that employed by the criminal law. The award is not *for* any particular work, but relates to the recipient's whole output. The person's most recent efforts may be given little weight, or even may be discounted entirely, if his or her earlier contributions are deemed more significant.

The criminal law is structured otherwise. The actor is punished *for* a particular crime – that for which he now stands convicted. The substantive criminal law defines, classifies, and prohibits *crimes*. (A career-oriented system would classify *persons* according to the frequency and gravity of their offending.) Existing trial and sentencing procedures are suited to determining the defendant's guilt or innocence for the current crime, and for evaluating extenuating and aggravating circumstances surrounding that crime. Without fundamental procedural changes, however, the criminal process does not have the means to inquire with even a modicum of care and discrimination into the degree of demerit of a person's whole criminal career. Evaluating a criminal's 'career-desert' would call for in-depth information about past crimes for which he was convicted. (One would, for example, need adequate information about any aggravating or mitigating circumstances that had been found to exist with respect to any such prior crime.) Existing sentencing procedures and record-keeping methods are not remotely capable of establishing such facts.

Once the Halliday Report's purported 'redefinition' of proportionality is understood for what it is, that is, not a modification of the proportionality principle but its abandonment for something else, then the real nature of these proposals becomes apparent. The principle of proportionality, which relates the seriousness of the current offence to the severity of the punishment, is largely being abandoned, save for some imprecise (and unexplained) 'outer limit' on severity based on current crime seriousness.

A career-oriented criminal law?

Might we wish, however, to try to reshape the criminal law so as to emphasise punishing criminal careers rather than crimes? I think not. The advantage of a criminal and sentencing law which focuses on crimes is that it provides a comprehensible valuation of conduct. What chiefly counts is what was done, not who did it. Penal sanctions thus furnish reasonably clear public expression of the degree of blameworthiness of various kinds of criminal acts. If that conduct is serious, the condemnation is severe, thereby recognising the importance of the rights of those affected; if it is not serious, the condemnation should be reduced accordingly. A career-based system would make the criminal law's public valuation of conduct much more diffuse. The focus would no longer be on what was done but rather on who did it and how frequently he had done it before. It is true that the law's rules or principles would have to be able to assess the gravity of crimes in order to set standards for criminal careers. However, the punishment – the public expression of penal censure that is the product of such reckonings[12] – would vary independently of the gravity of the current act, depending on the prior criminal record. As a result, the criminal sanction would no longer so clearly testify to the recognition of the degree of wrongfulness of the conduct, and to the significance of the rights that had been infringed.

A proponent of the Report's proposals might reply, however, that they do not seek to go to this length to create a career-based penal system. The aim, arguably, is to continue to give crime-seriousness an important role, but to give more prominence to the criminal record than a desert model would allow. But if that is the aim, the Report fails to implement it. The Report's 'illustrative examples' would seem to put primary stress on the record. The example is given of a middle-level offence, in which the 'entry point' is 18 months' imprisonment. Here, it is stated, a first offender could receive a non-custodial sentence, and a multiple recidivist a three-year custodial sentence (2.20). This would involve a 100 per cent adjustment in either direction of the starting point, thus giving the record considerably more leverage than the instant offence (see Roberts 2002).

The proponent might reply that these numbers are mere examples, and the panel or other body writing the sentencing guidelines[13] could opt for smaller recidivist premiums. The difficulty is, however, that this body would receive no principled guidance from the Report's proposals. Whether the criminal record should play a primary or more subordinate role is a crucial issue of principle for a sentencing system, with differing rationales pointing to differing degrees of emphasis.[14] It is not something that is merely a matter of drafting detail.

This problem of insufficient principled guidance is made all the worse by the Report's formulation of proportionality as including the record. Were proportionality defined according to its normal meaning

– as referring to the current offence – then the role and weight of the record could at least be made explicit. The desirability of a larger or more modest recidivist premium could be debated, drawing on the differing rationales on which such differing approaches would rest. However, if the record is lumped in with the current offence in defining proportionality, its role is obscured.

The Report also fails to address another important issue in its proposals for increasing the sentence premium for recidivists. That is the issue of how parsimoniously or prodigally that premium should be employed. Parsimonious use would mean building up the sentence increase slowly, with large increments reserved only for flagrant cases of multiple recidivism. A number of techniques would be available for this purpose, including (1) requiring very frequent reoffending before the large upward adjustments were invoked; and (2) applying such larger adjustments only to cases where both the instant conviction and the prior convictions were for rather serious offences.[15] Taking this approach would help preserve proportionality (in that word's normal meaning), as it would give the current offence the greater relative impact in ordinary cases, and reserve substantial recidivist premiums only for the most flagrant cases of reoffending. It might also help limit resorting to imprisonment for the more routine cases coming before the court, such as those involving repeat property offenders. Addressing this issue would call for a principled stance on the parsimonious use of prior-record increments, which the Report does not suggest.

Could giving greater emphasis to prior offending enhance crime prevention?

Let us turn next to the question of whether crime-prevention concerns could support the proposed increase in emphasis on prior offending.

Increased incapacitation or deterrence?

Could incapacitation or deterrence justify giving greater weight to the criminal record? There are grounds for doubt, supplied in the Halliday Report's own discussion.

Earlier Home Office documents (see, for example, Home Office 2001a) appear to suggest that emphasising the criminal record might have significant incapacitative benefits. Reference was made to a group of about 100,000 persistent offenders, whose criminal activities could be impeded by lengthier prison sentences for recidivists (ibid.: 1.28). The plausibility of this claim was marred by these documents' own admission that the composition of this group is continually changing – with new entrants into the cohort of active offenders, and with offenders leaving the cohort as their criminal careers decline (ibid.: 1.31). Those given the enhanced sentences thus may no longer constitute the group's most active offenders.

Does the existence of a cohort of active repeat offenders necessarily mean that extended sentences for recidivists will restrain crime more effectively? The history of 'Selective Incapacitation' in the 1980s in the United States points to reasons for doubt (see von Hirsch 1998a). Self-reports among robbers in confinement suggested that most such offenders offended only occasionally, but that a small subgroup offended with high frequency. The aim of the selective incapacitation strategy was to achieve incapacitation by targeting this subgroup – through use of predictive instruments emphasising prior arrests and convictions. Early projections suggested dramatic crime-reduction effects (Greenwood 1982), but a subsequent analysis by a National Academy of Sciences panel report (National Academy of Sciences 1986) showed the projected incapacitative effects to be rather modest, in part, because of the shifting composition of the subgroup of active offenders. A particular difficulty was making prediction-based terms of confinement coincide sufficiently with offenders' estimated residual criminal careers.

The Halliday Report, to its credit, refrains from basing its proposals regarding criminal record on claimed incapacitative effects. It notes the shifting composition of the group of active offenders, and points out that even modest increases in incapacitation would call for large increases in the prison population – up to 15 per cent population increase for every 1 per cent reduction in crime rates. While asserting that possible incapacitative benefits would be a welcome side effect of changes in the sentencing framework justified on other grounds, the Report admits that these would not themselves provide sufficient support for such changes (1.66–1.68).

Another possibility would be that sentence increases for recidivism could better deter crime: the potential recidivist would 'think twice' before reoffending, if he knew that this could attract much severer punishment.[16] The Halliday Report, however, is careful not to make such claims. Citing current research, including a review of recent deterrence studies commissioned by the Home Office and carried out by researchers from the Cambridge Institute of Criminology (von Hirsch et al. 1999), the Report notes the lack of strong statistical correlations between changes in penalty levels and crime rates, and the potential difficulties of deterring those who persist in the face of repeated punishment. The Report concludes that changes in the sentencing framework should make 'no new assumptions about deterrence' (1.62–1.64).

The recidivist premium and 'better opportunity for reform'

In addition to its basic claims about recidivists deserving more punishment, the Halliday Report offers another suggestion: that longer sentences for recidivists could afford more time (and hence better opportunity) for providing treatment (1.76). The repeat offender appears unresponsive to normally-used correctional measures, and thus arguably requires a longer sentence for treatment to be pursued. While sceptical about deterrence and incapacitation, the Report is most optimistic about treatment claiming that this is capable of yielding a (surprising) 5 to 15 per cent reduction in recidivism rates (1.49).[17] Could such treatment concerns really support an enlarged recidivist premium?

Treatment and longer time in prison

A major feature of the Halliday proposals is that they could greatly lengthen the periods that recidivists actually serve in prison. Consider the Report's 'illustrative example' of a relatively serious offence, for which the 'entry point' might be five years. Then, it is suggested, the sentence for extensive recidivism could be *double* that amount, or ten years[18] (2.20). As sentences over 12 months are to be served at least 50 per cent in prison (4.14), this means that duration of actual confinement will rise from two and a half years to five years.[19] However, it is extremely doubtful that the additional two and a half years of incarceration would have significant rehabilitative utility and, indeed, it may well have counterproductive effects. (Indeed, the Halliday Report itself points out that treatment is primarily to be delivered under supervision in the community, not inside the prison (4.15).)[20]

The problematic character of thus extending prison durations becomes all the more apparent, if we consider costs and benefits, as the Report attempts to do (ch. 9). The major financial and human costs of the Report's various proposals derive from the increased use of imprisonment, which stems mainly from the harsher penalties for recidivists. This, according to the Report, could result in prison population increases of 3,000–6,000, and associated costs in the range of about £500 million (9.6). The main claimed benefit is the potentially substantial reduction in recidivism that stems from more active treatment interventions. Yet it is not this costly aspect of the proposals (more imprisonment) that would yield the anticipated rehabilitative benefits!

Treatment and longer supervision time
The longer prison sentences for recidivists will also yield longer periods under supervision. In the above example, the extension of the recidivist's sentence from five years to ten years will also result in doubling the supervision period after release, from two and a half years to five years. Is this additional time likely to enhance the prospects for rehabilitative intervention? This 'more time' thesis becomes progressively more dubious the longer the terms of supervision involved. To take the just cited example, a five-year prison sentence with supervision in its second half should be ample to provide any rehabilitative guidance that could be realistically achieved. Doubling the supervision-in-the-community period from two and a half years to five years would not seem likely to enhance programme effects.

Were the more-time-for-treatment theory meant seriously, it could be implemented much more parsimoniously. The recidivist might face a somewhat longer supervision period, but not a longer initial stay in prison, and the extension of the supervision period would be kept within realistic limits.

Added time for treatment and proportionality constraints
The Report's more-time-for-treatment thesis would also need to be squared with proportionality constraints. It is not apparent how it could. On a just-deserts theory, the answer would be straightforward: rehabilitative concerns would not support increasing severity of sentence (see von Hirsch 1976: ch. 15). The Halliday Report's conception of desert is a much diluted one, as noted already, with severity much less strongly related to the seriousness of the current offence. Perhaps the Report's more-opportunity-for-treatment thesis might square with this conception, but the Report's suggested desert conceptions are not made any stronger through invocation of the treatment thesis: the justifications for diluting desert constraints remain the rather slender ones discussed in earlier sections, of the defiance theory and the redefinition of desert to include the record.

Might anything else help? Might support be drawn, for example, from the 'limiting retributivism' model developed by Norval Morris and Michael Tonry (see Morris 1982: ch. 5; Morris and Tonry 1990:

ch. 4)? According to the 'limiting retributivist' approach, desert – the seriousness of the current offence – would establish the permissible limits on the severity of punishment for a crime. Within those desert-based limits, however, the sanction could be determined on other (for example, crime-preventive) grounds.

The Morris-Tonry model differs somewhat from the Report's approach in that it permits increases above its lower desert bounds in individual cases, based on crime-preventive considerations, whereas the Report does not opt for such extensive individualisation.[21] That model also defines the desert limits in terms of the seriousness of the *current* offence.[22] However, it could possibly be argued that the model's general approach supports the Report's scheme. The seriousness of the offence, arguably, would supply an envelope of permissible severity; within that range, penalties could be set for other reasons. That other reason, in the case of recidivists, could be the Report's notion of 'opportunity for reform'.

There would, however, be significant difficulties in thus using 'limiting retributivism'. One difficulty concerns the extent of the sentence increase for recidivists. While limiting retributivism allows more scope for ulterior considerations than desert theory does, it still calls (at least in its more recent formulations) for substantial proportionality limits.[23] The Report's weak limits on severity in relation to the current offence, and its large penalty increases for recidivists (e.g. well over doubling of the penalty), would appear to breach these limits.

Another difficulty concerns limiting retributivism's requirements of 'parsimony'. While limiting retributivism would permit increases in severity (within the applicable desert ranges) for rehabilitative reasons, such increases are also subject to strong parsimony requirements. It would need to be shown why a severer sentence would better serve rehabilitative ends. That case is not made out by the Report, for the reasons just noted, namely: (1) it is not clear why the sharply increased durations of actual confinement for recidivists serve treatment goals; and (2) it is also not clear why substantially longer terms of supervision (especially with respect to lengthier sentences) are sufficiently related to rehabilitative success.

Concluding thoughts

The foregoing discussion suggests that the Report's proposed shift toward greater emphasis on the criminal record cannot be supported in the terms the Report suggests, either as reflecting what offenders deserve, or as a way of providing better opportunities for the reform of offenders. However, if there is little support for the proposals, are there reasons that strongly militate against the proposals' adoption, namely: that a more strongly record-driven sentencing system would entail unacceptable human and financial costs. Thus:

1. At a time when there reportedly is grave concern (even among Ministers) about escalating prison populations,[24] the proposals, by the Report's own calculations, could add a further prison population increase of 3,000–6,000 at a cost of about half a billion pounds. Besides the obvious financial costs, the human costs would be very great indeed – in terms of the added suffering inflicted on those involved.

2. The Home Office's 2001 policy paper made reference to 'a small group of hard core, highly persistent offenders, probably no more than 100,000 strong' (Home Office 2001a: 1.28), who may be responsible for more than half the crime that occurs, and seems to suggest that a more strongly record-driven sentencing policy may effectively reduce crime from this group. No basis has been offered for this supposition. A sentencing criterion based purely on prior convictions does not effectively discriminate between highly active offenders and those who actually offend less often but whose manner of offending leads to easy detection. Nor does such a criterion distinguish between those who now are at the most active phase of their criminal careers and those whose criminality has begun to decline. The Halliday Report's own caution about claiming substantial incapacitative effects confirms the validity of such doubts.

3. The rehabilitative benefits would be marginal at best. While the Report asserts that renewed treatment and reform efforts could reduce rates of return to crime by 5–15 per cent, no convincing explanation is made about how the provisions on tougher penalties for recidivists would aid this effort. Much of those provisions' impact on durations of imprisonment relates to longer stints of actual imprisonment for recidivists, but the Report, as noted in the previous section, fails altogether to explain how longer stays in prison would be more rehabilitative.

4. These manifest human and social costs and doubtful benefits would be achieved at a very substantial sacrifice of justice. No sentencing system that relies heavily on previous offending instead of on the degree of blameworthiness of the current offence can claim to be a

fair and proportionate one. The Halliday Report's assertion that recidivists somehow 'deserve' much more punishment rests on shaky propositions, indeed: on redefinitions of the notion of proportionality to mean something else, or on the theory that mere disobedience warrants much severer punishment. Such propositions would be acceptable only on assumptions that are more strongly authoritarian, and give much less weight to claims of individual justice than a free society should accept. There should be no place in England and Wales for a sentencing philosophy of incarcerating up the usual suspects.

Notes

1 This article appears by permission of SAGE Publications Ltd and is published in *Punishment and Society*, vol. 4 no. 4 October 2002. I am grateful for the comments of several readers of earlier drafts of this chapter – Andrew Ashworth, A.E. Bottoms, Sue Rex, Julian Roberts and Helen Weeds, and also for comments emerging during the Cropwood Conference on Sentencing Policies and Possibilities held at the Institute of Criminology in Cambridge in December 2001.

2 For a discussion of the overall sentencing philosophy of the Criminal Justice Act 1991, see Ashworth (2000: ch. 4); for the rationale of the Act's provisions regarding previous criminal record, see Wasik and von Hirsch (1994).

3 A useful discussion of the impact that this greater emphasis on the criminal record would have on patterns of sentencing is found in Julian Roberts's essay on the Halliday Report (Roberts 2002).

4 In the US in the mid-1900s, penologists also developed interest in a prediction-orientated rationale known as 'selective incapacitation', but enthusiasm soon waned (see p. 206). This approach never generated much interest in Britain.

5 For discussion of this model's elements, see von Hirsch and Ashworth (1998: ch. 4); and more fully, von Hirsch (1993).

6 See, for example, Straw (1996).

7 For a discussion of some of these developments, see Morris (1951: chs 2 and 5).

8 See Halliday Report (2.14–2.15) for a rejection of the 'cumulative approach', according to which each repetition would elicit a stated increment in sentence (thus possibly leading to lengthy sentences for minor offenders with sufficiently long criminal records).

9 Such a view was once put forward in von Hirsch (1976: ch.10), but subsequently disavowed (von Hirsch 1986: ch. 7).

10 On this point, see further von Hirsch (1986: 78–80); Fletcher (1982: 57). Infringement of a statutory criminal prohibition is, of course, a condition

precedent to criminal liability, on rule-of-law grounds. However, this does not mean that flouting a prohibition is an extra evil deserving of additional punishment beyond the harmfulness and culpability involved in the conduct itself.

11 The Report's relevant stated principles (2.40) are:

- severity of punishment should reflect the seriousness of the offence ... and the offender's criminal history;

- in considering the criminal history, the severity of the sentence should increase to reflect a persistent course of criminal conduct, as shown by previous convictions and sentences.

This formulation gives no guidance concerning the weight to be given to the seriousness of the current offence relative to the criminal record.

12 For further discussion of penal censure's role in providing such a public valuation, see von Hirsch (1993: 10–11; 1999: 78–9).

13 For the proposals on creating a system of sentencing guidelines, see the Halliday Report, ch. 8.

14 For discussion of the relationship between sentencing rationale and the relative emphasis given to the crime and the criminal record, see von Hirsch (1986: ch. 12).

15 The Oregon sentencing guidelines employ these techniques; see von Hirsch (1995: 154–6).

16 Home Secretary, David Blunkett, in his July 2001 statement releasing the Halliday Report, apparently adopts this view, stating that 'Sentencing should send a clear message that the more you offend the greater punishment you can expect, with longer and more demanding sentences' (Blunkett 2001); see also Straw (2001).

17 For a more sceptical assessment of treatment effects, see, however, Lösel (2001)

18 The Report gives serious burglaries as an example, but such lengthy sentences are likely to be a rarity for that offence. A more realistic example of an offence with a five-year 'entry point' might be certain types of robbery.

19 The increased duration of imprisonment becomes still more dramatic when the recidivist premium causes the prison sentence to rise from below to above 12 months. Suppose the 'entry point' for a given type of offence is set at nine months: in that event a normal sentence would consist of a prison phase between two weeks and three months, with the remainder of the term served under community supervision (3.12). The recidivist premium, however, could cause this sentence to double to 18 months. Under the proposed rules for sentences over 12 months, one half of this 18-month term would have to be spent in confinement. As a result, the recidivist premium would cause the duration of actual imprisonment to rise from no more than three months to nine months – or a tripling of prison time.

20 For sentences under 12 months, the Report recommends prison terms of up to three months followed by supervision. It is questionable whether such short stays in prison would have much rehabilitative utility. In the 1970s, Germany substantially restricted the use of short-term sentences (i.e. those under six months), on the grounds that – given the logistics of putting people into prisons, classifying them and so on – these periods of incarceration would be too short to provide adequate treatment, yet sufficiently long to cause damage to people's community and family ties and their employment connections (Albrecht 1997: 182).

21 For the ordinary prison sentence of 12 months or more, sentence duration according to the Report would be based on crime-seriousness and the criminal record, without provision for variation of sentence length on the basis of rehabilitative considerations. Half of that sentence would have to be served in prison.

22 Morris makes this point clear in a 1985 article where he compares the penalty for an offender with a 'clean' criminal record with that of an offender with extensive prior convictions (Morris and Miller 1985). There, he does not treat the latter's record as making him more deserving of punishment. If there is to be a penalty increase at all, it would have to be on risk-orientated and incapacitative grounds (that the latter offender constitutes a worse risk), but subject to the upper desert limits for the offence.

23 In Norval Morris's initial formulation the desert limits were quite broad and were to be based on what would be seen by community mores as excessive (Morris 1976). The difficulty of such a formulation was that it provided scant restraint: even draconian sentences might be permissible if community sentiment were to support them. Michael Tonry, more recently, has rejected the community-mores view and opted for desert constraints derived from normative arguments concerning the punishment's censuring implications (Tonry 1994). Tonry has also moved towards having narrower desert limits (see, for example, Tonry 1998). Crime seriousness would seem to retain pre-eminent weight in deciding penalties and reliance on other grounds would be subject to significant desert-based limits.

24 See *The Guardian*, 1 November 2001, p. 2.

References

Albrecht, H.-J. (1997) 'Sentencing and Punishment in Germany' in Tonry, M. and Hatlestad, K. (eds), *Sentencing Reform in Overcrowded Times*. New York: Oxford University Press, pp. 181–7.

Ashworth, A. (2000) *Sentencing and Criminal Justice*, 3rd edn. London: Butterworths.

Blunkett, D. (2001) 'Put Sense Back into Sentencing', Home Office news release 5 July.

Fletcher, G. (1982) 'The Recidivist Premium', *Criminal Justice Ethics*, 1(2), 54–9.

Greenwood, P.W. (1982) *Selective Incapacitation*. Santa Monica, CA: Rand Corporation.

Home Office (2001a) *Criminal Justice: The Way Ahead*. London: Home Office.

Home Office (2001b) *Making Punishments Work: Report of a Review of the Sentencing Framework for England and Wales*. London: Home Office.

Lösel, F. (2001) 'Evaluating the Effectiveness of Correctional Programs: Bridging the Gap between Research and Practice', in Bernfeld, G., Farrington, D.P. and Lescheid, A. (eds), *Offender Rehabilitation in Practice: Implementing and Evaluating Effective Programs*. Chichester: John Wiley.

Morris, N. (1951) *The Habitual Criminal*. London: Longmans, Green.

Morris, N. (1976) *Punishment, Desert and Rehabilitation*. Washington, DC: US Government Printing Office.

Morris, N. (1982) *Madness and the Criminal Law*. Chicago: University of Chicago Press.

Morris, N. and Miller, M. (1985) 'Predictions of Dangerousness' in Tonry, M. and Morris, N. (eds), *Crime and Justice: An Annual Review of Research*, vol. 6. Chicago: University of Chicago Press, pp. 1–50.

Morris, N. and Tonry, M. (1990) *Between Prison and Probation: Intermediate Punishments in a Rational Sentencing System*. New York: Oxford University Press.

National Academy of Sciences, Panel on Research on Criminal Careers (1986) 'Report', in Blumstein, A., Cohen, J., Roth, J. and Visher, C. (eds), *Criminal Careers and 'Career Criminals'*, vol. 1. Washington, DC: National Academy of Sciences.

Roberts, R.J. (2002) 'Alchemy in Sentencing: An Analysis of Reform Proposals in England and Wales', *Punishment and Society*, 4(4).

Straw, J. (1996) 'Honesty, Consistency and Progression in Sentencing', Paper for the Parliamentary Labour Party Home Affairs Committee.

Straw, J. (2001) 'Next Steps in Criminal Justice Reform', Speech before Social Market Foundation, 31 January.

Tonry, M. (1994) 'Proportionality, Parsimony, and Interchangeability of Punishments', in Duff, A., Marshall, S., Dobash, R.E. and Dobash, R.P. (eds), *Penal Theory and Practice: Tradition and Innovation in Criminal Justice*. Manchester: Manchester University Press, pp. 59–83.

Tonry, M. (1998) 'Interchangeability, Desert Limits and Equivalence of Function', in von Hirsch, A. and Ashworth, A. (eds), *Principled Sentencing: Readings on Theory and Policy*, 2nd edn. Oxford: Hart Publishing, pp. 291–6.

von Hirsch, A. (1976) *Doing Justice: The Choice of Punishments*. New York: Hill & Wang.

von Hirsch, A. (1986) *Past or Future Crimes: Deservedness and Dangerousness in the Sentencing of Criminals*. Manchester: Manchester University Press.

von Hirsch, A. (1993) *Censure and Sanctions*. Oxford: Oxford University Press.

von Hirsch, A. (1995) 'Proportionality and Parsimony in American Sentencing Guidelines: The Minnesota and Oregon Standards', in Clarkson, C.M.V. and

Morgan R. (eds), *The Politics of Sentencing Reform.* Oxford: Oxford University Press, pp. 149–67.

von Hirsch, A. (1998a) 'Selective Incapacitation: Some Doubts', in von Hirsch A. and Ashworth, A. (eds), *Principled Sentencing: Readings on Theory and Policy*, 2nd edn. Oxford: Hart Publishing, pp. 121–7.

von Hirsch, A. (1998b) 'Desert and Previous Convictions' in von Hirsch, A. and Ashworth, A. (eds), *Principled Sentencing: Readings on Theory and Policy*, 2nd edn. Oxford: Hart Publishing, pp. 191–7.

von Hirsch, A. (1999) 'Punishment, Penance and the State: A Reply to Duff', in Matravers, M. (ed.), *Punishment and Political Theory.* Oxford: Hart Publishing, pp. 69–82.

von Hirsch, A. and Ashworth, A. (eds) (1998) *Principled Sentencing: Readings on Theory and Policy*, 2nd edn. Oxford: Hart Publishing.

von Hirsch, A., Bottoms, A.E., Burney, E. and Wikström, P.-O. (1999) *Criminal Deterrence and Sentence Severity: An Analysis of Recent Research.* Oxford: Hart Publishing.

Wasik, M. and von Hirsch, A. (1994) 'Section 29 Revised: Previous Convictions in Sentencing, *Criminal Law Review*, 409–18.

Cropwood 26th Round Table Conference: Sentencing policies and possibilities in Britain – summary of discussions

David A. Green

Discussion 1 (following the Halliday Report)

The Halliday Report was published during a period in which, it was argued, public confidence in government institutions had diminished. A similar lack of confidence in the practical expertise of practitioners and academics had also been noted. Many of the proposals put forward by Halliday were meant to be instrumental in rebuilding this confidence by crafting sentencing measures that were systematic, rational and transparent. One discussant pointed out that the mere existence of the Halliday Report – that is, of a rational, systematic sentencing review and reform programme – might be enough to gain the support of politicians and the general public. There was a danger, then, that too lengthy a critical appraisal of the details of the plan by practitioners and academics might ultimately undermine public confidence by reinforcing the notion that the experts were out of touch with mainstream public opinion.

Numerous discussants were not fully convinced that the impact of the Halliday Report recommendations on the prison population would be neutral or that inflationary consequences would be averted. The effects the Halliday proposals would have on the prison population would depend, to a large extent, on the sentencing guideline framework that would be developed. For instance, allowing the judicial consideration of previous convictions when sentencing – a consideration that was disallowed under the Criminal Justice Act of 1991 – would ultimately lead to an increase in custodial disposals unless sentence tariffs were lowered significantly. As restoring public confidence was a key purpose of the sentencing review and its reform proposals, concern was expressed that 'sentencing on record', though popular with the public and politically desirable, would inevitably lead to longer sentences for repeat offenders and to consequent growth in the prison population. Furthermore, because sentencing reform proposals must be 'sold' by politicians to their constituents, most often the tendency had been to embrace custodial penalties rather than alternatives to custody. The former conveyed tough, punitive messages that resonated well with the public, whereas the latter were often construed as a 'soft' option. In practice then, the sentencing guidelines framework called for in the Report would be a crucial part of the provisions because it would ultimately determine the cumulative effects the reforms would manifest on the prison population.

Research suggested the public wanted predictability in sentencing. It might prove difficult to increase the number of tools in the sentencing 'toolbox' – that is, increasing the number of options available to sentencers – whilst simultaneously attempting to maintain predictable outcomes the public would support. The conditional sentence might pose similar problems. Members of the public in Australia and Canada, it was pointed out, had difficulty accepting the conditional sentence because it was not clear to them if the offender was serving a sentence in prison or in the community. The conditions of such a sentence would need to be very clearly stated in order to prevent confusion and misperceptions.

Concern was expressed about the unintended consequences of introducing effective rehabilitative programmes in prison. This could have the effect of making custody more attractive to sentencers and to the public at a time when the number of imprisoned offenders would need to be reduced for programmes to be possible. In addition, attempts to make short custodial sentences more constructive might divert attention away from the question of whether short prison sentences were – in light of their possible destructive and criminogenic effects – ever an effective sanction. Advocates for the increased use of custody, and for longer periods, might be enabled to further that agenda if this debate was abandoned. On the other hand, by recommending community penalties for all offences that would otherwise carry a custodial sentence of less than 12 months, the Halliday Report posed the danger that such an implicit discouragement of short prison sentences might ultimately lead to longer ones.

A safer way forward, it was suggested, might be to pursue the closer partnership between the Prison and Probation Services called for in the Report. This effective partnership could yield short prison sentences that were constructive – provided prison populations were at manageable levels, resources and infrastructure improvements were available to facilitate it and cultural change within prisons was evident. Most of the measures proffered in the Report would first require the relief of present overcrowded conditions to be effective. Many discussants were sceptical that change on so wide a scale could occur in the near future, but they agreed that such change was a prerequisite for effective implementation of the Halliday proposals. Pre-release review by the courts, for instance, would require solid, up-to-date information from the Prison Service and the Probation Service about what was possible, what had been achieved and what remained to be achieved by a particular offender.

Scotland chose a different route to achieve more systematic and rational sentencing by developing the Sentencing Information System (SIS), which allowed judges instantaneous access to information on prior sentencing practice in similar cases. Such a system took eight years to develop, and the scale of this commitment threw into relief the increase in resources, the improvement of facilities and the cultural shift among magistrates, judges, prison personnel and probation officers required to realise the Halliday recommendations.

The need for strong leadership by the government and the judiciary was an important consideration if Halliday was to succeed. For instance, the present Home Secretary had expressed concern about the expansion of prison populations. His leadership could facilitate down-tariffing that might help offset the effects of the judicial consideration of previous convictions during sentencing. Under the Halliday framework, judges and magistrates would be required to assess the needs of, and risks posed by, offenders in order to select the appropriate disposal, a skill that would require a significant amount of commitment, training and resources.

Discussion 2 (following Andrew von Hirsch)

As offender self-reports had shown that prior record could be a poor indicator of actual rates of previous offending, it was important to be aware that allowing prior record to bear prominently on sentencing decisions could amount to punishing incompetence. Those offenders that came before a judge over and over again had not necessarily represented the most prolific offenders, but rather those individuals most easily apprehended by the police. There was some advocacy indicated in discussion for attempts to engage the public in a dialogue about alternative, non-custodial means of dealing with persistent offenders (or at least with those offenders who were repeatedly caught). There was a need expressed for debate about the causes of persistent offending, such as addiction and mental illness, which could conceivably sway members of the public to embrace the notion of treatment over punishment.

The public expected and wanted prior record to matter. If the aim of the Halliday proposals was to strengthen public confidence, this fact must be taken into account. The question then was not whether previous convictions should count, but rather to what degree. One discussant indicated that, in current practice, consideration of an offender's prior record already affected the length of sentence imposed. Thus a sentencing framework which obligated sentencers to consider previous convictions could result in even longer sentences for reconvicted offenders. Given this, it was crucial to adequately define entry points and tariffs for offences on a nominal scale, and to commission research to determine the degree to which prior record was being taken into account in current judicial practice.

Criminal justice issues were political issues, so the proposals presented to government must attract politicians to find support. Proposals that are simply effective, or principled, or rational, or all three, would not succeed if they are not politically viable. At the same time, policy needed to be effective because votes could be lost if measures did not work. One opinion offered was that the most politically practical way to move forward would be to adjust tariffs down, rather than to attempt to engage the public and politicians in a debate about whether sentencing with prior record in mind was morally justifiable.

Another participant called attention to the uniformity of reconviction rates – 50–60 per cent cross-nationally – in order to suggest that prisons had criminogenic effects that contributed to patterns of recidivism. Support was expressed for sentences that omitted the use of custody entirely. In so far as prison was to be used, some suggested prison regimes should reflect an ethos of support and inclusivity, rather than an orientation toward punishment and exclusion. This shift was seen as fundamental if programmes aimed at preventing reoffending were to be effective.

Discussion 3 (following Julian Roberts)

It was noted that the issue of increasing public confidence was not mentioned in the speech Jack Straw made announcing the planned sentencing review. The focus instead was on the small number of persistent offenders believed to be responsible for the bulk of committed offences. It was only later on that the former Home Secretary mentioned his wish to raise public confidence in sentencing practice. This focus on public confidence troubled some discussants because the public was known to be ambivalent about criminal justice issues. Public opinion about sentencing was both difficult to assess and difficult to alter through specific sentencing policy changes.

Nonetheless, there was considerable discussion about ways to inform the public about sentencing issues. Recent Home Office efforts to educate the public about sentencing had been promising. However, some scepticism was expressed about whether the knowledge gained by the public through these latest initiatives could withstand the seemingly inevitable wave of emotive media coverage and misinformation likely to accompany the next crime scare.

Others questioned the ultimate effectiveness of programmes to inform the public and to build public confidence in light of current social, cultural, economic and political contexts. The inherent insecurities and ambivalence of 'late modernity' seemed likely to prevent any long-lasting assuagement of public anxiety. This ambivalence was perhaps most clearly illustrated in the tendency of the public to voice a great deal of support for the police, and yet to disapprove of the criminal justice system as a whole. The public similarly approved of the work of individual doctors and nurses, but simultaneously remained distrustful of the National Health Service in general. A lack of confidence in the criminal justice system might only be symptomatic of a larger cultural malaise, resistant to remedial measures intended to build public support in a particular policy area.

Although the wide and effective dissemination of knowledge might be a crucial part of a strategy to bolster public confidence in the criminal justice system as a whole, it was pointed out that the media presentation of an issue had more significant an impact on public opinion than the reality of that issue. For instance, the news media might create an impression that judges were overly lenient, an impression that might not adequately be dispelled by empirical evidence to the contrary. It was also argued that an individual's opinions were affected more by experience than information, and more imaginative ways of informing the public should account for this. For example, arrangements allowing offenders to work on community service projects and to interact with members of the public could transform how members of the public regarded offenders.

Questions about the degree to which public opinion should influence sentencing decisions were also raised. Though there was the conception that a sentencing magistrate or judge made a decision in a case with the will of the public in mind, the principle was also expressed that the will of the public should not bear directly on individual cases. The general approach to sentencing should be shaped by what the public want, but the offender in each individual case should be sentenced according to judicial principles.

Though a sentencer might not feel that the passing of a sentence in a particular case should communicate messages to the public, it was suggested that judges could do more to build public confidence if they articulated more clearly the factors contributing to a particular decision. One discussant wondered whether sentencing guidelines might serve the secondary function of communicating to the general public the reasons for decisions in particular cases. Rather than require a judge to speak directly to the media to explain the reasoning behind a decision, the judge's decision would speak for itself. The guidelines would be made available to the public and the judge's decision in a case could conceivably be explained by way of the guidelines. Guidelines could enhance predictability in many cases, and 'transparently' justify the actions of magistrates and judges.

Discussion 4 (following Sue Rex and Alison Liebling)

Explanations were offered for the frequent domination of community penalties by the threat of custody and the rhetoric of punishment. First, community penalties were depicted in punitive language to render them more politically attractive, as punitive rhetoric remained resonant with the public and popular with politicians. Using such language to describe a community penalty also made the disposal more attractive as a substitute for incarceration, and less likely to be regarded as a 'soft' option. As far as matters of proportionality were concerned, the terminology also prevented violations of parity of sentencing. In the case of offenders on the borderline between a custodial and a community sentence, a 'community punishment order' appeared suitably punitive and, therefore, closer in terms of severity to the custodial option.

One discussant argued that the components of 'pick and mix' sentencing, whereby sentencers choose from a menu of disposal options, might prove difficult to market to the public. Terminology like 'pro-social modelling' and 'cognitive behaviour programmes', for instance, were unlikely to appeal to a public whose confidence in existing sentencing practice was already lacking. Therefore, providing the public with information about actual practice carried the risk that it might weaken, rather than strengthen, public confidence.

Several discussants were concerned that 'pick and mix' sentencing would undermine the progress achieved by Pathfinder programmes and the 'What Works' agenda. Targeting interventions to particular offenders was a critical feature of these programmes. The danger of the 'pick and mix' sentencing approach was that sentencers could overuse some disposals intended for particular groups of offenders, thereby weakening the overall effectiveness of efforts to reduce recidivism.

Again, discussants were keen to emphasise the enormous scale of the changes called for in the Halliday proposals. It was argued that prisons were only able to cope with the current levels of overcrowding by providing no rehabilitative programming for short-term prisoners. Though some discussants expressed the view that short prison sentences did more harm than good, it was generally agreed that a substantial decrease in prisoner numbers was a prerequisite to making short prison sentences constructive.

New proposals for custody-minus and custody-plus would also require a reduction in the prison population. In addition, these new provisions risked creating net-widening effects, because sentencers might find the 'taste of custody' portion of the measure attractive and might use it for more offenders than was intended or advisable. This likelihood could be reduced if the sentencing guidelines clearly stipulated the conditions under which a sentence of this kind was appropriate.

It was suggested that the outcome-driven, managerial approach evident in England and Wales had caused policy-makers and practitioners to lose sight of the more important issues of principle underpinning penal practice. However, the determination of what was 'right' for criminal justice policy was not always clear, and questions of principle had to be balanced with those of both practicality and effectiveness.

Discussion 5 (following Michael Tonry)

Discussion produced considerable disagreement about the state of our knowledge of current sentencing practice. Some participants emphasised the need for research into current judicial practice, noting the traditional judicial resistance to efforts to study their decision-making. Others objected to the notion that little was known of current practice by pointing to the body of work on sentencing by David Thomas as an outstanding source of information. However, some mentioned the considerable disparity between judges regarding the weight given to previous convictions. It was argued that this disparity indicated much more needed to be learned in order to understand the degree to which prior convictions influenced sentences.

Once again the need for a review of current tariffs was stressed, because – as one discussant feared – instituting guidelines to limit judicial discretion could result in more custodial sentences if tariffs were not reconsidered. The guidelines were viewed to be the cornerstone of the entire sentencing framework proposed by Halliday.

There was also debate about how comprehensive the guidelines would need to be. Magistrates' courts already had sentencing guidelines, and there was some discussion of their sufficiency under the proposed framework. The point was made that if tariffs were changed, they would have to be changed across the board to cover tariffs in magistrates' courts.

Some believed that the question of how to ensure compliance with the guidelines was the most important one raised by the guidelines issue. Against doubts that guidelines would result in consistency of outcome, evidence from the United States and the Netherlands was cited which suggested guidelines could sharply reduce sentencing disparities. Others stressed the importance of defining a sentencing rationale and the principles upon which the guidelines would be based. It was not clear what coherent principles informed the sentencing guidelines presented by Halliday, and a consistent, effective sentencing framework required core principles to be reflected throughout every level.

Discussion 6 (following Shadd Maruna and Michael Smith)

Discussion pointed to the possibility that the lay magistracy might resist any plan to include the review of cases among their responsibilities. Some magistrates might believe that those responsibilities should lie with probation professionals. The difficulty of reconvening the same bench to review a case demonstrated additional problems of practicality with the plan. There also might be a resistance to learning the new skills necessary to review cases, skills not initially included among those necessary to fulfil the duties of a lay magistrate. Some might feel ill suited to carry out adequately such an expansion of responsibility.

However, there was considerable support for the proposal among other discussants. The re-entry court could be a major step forward, one participant pointed out, as it would allow court ceremony to accompany an offender's release from custody. Presently, this experience occurred only during the trial process and to signal the start of a sentence. This change would afford a judge the chance to officially express support and commendation for an offender's achievements in custody, the offender's experience of which could prove beneficial by aiding to remove the stigma attached to an offender upon release. The encounter could be constructive for judges as well, who currently lacked the opportunity to encourage motivated offenders to continue their progress after release. Additionally, advocates of restorative justice measures might find in re-entry courts the opportunity to introduce restorative programmes. For example, the victims in a particular case could be given the chance to contribute to the determination of whether or not the offender involved had been sufficiently reintegrated during the course of custody.

It was acknowledged that Halliday's proposals for a review court applied to cases in which release from custody was automatic, and the options open to judges during review would not include custody. However, numerous concerns were expressed regarding this process that might ultimately lead to an increase in custodial disposals. Depending upon the discretion available to and used by reviewers, breach of the conditions imposed during the review could have the effect of increasing the number of offenders resentenced to custody. One discussant stressed that probation officers already faced the challenge of getting offenders to comply with probation conditions. Offenders indicated a wish to be free of constraints upon release, and re-entry courts imposing further community sanctions upon those released might find the enforcement of compliance difficult and counter-productive.

An example from the United States was offered to illustrate some unintended consequences of the efficient enforcement of community orders in drug courts. It became possible in the 1980s for courts to cheaply administer urinalysis kits that provided indisputable evidence of a breach of probation or parole conditions. The result was a large influx of custodial recommitments. A similar result could be avoided in England and Wales, it was argued, if those officials presiding over review courts were able to exercise some discretion and a certain degree of flexibility. For instance, in the case of a drug-dependent individual, a judge could approach the case with a measure of tolerance for failure on the part of the addicted person, failure which is typical in the recovery period. In the absence of this tolerance and flexibility, condemnatory resentencing for violations could ultimately undermine an offender's willingness to alter his or her offending behaviour.

Some contended that additional guidelines would be necessary to secure consistency in the way discretion was exercised. However, allowing flexibility sat awkwardly beside the purpose of guidelines, which was to reduce disparities by limiting discretion. It might also prove difficult to construct rules to guide a judge deciding whether an offender was a plausible candidate for a particular treatment disposal. Furthermore, as evidence suggested some systemic bias within criminal justice institutions, some discussants raised the question of whether it was possible to construct these rules in such a way as to avoid discriminatory effects.

Discussion 7 (following Peter Jones and David Faulkner)

The cursory mention in the Halliday Report of racial, ethnic and religious discrimination in sentencing concerned a number of participants. More research was advocated in order to gain a better understanding of whether, and to what extent, sentencing disparities existed on the basis of race, ethnicity and religion. The need was asserted for a comprehensive study to understand current practice in magistrates' courts, where the great majority of criminal cases were adjudicated. Anecdotal evidence offered by one participant suggested that routine discrimination might occur during defendant encounters with court ushers. One suggestion was to replicate Roger Hood's study of the Crown Court in magistrates' courts. Another was for an impact analysis, or 'disparity audit', to be conducted routinely to check levels of disparity.

Again, the dilemma of balancing guidelines and discretion was discussed. One major concern of discussants was the potentially discriminatory impact of discretion. The review court proposal appeared to entail more discretionary decision-making, and its possible implementation made the question of discriminatory sentencing even more urgent. If judicial discretion did have discriminatory consequences, then it was reasonable to assume that such discrimination would pervade practice in review courts, and possibly even increase with the expansion of discretionary powers. Guidelines had been shown to reduce the occurrence of gross disparities, but discretion was still crucial for just decision-making in individual cases. Furthermore, as was highlighted in the previous discussion, it was unclear how restrictive or flexible to make the guidelines governing judicial decision-making in review courts.

Another danger raised by review courts was the degree to which the nuances of lifestyle and culture influenced judicial decision-making. One discussant warned that the review court could become analogous to the overbearing mother in Philip Roth's novel, *Portnoy's Complaint*. Though the maternal or paternalistic aspects of a review court could conceivably have a positive effect upon offenders actively trying to 'make good', they could also elicit hostile and defiant responses from other more recalcitrant offenders. More fundamentally, on principle, this paternalism would ultimately penalise lifestyle choices not themselves criminal.

Some discussion centred on the idea of positive discrimination or affirmative action to address disparities. It was noted that race was not granted the same degree of consideration as gender in such debates. It was also asserted that measures to ensure that social diversity was represented satisfactorily in the judiciary might have little impact on decision-making, and might amount to little more than tokenism. Though defendants and judges might feel better when there was a member of a racial group present on the bench when a member of that group was sentenced, such measures might not ameliorate, but rather gloss over, the class and cultural divisions between offenders and the judiciary.

There was some disappointment that the Halliday Report did not include a reconsideration of how young offenders were handled by the courts. This oversight amounted to a 'missed opportunity' to experiment with imaginative judicial structures that took account of youthfulness when sentencing. For instance, options could have been made available to divert more young offenders from custody between the ages of 18 and 21 perhaps, on the grounds that their youthfulness was a mitigating factor. This would simultaneously reduce prison overcrowding and provide opportunities to introduce constructive, less stigmatising sanctions in the community for young offenders.

Discussion 8 (following Rod Morgan)

Much of the discussion focused on explanations for the large disparity between the sentences passed by lay magistrates and those of district judges. District judges used custody for remand and at sentencing twice as often, proportionately, as lay magistrates. One suggestion was that this was a result of 'undersentencing' by lay magistrates and 'oversentencing' by district judges. Though the magistrates' guidelines applied to district judges, some resistance by district judges to abide by them was perceived, specifically in regard to the calculation of fines. Others suggested that, culturally, there might be antagonism between lay and stipendiary magistrates that might contribute to disparities, and that this relationship needed to be understood more fully.

There was some discussion of the inherent dangers of a sentencing system in which serious cases were adjudicated by a lone decision-maker, but decisions in lesser cases were reached by a panel. This practice was defended by one discussant on the basis that the rules provided by the sentencing guidelines actually made sentencing easier in the more serious cases in which the issues to consider might be more unequivocal. In the lesser cases, the need to consider the range of non-custodial penalties available to magistrates made a panel decision defensible.

Attention was drawn to another dilemma, one that arose when efforts were made simultaneously to render the lay magistracy both more representative of the community at large and more actively participatory in the review of cases. Pre-release case review would require a greater commitment in terms of training time and experience on the part of lay magistrates. Retired individuals or those from privileged backgrounds were, therefore, more likely to participate in the process. This would, it was argued, make the lay magistracy even less representative than it currently was, further filtering out those citizens unable to meet the taxing time commitments demanded by these new responsibilities.

Finally, the need for adequate resources was again stressed. Little interest had been shown by either Conservative or Labour governments to bring judicial practices in line with available resources. Halliday's proposals would require a mechanism to regulate the prison population, yet this concern had attracted little government attention.

Index

11 September terrorist attacks, 61–2
accreditation, of offending behaviour
    programmes, 131–2
active responsibility, 173
America *see* United States
Auld Report, 21
    costs, 49–52
    District Division, 52–7
    lay magistrates, 42–4, 58
    Magistrates' Division, 46–52
    representation of racial minorities,
        69

'belief rules', 122
black people
    discrimination in sentencing, 65–6
    experience of criminal justice, 63–5
    violence rates, 94
Blunkett, David, policies, 2, 13, 21
boot camps, 133
British Crime Survey (BCS) (1997),
    23–4
British Crime Survey (BCS) (1998), 27
British society
    debate on race, ethnicity and
        religion, 60–2
    nature of, 62–3
Brixton Disorders 10–12 April 1981, The,
    60

Canada
    conditional sentences, 22–3, 218
    public attitudes to sentencing, 26
Canadian Needs Identification and
    Analysis system, 113
career-oriented criminal law, 204–6
    see also persistent offenders; prior
        records; record-driven
        sentencing
carrot and stick models of re-entry,
    163, 166–7
certification processes, 174
chairs, of sentencing commissions,
    85–6
children, of prisoners, 172
Clarke, Kenneth, 1
Cognitive Skills programmes, 115–16,
    129t
combination-deficit narratives of
    re-entry, 166–7
Commission on the Future of
    Multi-Ethnic Britain (CFMEB),
    61, 64
    hostile reactions to, 63
commissions *see* sentencing
    commissions
communicative penal theory, 142–4
community penalties, 147
    and communicative theory, 143

229